THE GOSPEL ACCORDING TO ST. JOHN

NEW TESTAMENT FOR SPIRITUAL READING

VOLUME 7

Edited by

John L. McKenzie, S.J.

THE GOSPEL
ACCORDING TO ST. JOHN

Volume 1

John J. Huckle and Paul Visokay

CROSSROAD • NEW YORK

1981
The Crossroad Publishing Company
575 Lexington Avenue, New York, NY 10022

Copyright © 1981 by The Crossroad Publishing Company

All rights reserved. No part of this book may be reproduced,
stored in a retrieval system, or transmitted, in any form
or by any means, electronic, mechanical, photocopying,
recording, or otherwise, without the written permission of
The Crossroad Publishing Company.

Library of Congress Catalog Card Number: 81-68180
ISBN: 0-8245-0116-0

PREFACE

Most modern readers of the Bible are aware that the Gospel of John is not to be read like the Gospels of Matthew, Mark, and Luke. A full explanation of this difference demands a much more detailed commentary than this series is planned to be, and such a commentary would scarcely leave room in a volume of reasonable size for the purpose of this commentary, which is an exposition for spiritual reading. The alert reader would like some assurance that the problems of critical and historical interpretation posed by the Gospel of John do not make an exposition for spiritual reading impossible, and that these problems are not simply glossed over with pious platitudes in the present work. One does not wish to say that there is no place in Christian exposition for pious platitudes, but they should not be presented under the title of a commentary on the Gospel of John.

I wish to reassure the reader on both these counts, as far as a personal attestation can reassure. The authors have evaded no problem which they encountered in their set purpose of spiritual exposition. They have presumed that the reader who wishes to learn more about the modern scholarly handling of these problems is willing to go elsewhere for the kind of treatment in which they could not engage in this work. The reader may indeed wonder whether there is any easy way to read the Gospel of John, and it is no comfort to tell him or her that there is not. They must pursue the study involved in this reading in the assured hope that the effort is rewarding; I can tell them that their assurance will be fortified before they have worked through many pages.

The major problem for most readers will be the relation of the Jesus of the Gospel of John to history. It is a mistake to think without further discussion that anything but a stout affirmation of the historical reality of the Johannine Jesus is an implication that the Johannine Jesus is unreal. The reality of Jesus is far too large to be encapsulated in a historical description. The author of the Gospel of John was almost certainly acquainted with the other three Gospels and perhaps with other similar materials no longer preserved. The reader will see from the exposition that his refusal to employ these materials arose neither from any doubt in his mind about the historical reality of Jesus of Nazareth nor from doubts of the quality of

v

the memories preserved about him—the kind of doubt which so many modern scholars entertain. It is safe to assume that John's reception of his predecessors was by modern standards uncritical. John did not use this material because he thought that it did not present fully the reality of Jesus Christ.

The full reality of Jesus Christ is the risen and glorified Jesus, and that is the Jesus that walks and talks in the pages of John. Obviously this reality was not an object of historical experience, and it was not presented as such by the authors of the Synoptic Gospels, although modern scholars do not agree on the extent to which Jesus has been transfigured in the Synoptic Gospels. But there is no question that the Jesus of John was never experienced by any one prior to the resurrection. He is the Christ of faith in a way in which the Jesus of the Synoptic Gospels is not, yet no one denies that the Jesus of the Synoptic Gospels is also the Christ of faith. Certainly John attempted to present a reality which is not an object of historical experience. His own response, no doubt, would be that one who knew Jesus only by historical experience did not really know him and that he, John, attempted to present Jesus as he really is, not merely as he was remembered.

The same question can be asked about John's presentation of events which never happened and of words which Jesus never uttered. John calls the miracles of Jesus "signs." Interpreters have discussed at great length and with sufficient clarity the place and function of symbolism in the sign narratives of John, and the reader will have less trouble with them if he accepts the fact that John uses the sign narratives to instruct and not to communicate information about events. If the narratives are treated as historical sources, the problems become so monumental that the narratives become meaningless. Again, John knew the other Gospels. Some of the miracles in the sign stories can be found in these Gospels. Others cannot and no special source for them should be sought. For John's purpose it is immaterial whether they come from a source or not.

The discourses of John have nothing resembling them in style or content in the Synoptic Gospels. It is only honest to admit that the Jesus who speaks in John is not the same Jesus who speaks in the Synoptic Gospels, which are themselves compiled from various sources. In spite of this, a single personality clearly emerges. Without implying untenable claims about the accuracy of the quotations of the words of Jesus in the Synoptic Gospels, it is clear that the speaker who utters the words of Jesus in the Gospel of John is a Christian of the late first century. As happens often in the Synoptic Gospels, some Christian spokesman articulates what he believes to be the response of Jesus to a situation which Jesus never directly addressed.

The reader may wonder why John felt that it was necessary to present the risen glorified Christ where the Jesus of history had stood and thus create a new gospel form. Our authors tell us that he thought that this was the way in which he could make Jesus real and present to the community for which he wrote. The signs are chosen for their symbolic significance for this community. The discourses are addressed not to the disciples of Galilee or to Palestinian Jews but to this community. The problems and the needs of this community can thus be known only by deduction from the content of these discourses. The reader will sometimes feel that the identification of these problems and needs has been vague and unsatisfactory; he must allow room for the educated guesses of scholars. If these problems and needs were better understood, we would better understand the Johannine emphasis on the themes of light-darkness, life-death, and truth-life. It takes no prolonged study to recognize that the authors of the Synoptic Gospels did not know these themes.

It appears therefore that the authors of this work have been asked to produce a commentary for spiritual reading on a work which was written for spiritual reading. This task is fully as difficult as it appears. The authors must show that the needs and problems of the Johannine community are similar enough to those of the modern church to allow them to make the spiritual exposition of John meaningful to contemporary Christians. To do this demands extensive knowledge and profound understanding ot the Roman-Hellenistic world of the first century A.D. In addition, a similar knowledge and understanding of the Christian church of the period is required. The Johannine community has been neither identified nor located, and the antecedent difficulties of finding a common religious and cultural language for an obscure corner of the Roman Empire and the twentieth century western world seem unsurmountable. I stand in amazed admiration at the skill with which my colleagues have accomplished their task. The difficulties should not be stated in such a way as to imply that communication between us and the Johannine world is impossible. Expert interpreters are necessary, and they have done their work in this volume. Every student not only of the New Testament but of the Roman-Hellenistic world begins to sense a recognition of the familiar. That world in its achievements and in its failures was astonishingly like our world. The voice of John is not really as strange as it first sounds. Equally important, the task of interpreting John demands an insight into the contemporary world which is both sympathetic and critical. I am old enough to know that such insight is extremely rare.

I may conclude this preface with what I hope is a word of encouragement.

Readers of the Synoptic Gospels have found them more difficult than they appear to be. Readers of this commentary will find the Gospel of John easier than it appears to be. It is still more difficult than the Synoptic Gospels.

JOHN L. McKENZIE

PUBLISHERS NOTE

A word of explanation is owed the readers of the *New Testament for Spiritual Reading* for the significant differences in style and approach, let alone in authorship, between volume 1 and volumes 2 and 3 of this commentary. As Josef Blank, who was originally commissioned to write the entire work, makes clear in the Preface to volume 2, he actually began his treatment of the Fourth Gospel, not with chapters 1-12, but with chapters 13-21. The justification for this as well as for the overall differences in method may also be found in the Preface to volume 2. When, after considerable delay, Blank's first volume was not forthcoming in the German original (the complete text has not appeared to date), the American publisher felt constrained to complete the commentary by commissioning, in this case, a pair of authors.

OUTLINE

Prologue (1:1–18)

St. John's gospel begins with an introductory hymn of fascinating beauty. Throughout the gospel, persons and events will bear witness to the truth of the claims of Jesus Christ. Perhaps, in a sense, the prologue is the witness of human speech itself to the unspoken Word.

¹In the beginning was the Word, and the Word was with God, and the Word was God. ²He was in the beginning with God;

St. John's vision of the beginning of the announcement of the good news of Jesus Christ is overwhelming. In a new sense, the Gospel of Jesus Christ is an eternal Gospel. Jesus is *the* Word, absolutely and with no qualification. It is here that the Gospel of Jesus begins, in the mystery of God before anything came to be.

For Mark (1:1), the Gospel begins at the start of Jesus' public ministry heralded by the eschatological preaching of John the Baptist. Matthew and Luke, each independently, see in the events surrounding Jesus' birth the fulfillment of Old Testament promises of deliverance. Because Simeon, upon seeing the child Jesus, looked upon the Christ, the Messiah, the promised redeemer, he could sing, "mine eyes have seen thy salvation / which thou hast prepared in the presence of all peoples, / a light of revelation to the Gentiles, / and for glory to your people Israel" (Luke 2:30-32).

John, however, understands that all human history belongs and has always belonged to the good news of God's salvation. This insight of the evangelist requires a revision of the story of creation. For this purpose, John places us in the context of the Old Testament Book of Genesis: "In the beginning God created the heavens and the earth. . . . And God said, 'Let there be light . . . ' " (Gen. 1:1,3). Under the radiant light of the new creation in Christ John looks beyond time, beyond the beginning of anything at all, to the timeless beginning of the Word.

Before all things the Word existed. Nor is this Word a mere

1

attribute or expression of God. Independent and equal, the Word is himself God and, at the same time, in the presence of God. The Greek of the gospel makes these distinctions more clearly. *Theos*, the Greek word for God, when used with the definite article (*ho theos*) traditionally designates God the Father, the God who has made himself known through the Old Testament as well as through the Christ. However, faith in Christ has added dimensions to the divine mystery. The Word was in the presence of *ho theos;* the Word also is *theos.* How this is possible the evangelist does not attempt to explain or even to comment upon. John is writing confession not philosophy. Concise (if not necessarily illuminating) trinitarian formulas and speculations are the products of more sophisticated times.

The Greek substantive used by the evangelist, which is translated as Word, is *logos.* It carries the meaning not only of communication but also of order and reason. As such it is familiar to us in many English formations. Logic and sociology are but two instances. As used by the evangelist, surrounded by a Gentile world largely created by Greek culture, the title would resonate strongly in many Hellenistic philosophic and religious thought currents. As a title for the preexistent Christ, *logos* explicitly appears only three times in the fourth gospel; all three instances are confined to the prologue (1:1,14). In fact, John's special usage is not found throughout the rest of the New Testament writings. Since the title is not explained in the gospel, John presumably expected his readers to be familiar with this designation for Jesus. This would be very much the case if the prologue were originally a hymn to the Word with an established liturgical use in the Christian community. Although the specific meaning that John has attached to the title is unique, its rich allusive quality is only adequately grasped against a background of Christian and Old Testament images.

From one point of view, the Old Testament, as well as the New Testament, is very much a celebration of language, that special world of order and communication within our own world created by the unbelievable power of words. Through the Scriptures, human language uses itself as metaphor to speak about the speechless world of the divine reality. Words themselves, for the Old Testament, are instruments of power, dynamic beyond the simple fact of utterance. They can, especially when spoken in blessing or curse, become independent effective events, no longer under the control of the speaker or hearer. So when Isaac is tricked into bestowing his blessing, the prerogative of the first-born son, upon Jacob, he cannot call it back. Once spoken, its reality is out of his control (Gen. 27:32-38). Faint reflections of this forcefulness of words are familiar enough to us. We can be swayed by the power of a speaker's rhetoric (or in very rare cases, a forceful and concisely developed argument), or we may accept the authority of what is written in a book or newspaper merely because it is written. Various professions, like politics, realize this too. Presumably, if politicians use enough words, they hope eventually to find the right one. This technique calls to mind the worshiper in certain ancient religions who believed that if one called out all the names of god the right name which gave the power to command that god might eventually be found.

Understandably then, if human speech is in itself a source of power, how much more so is God's word. The universe is called into existence by the simple spoken command of God: "God said . . . 'Let there be . . .' and there was . . ." (Gen. 1:1f.). For God, in fact, word and event are inseparable and inevitable. As rain and snow water the earth and cause things to grow, so God's word never returns empty but accomplishes its purpose (Isa. 55:10-11). This same divine word effectively addresses itself to us, commanding, guiding, revealing—a saving as well as a creating word. Later Judaism, using an Aramaic expression, will, in fact, speak of the *Memrah (word) of* God in much the same way as the Old Testament spoke of his messenger or his name, as surrogates for the divine presence or activity.

Neither Judaism nor the Old Testament writers, however, developed a notion of a fully personified word, distinct from God himself and established as a separate living intermediary between God and the world. Indeed, the intolerant and hard-won monotheistic faith of Israel makes this virtually unthinkable. However, many word-images do abound which poetically represent aspects of God or his activity under personified forms. We have already seen something of this in speaking of the creative word. This tendency toward poetic personification is especially evident in the portrayal of personified wisdom in the Old Testament and provides striking parallels with John's description of the divine *logos* in his prologue.

3

Through wisdom we may order our lives on the paths of the Lord and achieve happiness. Though wisdom is such a quality of mind and heart in our possession, it is also much more. Groping to understand more completely the reality of God, the sages who developed the sapiential literature of the Old Testament understood wisdom itself as a divine reality. The Book of Proverbs, which is an early representative of this wisdom speculation, already portrayed wisdom (Hebrew, *hokmah;* Greek, *sophia*) as a preexistent being, brought into existence as the first of God's works and who is present with God at the creation of the universe (Prov. 8:22-31). It is by the wisdom of God, in fact, that the world is founded (Prov. 3:19). Though sharing the divine presence, she (personified wisdom) is also intimately involved with the world, both in the act of its creation and in the lives of its people. She addresses people directly, instructing them in knowledge and discretion (Prov. 8:16). She calls them to God. In later sapiential literature, the role of wisdom as creator and savior is even more dramatically stated (e.g., Wisd. of Sol. 9:1f.). At the same time, like God's word, wisdom came forth from his mouth (Sir. 24:3). In later Judaism, the figure of wisdom will provide the basis for the personification of Torah (law), which will be described in similar terms.

In the New Testament, the power of God's word is not diminished. On the contrary, the word of God is the Gospel itself, the announcement of salvation in Jesus Christ, which calls a new creation into being. If Jesus brought this word throughout the period of his earthly ministry, at the same time, he himself is this word. His person, his work was this Gospel (2 Cor. 4:1-6).

For the fourth gospel especially, Jesus is his own message. In fact, he was from eternity his own message, total identity of word and event, himself God. With the opening words of the fourth gospel, then, we have been introduced to the foundation of the claim of Jesus Christ: God cannot lie.

³*all things were made through him, and without him was not anything made that was made.* ⁴*In him was life, and the life was the light of men.* ⁵*The light shines in the darkness, and the darkness has not overcome it.*

Revelation is not something imposed upon creation, for it is through the Word that all things came to be. The Word is God directed outward. As Word, God is already in relation to creation, addressing humankind, revealing himself as the Father (*ho theos*). As such, salvation and creation are twin aspects of God's activity.

The Word is the source of all life—in fact, it is life, and it is only through him that creatures are made alive. Much more though, it is through him that life is expanded to its fullness—life like God's, eternal life. It is this which enlightens the darkness of the world and illumines humankind.

With the images of life and light we encounter two major themes of John's gospel which are repeatedly intertwined. Jesus himself will claim to be the "light of the world" who gives to his followers the "light of life" (8:12). Indeed, he is life itself (11:25). This life which Jesus is and which he will bring to people has, the prologue reminds us, been from the beginning in the world through the Word. Always in opposition to darkness, to the world as it turns from God, the light has never been completely overcome. The Greek verb which the RSV has translated as "overcome" (v. 5) can bear two meanings, "understand" or "overcome." Both of these should probably be understood here. Darkness neither apprehended nor extinguished the light of life. Jesus as lightbearer and lifegiver is identical with the divine life of the creative Word and is the fulfillment of the lifegiving creation. Again we are reminded of the Book of Genesis. God first gave to the world light (Gen. 1:3); as a direct and special divine gift, life was given to humanity (Gen. 1:27; 2:7). John knows the deeper significance of both because he has looked upon the new creation and grasped it: that life was the light, which shone brightly in the face of the Christ and, at the same time, eclipsed the brightness of wisdom and Torah.

6There was a man sent from God, whose name was John. 7He came for testimony, to bear witness to the light, that all might believe through him. 8He was not the light, but came to bear witness to the light. 9The true light that enlightens every man was coming into the world.

The focus of the prologue breaks sharply and suddenly. From the great cosmological vision of eternity and creation, the evangelist turns to Gospel and the story of salvation in Jesus, anticipating the majestic statement of the unity of Word and history in verse 14.

With the introduction of John the Baptist we are called to history and the plane of humanity.

The gospel traditions record the prominence of the Baptist in the announcement of the good news, whose ministry found a place in the recounting of the apostolic kerygma (Acts 10:37). Here, in fact, as the synoptics record, was the forerunner of the Christ (Mark 1:2f.). For the fourth gospel, however, the greatness of the Baptist is seen from a different perspective, one that entirely subordinates him to the single unique event of Jesus Christ. The purpose of the gospel, as well as of the events and persons in the gospel, is to bear witness to the incarnate Word who is himself the Gospel and the supreme witness testifying to the Father. For this purpose, the Baptist is raised up by God and divinely commissioned: to testify to the genuine light, the divine Word, and to bring all to belief through this testimony.

The prologue, as the gospel, is especially emphatic in contrasting the Baptist with Jesus (v. 8). It is quite probable that this contrast is further motivated by the existence of a sect of the Baptist's followers in the early Church, which accepted him and not Jesus as the true light. Acts 19:1-7 records the meeting of Paul at Ephesus with some disciples of the Baptist who had received his baptism of water but did not even know of the Holy Spirit.

As the rest of the gospel makes clear, though everyone is "enlightened" by the real light, this enlightenment brings confrontation and judgment (see 3:19-21), not universal knowledge and inner illumination. The Word is not a message; the message is the Word.

[10]*He was in the world, and the world was made through him, yet the world knew him not. [11]He came to his own home, and his own people received him not. [12]But to all who received him, who believed in his name, he gave power to become children of God; [13]who were born, not of blood nor of the will of the flesh nor of the will of man, but of God.*

If verse 9 is to be translated as the RSV does ("the true light . . . was coming into the world"), our eyes are already directed to the incarnation. Verses 10-13 summarize the ministry of the incarnate word as it is told in the gospel.

The mission of the true light was to humankind, the world (John uses the Greek word *kosmos*). Again and again throughout the gospel, the "world" or "this world" is the sphere of human history where the struggle between the light and the power of darkness goes on continuously. It is mysteriously both the world that, in the main, turns away from God and yet the world to which he has sent his saving love.

It is this world which rejected Jesus, irresponsibly failing to understand and embrace him. The knowledge that the world lacks of Jesus describes a comprehensive personal attitude: it is a denial of the claim of the Word rather than an intellectual oversight.

The bitterness of this rejection by the world is dramatized by the particular historic circumstances of the ministry of Jesus. Israel was the particular possession of God, a nation called from all the nations of the earth for his special favor. Between God and Israel was *hesed*, a Hebrew word defining their privileged covenantal relationship of love and loyalty. Yahweh was a God of *hesed*, of lovingkindness; Israel was expected to respond in faithful love and obedience. Through Israel, this divine favor of salvation was to be brought to all other peoples. From Israel would come the savior. To Israel, then, God's own property, his home, the light of Jesus first came and was refused. Israel proffers the first of the world's rejections.

This rejection, however, was not total. History will remain in conflict about the person of Jesus. Whether or not to believe in his name constitutes the crucial decision. This is not a question of debating the pros and cons of his credibility, but of surrendering oneself to Jesus as he is, as he has revealed himself; what he is is his name. From such acceptance comes a transformation of human life. He gives humankind the power to possess divine life—in the intimate metaphor of verses 12-13, to be born again as children of God. Though acceptance of Jesus is the condition for this power, it is a divine gift, unnecessary and unconstrained. People neither deserve it nor can they demand it. This new divine birth is emphasized by the three images of verse 13. The children of God are born of no human means whatever, neither of blood (perhaps reflecting an ancient belief about the function of blood in procreation), nor of natural sexual desire in general, nor of the initiating desire of any single person.

[14]*And the Word became flesh and dwelt among us, full of grace and truth; we have beheld his glory, glory as of the only Son from the*

Father. ¹⁵*(John bore witness to him, and cried, "This was he of whom I said, 'He who comes after me ranks before me, for he was before me.'") ¹⁶And from his fullness have we all received, grace upon grace. ¹⁷For the law was given through Moses; grace and truth came through Jesus Christ. ¹⁸No one has ever seen God; the only Son, who is in the bosom of the Father, he has made him known.*

In a sense, the opening phrase of verse 14, almost bland in its simple majesty, is at once the center and climax of the prologue. Everything else moves around and out from this celebration of eternity and time: the Word became flesh. The divine rebirth of humanity rests upon the human birth of divinity. God did not diminish himself, but rather expanded beyond all natural bounds the possibilities of human existence. The age-old dream of the human race for god-likeness becomes a reality by a paradoxical reversal. In Jesus, the meeting of God and humanity renders both truly visible to human-kind for the first time. What God is, Jesus is; what Jesus is, each of us in our own uniqueness can become. Through Jesus God and humanity meet also in each of us.

When John speaks of flesh, he is not conjuring up a picture of a sordid humanity hostile to God. Rather, flesh, as it is often used in both Old and New Testaments, represents the whole human being with all its limitations in relation to the divine. It emphasizes the fragility of human existence, its weakness and mortality. Humans on their own are flesh.

The mystery is that humanity is chosen as the supreme expression of the Word. The scandal of Christian belief, if we would hear John and the New Testament, remains the same today as in the past: God and humanity were united in one particular man at one specific time in one circumscribed place. Through this one human history all human history is changed. In essence, Christianity does not confront us with dogmas, philosophies, or creeds, but with the life, and death, and resurrection of Jesus Christ. To this person who was and is, this Word spoken and speaking to us in history, all theologies and theologians are mere addenda.

If the Word has become human (and for the evangelist this is no dumb show), John makes it clear that he is no less God. The dwelling of the Word with humankind recalls the dwelling of Yahweh with Israel. The Greek verb used by John means "to make a dwelling,"

8

"to pitch a tent." After the exodus from Egypt, the Hebrews are instructed to build a sanctuary, the tabernacle where God will "tent" with his people during their desert sojourn (Exod. 40:34). As Jesus is the true wisdom dwelling in the world, so he is also, as the enfleshed Word, the locus of the divine presence for humanity. Indeed, as the gospel will make clear, the person of Jesus will replace the Jerusalem temple which the Jews believed to be the permanent dwelling-place of Yahweh among his people.

John may further be suggesting that Jesus himself is the *Shekinah* of God. In Rabbinic theology, the *Shekinah*, like the *Memrah* discussed previously (vv. 1-2), was a surrogate for God himself. God localized his presence by his *Shekinah*. Intimately associated with the presence of God is his glory (Hebrew, *Kabod*; Greek, *doxa*). God often manifested his glory to Israel by his saving interventions on their behalf (Exod. 17:7). As we have seen, both closely associated with the exodus and the tabernacle is the glory of God as an epiphany of light. The desert sanctuary is consecrated by Yahweh's glory (Exod. 29:43). The glory of Yahweh which settled on Mt. Sinai had the appearance of a devouring fire (Exod. 24:16–17); contact with this glory filled the face of Moses with blinding radiance (Exod. 34:29). It is this divine glory exposed in the works and person of Jesus that John testifies is visible to those who have come to him in faith. This is the glory of Jesus who exists in relation of unique sonship to God, the Father, whose actions are God's actions. Jesus is the Son; because of his relation to the Father, Christian believers are empowered as children of God. The incarnate Word has the fullness of grace and truth. John's phrase recalls a Hebrew expression which refers to God's faithfulness to his covenant promises (Exod. 34:6); he is a God whose *hesed*, whose lovingkindness, never wavers.

The Old Testament themes of verse 14 which converge in the Word made flesh are reemphasized in the remainder of the prologue. John the Baptist, the epitome of the Old Testament prophet, himself testifies to the preexistence of the Word. That fullness of grace and truth in Jesus overflows into the life of the Christian community continuously.

Verses 17-18 conclude the prologue with a sharp contrast between the Old Testament and the New Testament, between law and Gospel—a contrast which reasserts the supreme superiority of the Christ. No human being, not the greatest figures of Old Testament

9

faith, has ever had direct vision of God. Moses was refused the vision of God's face, for no one can see God's face and live (Exod. 33:20f.). But Jesus, the unique Son, in intimate relation to the Father, knows the invisible God. Jesus, the Word of God, the supreme revealer, makes known himself.

The Witness of the Baptist (1:19–34)

More than just a specific event which resulted in his condemnation
and death, the trial of Jesus becomes a metaphor which influences
the whole of the fourth gospel. To this end, Jesus is, at the very
start of his ministry, locked in contention with forces which question
his authority and negate his validity. Unable or unwilling to understand, they only hasten their own destruction by moving toward
his. For Jesus' trial is not an ordinary trial, but one in which the
defendant is accuser and the condemned already vindicated.
Throughout the gospel, many witnesses step forward to testify on
Jesus' behalf. John the Baptist is the first of these.

[19]*And this is the testimony of John, when the Jews sent priests and
Levites from Jerusalem to ask him, "Who are you?"* [20]*He confessed,
he did not deny, but confessed, "I am not the Christ."* [21]*And they
asked him, "What then? Are you Elijah?" He said, "I am not." "Are
you the prophet?" And he answered, "No."* [22]*They said to him then,
"Who are you? Let us have an answer for those who sent us. What
do you say about yourself?"* [23]*He said, "I am the voice of one crying
in the wilderness, 'Make straight the way of the Lord,' as the prophet
Isaiah said."*

[24]*Now they had been sent from the Pharisees.* [25]*They asked him,
"Then why are you baptizing, if you are neither the Christ, nor
Elijah, nor the prophet?"* [26]*John answered them, "I baptize with
water; but among you stands one whom you do not know,* [27]*even
he who comes after me, the thong of whose sandal I am not worthy
to untie."* [29]*This took place in Bethany beyond the Jordan, where
John was baptizing.*

With the appearance of John the Baptist, the public proclamation
of the good news begins. The fourth evangelist tells us little if
anything about him and his activity. He appears here first in the
Trans-Jordan, outside the land of Judea, perhaps signaling a sym-

bolic reentry into the promised land. No doubt the first readers of the gospel would have been familiar with New Testament, especially synoptic, traditions about the Baptist who came in the guise of the Old Testament prophets "preaching a baptism of repentance for the forgiveness of sins" (Mark 1:4); in fact, who was sent as herald to Israel to announce the coming of the savior. John, however, tells us nothing of this; even the account of Jesus' baptism, which in the synoptics marks the beginning of his public ministry, is presumed rather than described (1:32).

If then, in a certain sense, the fourth gospel downplays the person of the Baptist, it should no longer be surprising to us. Whether or not the evangelist was also interested in polemicizing against a Baptist sect known to his first century audience, which exalted John at the expense of Jesus, we have already been prepared by the prologue for John's understanding (1:6-8). The Baptist is presented as first witness to the light, first in a long line of witnesses reaching into the Christian community of our day and onward. Why someone is important is reexamined and reassessed by John in the light of Christ.

As the Word of God is Jesus, so, in a similar sense, the Baptist's word (his witness) about Jesus is who he is. Nor is this word apart from God, a mere human word.

At first the Baptist's word is largely negative. He was not himself the light. John presents this testimony in the context of a series of interrogations put to him by representatives of the Jews. For the fourth gospel, this term has a special meaning. The Jews usually refers to the ruling authorities in Jerusalem, who are consistently placed in opposition to Jesus. The usual distinctions among the groups that composed first-century Judaism and which are found in the synoptics are almost entirely absent from this gospel. This fact probably reflects the condition of late first-century Christianity. Judaism had by then become largely identified with the Pharisees organized under a central authority in Jerusalem and in active opposition to the emergent Christian Church. For John, the Pharisaic Judaism of his time symbolizes the world which, in rejecting the emissaries of the Christian faith, has in turn rejected Jesus. The struggle between Christian faith and the world, between belief in Jesus and rejection of Jesus, is historicized in the gospel as a bitter

12

struggle between Jesus and the Jews. John's dualistic perspective of all or nothing for Jesus allows him to speak of the Jews as an alien people even when it is Jews who are speaking or being referred to. So here it even appears that the Baptist is not also a Jew.

Asked who he is, and, presumably, what is the authority for his ministry, the Baptist replies with an emphatic and solemn denial, "I am not the Christ." Israel's hope for deliverance and for the inauguration by God of a final age of salvation (the *eschaton*) took many forms in first-century Judaism. Perhaps the most widespread was the expectation of the Messiah (Hebrew, *Mašiah;* Greek, *Christos*), the anointed king of David's line through whom God was to exalt his people. Although Jesus never claimed this title for himself and accepted it from others only with reluctance, it became among early Christians his primary title and quickly part of his proper name. Jesus may have avoided the title because of its close association with the establishment of a narrowly nationalistic and materialistic kingdom; after his death and resurrection, the notion of royal messiah underwent reinterpretation.

The Baptist further denies that he is any kind of messianic figure, even broadly speaking. He is not Elijah. Based upon the belief that the prophet Elijah did not die but was taken to heaven in a fiery chariot (2 Kings 2:11), postexilic Judaism held that Elijah was being kept in heaven until the day of the Lord. At that time, when Yahweh would make known his judgment and salvation decisively in the world, Elijah would be sent as a herald to Israel (Mal. 3:1-3; 4:5f.).

Nor is he the eschatological prophet. Based upon an interpretation of Deuteronomy 18:15-18, Judaism contained belief in a prophet like Moses, the Old Testament prophet without equal, who would be raised up in the last days. The New Testament identifies Jesus as this new Moses (Acts 3:22).

The Baptist completely removes himself from any messianic function. If the expectations are to be fulfilled, they are only to be fulfilled in Jesus. John's claim, in the words of Isaiah (40:3), is to be a "voice" whose testimony will prepare the way for God to come to his people. The Baptist has been called as the Word's first witness in the trial between light and darkness.

His very baptizing ministry is provisional as he himself is provisional. Hidden, waiting to be revealed, is the savior. In relation to the one who comes after him, the Baptist is completely self-effacing, declaring himself unworthy even to act the slave toward Jesus, "the thong of whose sandal I am not worthy to untie."

[29]The next day he saw Jesus coming toward him, and said, "Behold, the Lamb of God, who takes away the sin of the world! [30]This is he of whom I said, 'After me comes a man who ranks before me, for he was before me.' [31]I myself did not know him; but for this I came baptizing with water, that he might be revealed to Israel." [32]And John bore witness, "I saw the Spirit descend as a dove from heaven, and it remained on him. [33]I myself did not know him; but he who sent me to baptize with water said to me, 'He on whom you see the Spirit descend and remain, this is he who baptizes with the Holy Spirit.' [34]And I have seen and have borne witness that this is the Son of God."

A second scene, as stylized as the first, is set by the evangelist on the following day (presumably the day after Jesus' baptism). The Baptist now delivers his major positive testimony. Having denied that he was the light, he now gives direct witness to the light (1:8), this time, in the presence of Jesus. Again, the Baptist reaches into the Old Testament: Behold, Jesus, the lamb of God, who will remove the sinful condition of the world. The reference here is not to particular individual sins but to the world as alienated from and antagonistic to the Father. To this wounded humanity, estranged from God, comes the lamb. A multiplicity of allusions may underlie this title spoken by the Baptist.

In the Book of Isaiah (in that section which comes from a later prophet usually identified as Deutero-Isaiah) there is an enigmatic figure identified as the servant of Yahweh (42:1-4; 49:1-6; 50:4-9; 52:13-53). Chapter 53 describes the sufferings of this servant-figure who takes upon himself the "sins of many" and whose life and suffering are understood as an expiatory sacrifice. In his affliction, he is like "a lamb that is led to the slaughter, and like a sheep that before its shearers is dumb" (53:7). This text is directly applied to Jesus by the early community in Acts 8:32. The gospel may well be identifying Jesus with the suffering servant of Yahweh.

Again, it is difficult to avoid paschal symbolism in the interpretation of the lamb of God, especially considering the importance of

14

such symbolism in the fourth gospel. Is Jesus being identified with the paschal lamb slain for the Jewish Passover meal celebrating the exodus from Egypt? Though the Jewish paschal lamb was not considered sacrificial, Christians would have reinterpreted the new Passover in the light of Jesus' sacrificial death through which the world's sin was removed. In Paul this new interpretation is already present: "Christ our paschal lamb has been sacrificed" (1 Cor. 5:7).

Whether servant or pasch, or perhaps both, underlie the lamb of God symbol, both highlight the scandal of the incarnation, the subjection of the Word to the fragility of human life and to the renunciation of earthly power. The lamb expresses being-unto-death, like us but with a purpose and an authority beyond ours.

Paradoxically, a completely different and startling image may stand behind the lamb of God: that of a victorious conquering lamb who will take away sin by destroying evil in the world; who will come in power rather than silent renunciation. Such a figure is present in Jewish apocalyptic expectation, a tradition of thought and literature which expected the age of salvation to come violently and cataclysmically in a decisive struggle between good and evil. This picture of the victorious lamb appears in New Testament apocalyptic thought in the Book of Revelation (7:17; 17:14).

Is it possible that John means to invoke all three images, servant, sacrifice, and conquerer, and, thereby, expose the ultimate paradox of Jesus, the lamb of God, in whose death is our life?

The Baptist continues his witness with a statement of the preexistence of Jesus, applying specifically to Jesus the testimony already introduced in the prologue (1:15). Contained in the acknowledgement is clear evidence of the superiority of Jesus to John the Baptist. Both John and his baptism have no independent importance, but exist to reveal the Messiah to Israel. This Messiah was revealed to John in a vision much like that described at the baptism of Jesus in the synoptics. Like the servant of Yahweh, Jesus is invested with the Spirit of God (Isa. 42:1)—that same Spirit which would be poured out upon Israel in the messianic age (Joel 2:28f.). It is now Jesus' permanent possession; through him, after his death and resurrection, to be poured out on humankind. Jesus, the new Israel, the *eschaton* in the midst of this world, will remake the world by a new baptism through the Holy Spirit. Jesus stands revealed at the conclusion of this first testimony of the Baptist as the "Son of God."

It would be fitting here to see an echo of the heavenly voice in the synoptic scene of Jesus' baptism: "Thou art my beloved son; with thee I am well pleased" (Mark 1:11). There Jesus stands portrayed as the Lord's royal anointed and prophetic servant (recalling Ps. 2:7 and Isa. 42:1 respectively). Jesus is commissioned as servant-Messiah to Israel. The fourth gospel can invest this title with the deepest significance. Jesus is the unique son of God, one with the Father in substance as well as purpose.

The Witness of the Disciples (1:34–51)

Like the previous scenes with John the Baptist, John's account of the calling of the first disciples is stripped to bare theological bones. He has telescoped into a few short days an understanding of and a faith in Jesus (reaching its conclusion in the first Cana miracle), which, in the synoptics, is spread throughout the period of his ministry. For John, Jesus is recognized for what he is at the very start, for it is the presence of the risen Lord in the midst of his followers that illumines and interprets all the events of his earthly ministry.

There is little point in attempting to reconcile or contrast Johannine and synoptic reports. Though elements of the traditions recorded in the synoptics are contained in the fourth gospel, they are entirely subsidiary and subordinate to the evangelist's christological interests. (So, though John details the name change of Simon to Cephas/Peter in v. 42, there is no reason or explanation given for the name.)

This section, as well as the following episode at Cana (2:1-11), reintroduces into the gospel the motif of Jesus as true wisdom. Wisdom comes among humans in search of disciples, crying aloud in the streets her invitation and instruction (Prov. 1:20f.). Wisdom brings happiness and life to those who accept her instruction, who dwell beside her "watching daily at [her] gates, waiting beside [her] doors" (Prov. 8:34f.). She is available to those who love her; she "goes about seeking those worthy of her, and she graciously appears to them in their paths, and meets them in every thought" (Wisd. of Sol. 6:15f.). The man who finds and lives with wisdom is loved by God (Wisd. of Sol. 7:28).

In a similar manner, Jesus confronts his disciples. He is easily available to those who seek him. Where he dwells, his disciples dwell. His presence and instruction open the eyes of disciples to his true nature. At Cana Jesus provides the eschatological wine as wisdom prepares the wine of her instruction at her banquet (Prov. 9:1f.).

17

³⁵*The next day again John was standing with two of his disciples;* ³⁶*and he looked at Jesus as he walked, and said, "Behold, the Lamb of God!"* ³⁷*The two disciples heard him say this, and they followed Jesus.* ³⁸*Jesus turned, and saw them following, and said to them, "What do you seek?" And they said to him, "Rabbi" (which means Teacher) "where are you staying?"* ³⁹*He said to them, "Come and see." They came and saw where he was staying; and they stayed with him that day, for it was about the tenth hour.* ⁴⁰*One of the two who heard John speak, and followed him, was Andrew, Simon Peter's brother.* ⁴¹*He first found his brother Simon, and said to him, "We have found the Messiah" (which means Christ).* ⁴²*He brought him to Jesus. Jesus looked at him, and said, "So you are Simon the son of John? You shall be called Cephas" (which means Peter).*

The witness of John the Baptist to Jesus, the eschatological bringer of salvation, at once marks the end of the Baptist's role for Israel and the beginning of the world's renewal. The history of salvation, contained from all eternity in the Word, is interlocked with the history of the Word. From John himself Jesus receives his first disciples. In two greatly condensed and stylized scenes (vv. 35-42; 43-51), the fourth gospel presents us with a summary paradigm of Christian discipleship. Who Jesus is becomes known through the testimony of those who follow him.

The image of "following Jesus" throughout all four gospels carries us deeply into the significance of discipleship. If discipleship goes hand in hand with deepening insight into the reality of Jesus and the demands of his own mission, it, at the same time, finds neither rest nor comfort in spiritual enlightenment. The basis of discipleship is neither privileged gnosis nor solipsistic peace. Rather, it is a call to life after and in the manner of Jesus. It does not extinguish individual uniqueness; on the contrary, that uniqueness itself is part of the responsibility of discipleship. The disciple is not a copy of Jesus but an original expression of the enfleshed Word whose call to discipleship and whose own confrontation with the world lays down the cost of that expression. The follower of Christ is not xeroxed but created.

The synoptics make clear the urgent and difficult claims made by Jesus of those who would follow him. They, in fact, must be prepared to recenter their lives and cast off their old securities (Matt. 8:19-

22; Luke 9:57-62). To follow Jesus leads necessarily to the mystery of his cross in our lives, the mystery of our own life and death which we are called to accept: "If any man would come after me, let him deny himself and take up his cross daily and follow me." (Luke 9:23; cp. Matt. 16:24 and Mark 8:34. Luke's version of this saying emphasizes the constant daily activity of discipleship.)

The first words spoken by Jesus in the fourth gospel are deceptive in their simplicity. "Jesus turned, and saw them following, and said to them, 'What do you seek?' " Ostensibly addressed to the Baptist's disciples, they may well be addressed to every reader of the fourth gospel, to everyone who turns to Jesus. The question resonates at the deepest level of human desire and need. Addressed at this level, the disciples reply for all those who seek God. Jesus is confessed as Rabbi (a Hebrew word literally meaning "my great one"), the teacher, from whom the disciples will learn the answer to Jesus' question as well as to their search. In this light, the reply of the disciples, "Where are you staying?" is hardly a request for Jesus' street address. Rather, it expresses a desire to share Jesus' teaching and life. The Christian believer, the one who has come and seen, stays with Jesus (John uses the Greek verb *menein*, "to dwell," "to abide"). Disciple and master are in some sense one. This theme, of abiding, is developed extensively throughout the gospel (see especially chapter 15).

Staying with Jesus brings a deepening of the function of discipleship and a further understanding of the nature of Jesus. As Andrew to his brother Simon, the disciple makes Jesus known to others through ever-compelling testimony: "We have found the Messiah," God's anointed regent.

[43]*The next day Jesus decided to go to Galilee. And he found Philip and said to him, "Follow me."* [44]*Now Philip was from Bethsaida, the city of Andrew and Peter.* [45]*Philip found Nathanael, and said to him, "We have found him of whom Moses in the law and also the prophets wrote, Jesus of Nazareth, the son of Joseph."*
[46]*Nathanael said to him, "Can anything good come out of Nazareth?" Philip said to him, "Come and see."* [47]*Jesus saw Nathanael coming to him and said of him, "Behold, an Israelite indeed, in whom is no guile!"* [48]*Nathanael said to him, "How do you know me?" Jesus answered him, "Before Philip called you, when you were under the*

fig tree, I saw you." [49]*Nathanael answered him, "Rabbi, you are the Son of God! You are the King of Israel!"* [50]*Jesus answered him, "Because I said to you, I saw you under the fig tree, do you believe? You shall see greater things than these."* [51]*And he said to him, "Truly, truly, I say to you, you will see heaven opened and the angel of God ascending and descending upon the Son of man."*

Verses 43-51 conclude the account of the calling of the first disciples and expand the list of christological testimonies made in response to that calling. They in turn look forward immediately to the "greater things" which the disciples will see in Cana of Galilee (2:1-11). There John will describe the first sign performed by Jesus through which he manifested his glory. The events of the Baptist, the disciples, and Cana are organized in a progressive chronological sequence extended over a period of six days (vv. 29, 35, 43; 2:1), culminating in the scene at Cana "on the third day" (2:1). This last temporal identification may well be a symbolic reference to the resurrection as Cana itself foreshadows that event. That Jesus was raised from the dead on the third day is an element of the earliest Christian preaching (Acts 10:40).

This scene of the calling of the disciples dramatizes more emphatically the superhuman presence of Jesus—a presumption which runs throughout the gospel. Jesus, as human, is always more than human in the commanding force of his person as well as in his knowledge of people and events. To Philip a simple personal command from Jesus is sufficient; Philip follows. With Nathanael it is evident that Jesus sees not only into the hearts of all but also knows their actions when they are away from him. It is, after all, Jesus as the risen Lord who dominates the gospels of John and colors every description of him.

In a sense, the context of the fourth gospel is a total irony: The risen Jesus, the Jesus living and present to the evangelist, is progressively revealed in his portrait of the historic Jesus. However, it is not only the eye of faith that sees the risen Lord in every scene of the gospel and understands the deeper significance of surface events and speech. If Jesus, like all humans, can be identified by a certain place, by a certain family ("Jesus of Nazareth, the son of Joseph"), Philip can yet know him as the one "of whom Moses in the law and also the prophets wrote." He is the fulfillment of the entire Old Testament. At the same time, this "son of Joseph" is immeasurably more than this as the prologue of the gospel has already made clear.

Nathanael can disparagingly ask if anything of significance can come out of an unimportant village like Nazareth. Yet, in symbolic contrast to the Jews, he is a genuine Israelite and can finally confess Jesus as Son of God and king of Israel, two titles which are equivalent to Messiah. The readers of the gospel may themselves see a deeper mystery in the divine Sonship of this man of Nazareth.

This section is concluded by a solemn declaration of Jesus introduced by "Amen, amen," which is characteristic of Jesus' speech in the fourth gospel and assertative of the divine authority behind his pronouncements. A vision is promised to Nathanael similar to the vision of Jacob described in Genesis 28:12 of angels ascending and descending on a ladder between heaven and earth. Jesus, as the Son of man, takes the place of this ladder and himself becomes the means of intersection between heaven and earth, God and humanity. Jesus, the incarnate Word, through the resurrection is the locus of divine glory.

The title "Son of man" is characteristic of Jesus' self-designation in the synoptic gospels. At times it may mean no more than simply "person" and may be used as an equivalent of the personal pronoun "I." At other times, it may designate a definite figure: either one who suffers or who will come in glory at the end of the world. The figure of the Son of man seems to have its basis in Jewish apocalyptic expectation of a mysterious glorious savior (Dan. 7:13. The non-biblical Book of Enoch describes this Son of man as preexistent, hidden with God until the end of the world.). As Jesus used the title it underwent a reinterpretation. In the gospel of John, the Son of man is usually associated with future glory. It is that vision of future glory that Jesus may well be promising to Nathanael here, a future glory to be prefigured at Cana.

The First Miracle at Cana (2:1–12)

The synoptic gospels record many miracles of Jesus. In distinction, the fourth gospel recounts only seven, all of them contained in the first eleven chapters: the changing of the water into wine (2:1-11); the healing of the official's son (4:46-54); the healing of the man at the pool of Beth-zatha (5:2-9); the feeding of the five thousand (6:4-13); the walking on the water (6:16-21); the curing of the man born blind (9:1-7); the raising of Lazarus (11:2-44). All of these can be paralleled in some form or other by the synoptic miracle stories except for the changing of the water into wine. Unlike the synoptic stories, however, which generally relate to the coming of the kingdom of God and to Jesus' victory over the devil, the Johannine miracles are specifically christological in intention: they reveal something about the person of Jesus. As "signs" (the Greek word, *sēmeia*, is the word the evangelist uses to describe the miracles), they say more than they are. To the believer they describe two planes of reality: physical and spiritual or perhaps better, past and present. On one hand, the miracles acknowledge Jesus, the wonder-worker invested with divine power, who throughout his earthly ministry commanded physical reality. On the other hand, they are epiphanies of the risen Lord, signs anticipating the ultimate truth about Jesus which will only be fully revealed when his hour has been achieved. For John, the miracles further serve to stress the continuity between the earthly and risen Jesus: who he is now revealed as who he was also then, the incarnate Word, full of grace and truth.

At the first sign of Jesus at Cana in Galilee, John presents us with the charter that underwrites all of his signs: he "manifested his glory; and his disciples believed in him" (2:11).

[1]On the third day there was a marriage at Cana in Galilee, and the mother of Jesus was there; [2]Jesus was also invited to the marriage, with his disciples. [3]When the wine failed, the mother of Jesus said to him, "They have no wine." [4]And Jesus said to her, "O woman,

22

what have you to do with me? My hour has not yet come." [5]*His mother said to the servants, "Do whatever he tells you."* [6]*Now six stone jars were standing there, for the Jewish rites of purification, each holding twenty or thirty gallons.* [7]*Jesus said to them, "Fill the jars with water." And they filled them up to the brim.* [8]*He said to them, "Now draw some out, and take it to the steward of the feast." So they took it.* [9]*When the steward of the feast tasted the water now become wine, and did not know where it came from (though the servants who had drawn the water knew), the steward of the feast called the bridegroom* [10]*and said to him, "Every man serves the good wine first; and when men have drunk freely, then the poor wine; but you have kept the good wine until now."* [11]*This, the first of his signs, Jesus did at Cana in Galilee, and manifested his glory; and his disciples believed in him.*

[12]*After this he went down to Capernaum with his mother and his brothers and his disciples; and there they stayed for a few days.*

This incident is deceptive in its apparent simplicity, almost in its naiveté. Jesus, his mother, and his disciples are guests at a Jewish wedding feast. The wine runs out, then as now, a blow from which parties rarely recover. The mother of Jesus (concerned to relieve the embarassment of her hosts?) seems to request of her son some miraculous remedy for the situation. After an initial, apparently harsh refusal, Jesus complies with his mother's request (which she obviously expects him to do all along). In short order, Jesus produces an enormous amount of wine (between 120 and 180 gallons, which alone could keep the party going for another week), and of such quality that the steward of the feast is amazed. When the narrative is described in the above fashion, which admittedly introduces into the text a number of psychological connectives which are lacking, the question can easily be asked, how has this miracle manifested Jesus' glory and elevated the faith of his disciples? For John, the significance of Cana is to be found neither in the mere appearance of Jesus as a powerful worker of wonders nor in a banal sentimentalizing of motives and actions centered around a human mother/son relationship. It is at a properly christological level that Cana speaks even now to the reader of the gospel.

The setting of the miracle, at a wedding, is suggestive. In the Old Testament the image of marriage between Yahweh and Israel is

23

often used to describe the covenant relationship (e.g. Hos. 2:7f.). This image is extended to the messianic age, the time of completion and vindication, when God will rejoice over Israel "as the bridegroom rejoices over the bride" (Isa. 62:2-5). This imagery is present also in the New Testament. A particularly vivid and pertinent example dramatizing messianic completion appears in the Book of Revelation: "Hallelujah! For the Lord our God the Almighty reigns./ Let us rejoice and exult and give him the glory,/ for the marriage of the Lamb has come,/ and the Bride has made herself ready" (19:6-7).

The eschatological intention of the Cana story is deepened by the nature of the miracle itself: the provision of wine in great abundance. To refer again to the Old Testament, wine is symbolically connected with portrayals of the final days. On the one hand, God visits punishment on a sinful people by depriving them of wine (Deut. 28:39). The day of the Lord which is seen by the prophet Amos as a time of destruction and retribution will be a day of wailing in the vineyards whose wine the house of Israel shall never drink (5:17,11). On the other hand, the abundance of wine is a promise of happiness and deliverance. Amos's vision of the restoration of Israel sees a land where "mountains shall drip sweet wine, and all the hills shall flow with it" (9:13). Isaiah announces a "feast of wine" to be made for all peoples on Mount Zion (25:6).

With this background in mind, the miracle at Cana is the miracle of the messianic wine, the good wine which as the steward comments, has been held back "until now," the abundant wine to be poured out in the *eschaton*. The glory of God hidden in the incarnation of the Word and to be made fully visible when the hour of Jesus has been accomplished is prefigured in the sign of the eschatological wine. At the same time, the end of the old dispensation is graphically conveyed. The time of Judaism is over; its major institutions and figures are replaced by Jesus himself. This theme, already evident in the prologue and in chapter 1, will be continued throughout the gospel. At Cana, the water changed by Jesus was water set aside for Jewish purificatory washings, religious rituals now rendered meaningless by the presence of Jesus who is the bringer of the messianic wine. He himself will purify a new people of God. In this light, the request made of Jesus by his mother is both sad and cutting: "They have no wine." They have only water.

24

A saying of Jesus recorded in the synoptics is especially pertinent here: "And no one puts new wine into old wineskins; if he does, the wine will burst the skins, and the wine is lost, and so are the skins; but new wine is for fresh skins" (Mark 2:22; see also Matt. 9:17; Luke 5:37-39). Judaism cannot contain the Christ.

Read as part of the eschatological significance of the Cana miracle, the conversation between Jesus and his mother is neither inconsistent nor enigmatic. Both Jesus and his mother stand in the narrative as figures of the final age. Her request arises from profound spiritual need, at once a statement of the impoverishment of the old covenant and a petition for the new messianic wine, for the fulfillment of the hopes of Israel. It may well be that she symbolizes that faithful remnant of Israel, described in the Old Testament, who waited in humble and loyal expectation for the coming of God's deliverance. A similar though deepened representative role is given Jesus' mother in 19:26. There at the foot of the cross she appears as a figure of the Church, the new people of God. In both instances (2:4; 19:26), Jesus addresses his mother as "woman." Though his usual mode of address to women in the gospel, used of his mother it may well be a title expressing her eschatological role. (In chap. 12 of the Book of Revelation the Christian Church is symbolized by the image of "woman.")

In any case, the response of Jesus is neither harsh nor rebuking. Rather, it is a denial of involvement in her concern. A common Semitic expression underlies Jesus' answer (literally translated, "What to me and to you?") which indicates some separation of interest between two parties. The RSV's "What have you to do with me?" might be more clearly expressed by "What has this concern of yours to do with me?" Jesus understands the request of his mother for what it is, yet is has no claim on him. His times have been set by another, the Father, and no agency whatsoever can alter or supersede those commands. At present, his mother's request cannot concern him for his "hour has not yet come." Throughout the gospel the hour of Jesus is the hour of his passion and glorification when he will reascend to the Father. It is only then, when Jesus is glorified, that the time of salvation will be fulfilled. This hour is neither known to nor controllable by humans.

Understanding all too well the response of Jesus, his mother, as faithful Israel, can only submit to the mysterious will of God. Her

injunction to the servants, "Do whatever he tells you," recalls the
submission of Pharoah and all Egypt to Joseph in the Book of Genesis. When the people cry to Pharoah for bread because famine has
come upon the land, he tells them, "what he (Joseph) says to you,
do" (Gen. 41:55).

In response, Jesus performs a sign filled with promise, promise
that the yearnings of his mother and of the faithful of Israel will be
fulfilled in the new age to be inaugurated by his death, resurrection,
and ascension. Then he himself will purify his people; the symbol
of the messianic wine will be continued in the Eucharistic wine
when the living sacrament dwells in his Church.

The Cleansing of the Temple (2:13–25)

The incident of the cleansing of the Jerusalem temple by Jesus is found in all four gospels. Some understanding of the significance of this dramatic action of Jesus' ministry in the synoptic gospels will help to highlight the fourth gospel's account of the episode. It will also serve as an example of the way John consistently uses and transforms elements found in the synoptic tradition in order to bring out their christological significance. That same tendency, at work in John's portrayal of the role of the Baptist, and of the calling of the disciples, as well as of the "new wine (which) is for fresh skins" of Cana, turns his cleansing narrative into a christological sign.

The synoptics place the episode of the cleansing of the temple during the culminating days of the ministry of Jesus, after his entry into Jerusalem where he is to prepare for his passion (Mark 11:15-19; Matt. 21:10-17; Luke 19:45-48). For Mark the account seems to center on Jesus as the Messiah who comes to the temple to begin the fulfillment of Isaiah's prophecy (56:7) that the purified and spiritualized temple of the eschatological days would become "a house of prayer for all peoples," Gentile as well as Jew. For Matthew, on the other hand, Jesus comes as messianic king to bring an end to the temple cult. The eschatological age is properly the age of the Christian Church. Already in the course of his ministry, Jesus announces (Matthew alone reports these words) that "something greater than the temple" is in the midst of the Jews (Matt. 12:6). In the Lukan gospel, Jesus cleanses the temple as a stage in the historical process of salvation. Christ's death and resurrection will definitively establish the time of the Church and at once look to the parousia, the final coming of Christ in glory.

John's account of the cleansing is not so much a revision of as a meditation upon the event. In this gospel, the incident takes place at the beginning of Jesus' public ministry rather than at the end. It is from the beginning then that Jesus makes himself known as the master of Judaism as well as its consummation. The "Word was

27

God" and became incarnate in a man; the divine promise dwells in and fulfills itself in the person of Jesus of Nazareth. Divine authority resides only in Jesus; in the face of this authority, no institution of the old law, however great, can stand. In John's account of the cleansing then, Jesus decisively reveals himself as the fulfillment of the religion of Israel. Its institutions are not to be reformed and purified but replaced. Having looked upon the face of God, Judaism must die.

This theme of replacement is prominently developed throughout chapters 1–4. Previous to the cleansing of the temple, John had already introduced Jesus as the counterpoint to the ancient covenant. From the prologue we learn of the divine credentials of Jesus who, as incarnate Word, true wisdom dwelling among humans, is himself the tabernacle of God, the divine presence on earth. As the one true revealer of the Father, he surpasses both Moses and the Torah. John the Baptist himself gives testimony to Jesus as the eschatological redeemer whose presence already contains the death of the old order. His disciples recognize and confess him as the hope of Israel; through their vision of his glory at Cana they believe in him as dispenser of the messianic wine. For John, the truth about Jesus, which is only finally revealed in his glorification, is, in some sense, present throughout all the events of his life.

The incidents that follow the temple cleansing both proceed from it and refer back to it. Jesus lectures Nicodemus, a representative of Pharisaic Judaism, on the necessity of rebirth into the kingdom of God through water and the Spirit and on the meaning of eternal life (3:1-21). If the Jerusalem temple is no longer valid, certainly the teachers of Judaism no longer have standing. John the Baptist completes his testimony to Jesus as the perfect fulfillment of his own prophecies (3:22-36). To the Samaritan woman at the well, Jesus, the bearer of living water, reveals the nature of true worship "in spirit and in truth" (4:1-42). To the Gentile official Jesus shows himself as the bringer of life (4:46-54).

[13]*The Passover of the Jews was at hand, and Jesus went up to Jerusalem.* [14]*In the temple he found those who were selling oxen and sheep and pigeons, and the money-changers at their business.* [15]*And making a whip of cords, he drove them all, with the sheep and the oxen, out of the temple; and he poured out the coins*

of the money-changers and overturned their tables. [16]And he told those who sold the pigeons, "Take these things away; you shall not make my Father's house a house of trade." [17]His disciples remembered that it was written, "Zeal for thy house will consume me." [18]The Jews then said to him, "What sign have you to show us for doing this?" [19]Jesus answered them, "Destroy this temple and in three days I will raise it up." [20]The Jews then said, "It has taken forty-six years to build this temple, and you will raise it up in three days?" [21]But he spoke of the temple of his body. [22]When therefore he was raised from the dead, his disciples remembered that he had said this; and they believed the scripture and the word which Jesus had spoken.

[23]Now when he was in Jerusalem at the Passover feast, many believed in his name when they saw the signs he did; [24]but Jesus did not trust himself to them, [25]because he knew all men and needed no one to bear witness of man; for he himself knew what was in man.

Few institutions were closer to the heart of Judaism than the Jerusalem temple. Its origins, as recorded in the religious traditions of Israel, reached back to its very foundation as the people of God. The temple itself was heir to the tabernacle, the portable desert sanctuary which the Hebrews carried with them in their desert wanderings and which housed the ark of the covenant. The ark, which contained the stone tablets of the law given Moses by God, was itself the seat of Yahweh upon which, between the figures of the cherubim, the invisible God was enthroned.

As the Book of Exodus records, Yahweh himself commanded the building of the sanctuary and its ritual apparatus, even to drafting detailed architectural plans (Exod. 25:8-9). By means of this sanctuary, it was believed, God would reside in the midst of his people during the desert sojourn, at once revealing himself and cloaking himself in his glory and in the cloud. After the desert period, the sanctuary with the ark of the covenant was, during the initial days in Canaan, the sign of unity and the rallying point of the twelve tribes.

Tabernacle began to cede to temple when David, following God's instruction, had the ark transferred to Jerusalem which became the capital city of his kingdom. By one stroke, Jerusalem became the national as well as the religious center of the tribes. The construction of the temple by Solomon—again at God's command (2 Sam. 7)—brought this movement to completion. Eventually the entire legitimate sacrificial cult of Israel was centralized in the temple. Both practical center of worship and religious symbol par excellence, the temple stood in the midst of Israel invested with all the prerogatives of the tabernacle. It was the house of God, an earthly counterpart of the heavenly sanctuary (Exod. 25:40). It was here that God made his presence visibly manifest by his glory in the midst of the cloud (1 Kings 8:10-13). He dwells in the temple by his name (1 Kings 7:16-21).

The fact that the temple edifice itself was rebuilt three times well attests to the importance of its material presence within the religion of Israel. At the time of Christ, the third temple begun by Herod the Great (ca. A.D. 20) was still in the process of construction. Perhaps even more significant is its importance as a quasi-archetypal religious symbol. Within the religion of Israel itself there was sharp protest against excessive attachment to the material temple and a turning toward greater spiritualization of religious practice. However, in one instance among many, it is interesting to find that a prophet who could make such protest (Isa. 66:1f.), could also couch his universalistic vision of the age of salvation in strong cultic imagery: "and they [Gentiles] shall bring all your [Israel's] brethren from all the nations as an offering to the LORD . . . to my holy mountain Jerusalem, says the LORD, just as the Israelites bring their cereal offering in a clean vessel to the house of the LORD. And some of them also I will take for priests and for Levites, says the LORD" (Isa. 66:20-21).

It is only within this context of the sacrality of the Jerusalem temple that Jesus' action can be adequately understood and appreciated within the perspective of the gospel. The action of Jesus is awesome, for it is not directed to the reformation of a decadent system of worship; nor is it simply a violent protest against the superstitious security bred by the possession of a religious talisman. Rather, Jesus announces without reservations the extinction of a way of thought and life, which was his as well as Israel's. The temple is of God; it is his "Father's house"; its material presence consecrated the city of Jerusalem to which, as a Jew, he went in ritual pilgrimage to celebrate the Passover. In a certain sense, the incident of the cleansing of the temple confronts every reader of the gospel with the question, "In the presence of Jesus, what do we hold onto?"

Entering the outer court of the temple, Jesus finds the normal commercial business of the temple being conducted. Whether there were abuses or not in the temple trade is not the point of the account. Judaism, indeed, would have been a unique religion if there were not. On the contrary, the trade itself was necessary to the cultic life of the temple, making conveniently available to the worshiper, who sometimes travelled long distances, the animals for sacrifice. Jesus' response is not one of surprise and shock at a degraded worship but rather a sign of God.

Acting with great authority (only John mentions the whip of cords), Jesus drives *all* the elements of the cult out of the temple, making the normal business of sacrifice impossible. There is no reference in John's account (as there is in the synoptics) to the effect that the temple will become a future house of prayer or that the temple has become a den of robbers which must be reformed. Rather, Jesus declares, "you shall not make my Father's house a house of trade," which seems to allude to the writings of the prophet Zechariah. The day of the Lord will bring to an end (not bring about a reform of) temple commerce so that "there shall no longer be a trader in the house of the LORD of hosts on that day" (14:21). (This alone, one would think, should be sufficient incentive for all believers to pray for the *eschaton*.) Jesus' action is an announcement that that day has dawned. In retrospect, his disciples see in the cleansing a direct relation to Jesus' death, for he appears as the fulfillment of what was predicted in the Psalms (69:9): "Zeal for thy house will consume me." This psalm, which speaks of the righteous sufferer, was applied by the early Church to the passion of Christ (Acts 1:20; Rom. 15:3).

In the dialogue that follows the cleansing, Jesus speaks with even greater authority and boldly interprets his action. He now comes into open conflict with the Jews, representatives of the old order, defenders of the ancient faith, reflections of the world's rejection. Explicitly hostile, they understand that Jesus has attacked the temple and what it represents, and demand a sign as warrant for his action. This sign is far from John's understanding of Jesus' miracles. Of course, no sign is given: Jesus does not perform tricks on request, feeding humans' silly passion for miracles. Nor can any sign be given that those in darkness would see: "He came to his own home, and his own people received him not" (1:11).

Instead, Jesus replies with a cryptic statement which is immediately misunderstood by the Jews: "Destroy this temple, and in three days I will raise it up." Jesus is speaking of himself, the new temple, the living presence of God among his people. So that there should be no doubt for every reader of the gospel, John highlights the meaning of Jesus's statement, "But he spoke of the temple of his body . . . " By cleansing the temple, Jesus has already proclaimed that God's *eschaton* has struck down the old worship. Hereafter the only temple is Jesus glorified. The reply of the Jews (incredulous? mocking?) understands Jesus only on the level of the superficially visible, the narrowly rational. To rebuild in three days what it took forty-six years to build! Impossible! The irony of the scene will be repeated again and again throughout the gospel, an irony based on irreconcilable opposition between light and darkness. Those who are of the light recognize the light. Others demand signs and wonders to coerce their understanding and belief. Distracted from the presence of Jesus by their demands, their expectations, their categories, they lose him in the miracle.

The Meeting with Nicodemus (3:1–21)

Chapter 3 introduces us to a discourse of Jesus, the first of many to be delivered throughout the gospel. Through them Jesus speaks his revelation, often as interpretations prompted by some previous situation or sign. In essence, they are self-commentaries, words of God's incarnate Word. Though longer discourse is not absent from the synoptic gospels, the teaching of Jesus is characteristically couched in parables and epigrams. John, on the contrary, shows us a Jesus who speaks in solemn and hieratic monologues whose tone blends well with the transcendent character of Jesus consistent throughout the gospel: the risen Lord walks the earth.

The occasion for this first discourse is a visit to Jesus by one Nicodemus whose credits read as if they came out of the Jerusalem *Who's Who:* a member of the influential religious party, the Pharisees; a member of the Jerusalem ruling body, the Sanhedrin; a teacher of Israel. Impressed by the signs Jesus performed while he was in Jerusalem (2:23), Nicodemus is obviously well-disposed to Jesus as a teacher who has God's approval. (John, of course, does not describe these signs. Within the scheme of his gospel, Jesus' second sign occurs in chap. 4.) If Nicodemus is well-disposed toward Jesus, the episode makes it clear that Jesus is not greatly impressed by Nicodemus. In fact, he seems to represent a kind of in between faith motivated by miracles like the faith of those in Jerusalem to whom "Jesus did not trust himself" (2:24). A step ahead of the Jews who hostilely reject Jesus, Nicodemus as yet belongs too much to himself and to his world to profess the all-or-nothing belief of the disciples. Consequently, as part of the darkness, he comes "by night" into the presence of Jesus, the light. Nor is he able to understand the words of Jesus.

Recalling that the Judaism of John's time represented primarily the triumph of Pharisaism, we might also find in this scene a conversation between Church and synagogue.

33

¹Now there was a man of the Pharisees, named Nicodemus, a ruler of the Jews. ²This man came to Jesus by night and said to him, "Rabbi, we know that you are a teacher come from God; for no one can do these signs that you do, unless God is with him." ³Jesus answered him, "Truly, truly, I say to you, unless one is born anew, he cannot see the kingdom of God." ⁴Nicodemus said to him, "How can a man be born when he is old? Can he enter a second time into his mother's womb and be born?" ⁵Jesus answered, "Truly, truly, I say to you, unless one is born of water and the Spirit, he cannot enter the kingdom of God. ⁶That which is born of the flesh is flesh, and that which is born of the Spirit is spirit. ⁷Do not marvel that I said to you, 'You must be born anew.' ⁸The wind blows where it wills, and you hear the sound of it, but you do not know whence it comes or whither it goes; so it is with everyone who is born of the Spirit."

As is so often the case in the Johannine gospel, this dialogue between Jesus and Nicodemus develops by means of misunderstanding. Jesus speaks at one level of reality, revealing intimate knowledge of God; he is heard and understood (misunderstood) at another level determined by the self-limitations of his hearers. As in this conversation, the conflict of interpretations is not so much of spiritual vs. materialistic understandings as it is of Spirit vs. flesh.

As Jesus' answer seems to indicate, Nicodemus has come to him with a query about conditions for entrance into the kingdom of God. The phrase "kingdom of God" or "kingdom of heaven," common in the synoptics, appears only twice in the fourth gospel, both of them in this scene. In Jewish eschatological thought, the notion of the kingdom takes on many forms. Underlying them all, however, is the expectation that God, the ruler of the world, will some day definitively and universally manifest his sovereignty. As it is usually developed in the apocalyptic literature, the kingdom will establish a permanent era of peace and prosperity after a final battle between the armies of good and evil and the complete destruction of the power of the devil. In the synoptic gospels, Jesus' teaching centers upon the kingdom of God, and the mystery of its coming is intimately associated with his words and works. The casting out of devils, especially, is visible evidence of the fact that Satan's power over the world has been broken. As Jesus declares, "If it is by the finger of

God that I cast out demons, then the kingdom of God has come upon you" (Luke 11:20). Though the kingdom is a present reality in the ministry of Jesus, its ultimate victorious realization is future. The synoptics present side by side these two aspects of Jesus' thought on the kingdom, on the one hand a realized eschatology, on the other a futuristic eschatology. In both cases, the entrance requirements of this kingdom are based upon acceptance or rejection of Jesus. Nor can it be coerced or hastened by humans; it is, in fact, God's miracle of salvation.

The imagery of the kingdom of God plays no real role in the fourth gospel; rather, John focuses on the gift of eternal life and the divine miracle of rebirth. The prologue has already prepared us to hear Jesus' answer to Nicodemus. We are reborn "not of blood nor of the will of the flesh nor of the will of man, but of God" (1:13). To experience this kingdom is not dependent upon membership in the people of Israel or upon the the proper performance of Torah or, in fact, upon any human activity. With solemn authority, Jesus informs Nicodemus that one must be born anew. The Greek word that the RSV translates "anew," *anōthen*, can mean both "anew," or "again," and "from above." Both of these meanings should probably be understood in Jesus' statement. Rebirth is from above as human life is touched and transformed by God's power. Nicodemus's reply is almost too crude in its misunderstanding: Can a person "enter a second time into his mother's womb and be born?" It is not that Nicodemus is hopelessly befuddled because he forgot the double meaning of the word used by Jesus or that he is stupid. Rather, his reply dramatizes the condition of humans apart from God. Two completely different and irreconcilable orders of reality are in question here and, because of that, two distinct unbridgeable modes of understanding: flesh and Spirit.

In Johannine thought, flesh (Greek, *sarx*) is synonymous with the natural human condition. Humanity in its isolation, alienated from its destiny in God, in its weakness, in its being-unto-death, is *sarx*. Flesh does not condemn human sinfulness or deny its highest spiritual aspirations; it defines humankind's fragile existence and pathetic mortality. It is at once a statement of helplessness and a cry for help. Jesus himself, the Word made flesh and thus joined to humanity's natural fate, lived under this sentence of weakness and death. Without God, wounded humanity is under the power of its

35

fate. Its understanding, like that of Nicodemus, can move only within a world of categories and interests circumscribed by itself. Flesh builds its own prisons and trivializes its own mysteries. Both imprisoned and demystified, Nicodemus cannot hear Jesus; he listens only to himself.

Human existence as flesh is changed by the power of God. It lives in a new order of reality as Spirit (Greek *pneuma*, like Hebrew *ruah*, can also mean "wind" or "breath"). Spirit does not cancel out humanity's existence as flesh. Rather, it transforms humanity's source of life, freeing it from the power of fate and raising it to a divine destiny. John's language contrasts two ways of life, one a burden, the other a grace: humanity for and of itself; humanity for and of God.

If we keep in mind the meanings of *pneuma* as "breath," "wind," and "spirit," the impact of rebirth through the Spirit can become clearer. Humans' first birth is also of God. They live because they possess the breath of life. In Genesis, the essential connection between God and human life is described under the image of a potter and his work: God molded humanity from the earth's clay and "breathed into his nostrils the breath of life" (2:7). The very existence of humanity as flesh is a miracle. However, this miracle is less than a pale shadow of the new *pneuma* of life, which is irresistable and mysterious. The statement of Jesus in verse 8, a play upon the different meanings of *pneuma*, emphasizes this. To the ancients the wind (*pneuma*) was an enigmatic force revealed by its sound and its effect, its origin and destination unknown. So also the Spirit (*pneuma*) breathes where it will, its coming and going hidden in God, its voice calling us to rebirth.

In verse 5, a solemn saying of Jesus associates this rebirth with the Church's sacrament of baptism: "Truly, truly, I say to you, unless one is born of water and the Spirit, he cannot enter the kingdom of God." With "water" and the "Spirit" we have two images of eschatological consummation combined in the Christian sacrament. Water is a common image in the Old Testament for a blessing or for rebirth, and the promise of flowing water or rain is used to describe the fertility and regeneration of the land in the messianic age. Chapter 47 of Ezekiel is especially famous for its description of eschatological revitalization of the land by streams of living water that flow from the temple. Added to this water image are a number of passages which speak of the effusion of the Spirit in terms associated with the metaphor of the pouring out of water. Through the prophet Isaiah, for one, Yahweh announces, "I will pour water on the thirsty land/ and streams on the dry ground;/ I will pour my spirit upon your children" (44:3). Through the prophet Joel, he promises, "I will pour out my spirit upon all flesh . . ." (2:28).

Through the glorified Jesus, the outpouring of the Spirit turns promise into reality.

⁹Nicodemus said to him, "How can this be?" ¹⁰Jesus answered him, "Are you a teacher of Israel, and yet you do not understand this? ¹¹Truly, truly I say to you, we speak of what we know, and bear witness to what we have seen; but you do not receive our testimony. ¹²If I have told you earthly things and you do not believe, how can you believe if I tell you heavenly things? ¹³No one has ascended into heaven but he who descended from heaven, the Son of man. ¹⁴And as Moses lifted up the serpent in the wilderness, so must the Son of man be lifted up, ¹⁵that whoever believes in him may have eternal life."

Nicodemus puts his second and final question to Jesus and then fades forever from the scene of John's gospel. By the end of verse 11 and in verse 12 the Greek of the gospel has replaced the singular "you" previously addressed to Nicodemus with the plural "you" indicating a more general audience. The discourse that follows can have no focus other than that of the revealer and his revelation. Nicodemus's inability to comprehend the words of Jesus contains his own dismissal. In a way, he is a shadow-figure, coming by night and dissipating when faced with the light.

His question expresses bewilderment and, at the same time, puts Jesus into question. Nicodemus came to Jesus expecting to find an orthodox teacher willing to give him the answers he wished to hear. Jesus, instead, challenges him with a puzzling rebirth in the Spirit. "How can this be?" Yet Nicodemus should have understood. As a teacher of Israel he knew the Old Testament and the prophecies. Obviously, as a teacher he compares more than unfavorably with Jesus. In fact, for Nicodemus to so question Jesus smacks of arrogance. Many may bear witness to Jesus in the gospel, but it is his own witness that is paramount. To reject his testimony is to reject what he can uniquely witness to—direct knowledge of heavenly things, which is also self-knowledge and self-experience.

To call into question the testimony of Jesus is to fail completely to comprehend who he is. No acknowledgement of his learning or of his insight is adequate. No homage paid to his manner of life or to his demanding vision of human existence does more than impose humanistic embellishment on an already distorted Christ. He is neither a man gifted with extraordinary powers nor a god in disguise. He is *the* revealer, unlike all other persons, because he is preexistent Son of man, speaking of heavenly things since his origin itself is of heaven. Already Jesus spoke of himself as the Son of man who, through his glorification, becomes the effective nexus between heaven and earth, between God and Humanity (1:51). This is not the first time (nor will it be the last) that John's gospel employs the spatial imagery of heaven and earth, ascent and descent to communicate the truth of Jesus. Subjection to human concepts and language is itself part of the enfleshment of the Word. Repeating this imagery, Jesus affirms that he is the Son of man who alone has direct vision of God: "No one has ascended into heaven but he who descended from heaven." The Old Testament is quite emphatic that direct experience of God is beyond the scope of mortals: "Who has ascended to heaven and come down? Who has gathered the wind in his fists? Who has wrapped up the waters in a garment? Who has established all the ends of the earth?" (Prov. 30:4). It belongs only to the Word who, in Jesus, traced the arc of salvation, descending to the world, ascending to the Father. Jesus' saying in verse 13 speaks as if the moment of the Word in the world were already consummated. From the post resurrectional perspective of the gospel, this is so. However, the ascent of the Son of man must await the fullness of the glorification when Jesus returns to the Father.

Jesus finally explains how rebirth through the power of the Spirit can come about: the Son of man must be "lifted up." Behind his words stands an incident from the story narrated in the Book of Numbers (21:4-9). To punish the people of Israel for their grumblings against him in the desert, Yahweh sends against them a plague of lethal fiery serpents. Eventually responding to the people's repentance and to Moses' prayer on their behalf, he then instructs Moses to make a bronze serpent and set it on a pole. Thereafter, any of the Israelites who were bitten by the fiery serpents need only look upon the serpent raised up on the pole and live.

Jesus compares the lifting up of the Son of man with the lifting up of the bronze serpent. The raised serpent brought physical life to those who looked upon it. The Son of man lifted up is to be the source of salvation for those who look upon him in faith. John tells up quite explicitly that this lifting up refers to Jesus on the cross: lifted up from the earth Jesus says he will draw all to himself and so indicated "by what death he was to die" (12:32). However, this is not the total content of "lifted up." The Greek word in the gospel (*hypsoun*) has a double meaning. For when the Son of man is lifted up his true nature will be revealed (8:28) and he will draw all to himself, dispensing eternal life. Jesus will be lifted up not only in death but in his glorification when he is lifted up to the Father. The image of the suffering servant in Isaiah seems to inform this notion. The faithful servant who suffered for the sins of many (perhaps even to death) was also vindicated: "Behold, my servant shall prosper, he shall be exalted and lifted up, and shall be very high" (Isa. 53:13). If the Son of man, then, shall be lifted up on the cross in death, it is as the first movement of a three part symphony of glorification: death, resurrection, and ascension. His suffering and death is both the necessary condition for his glorification and the first stage of it. The cross also is revelatory of the glory of God. As John will tell us, Jesus is also victorious king on the cross. Though sometimes belied by an atmosphere of morbid sentimentality, the Church's solemn liturgy of Good Friday knows this truth and celebrates not a funeral but a triumph of life.

If humanity is to partake of the source of salvation, it must believe in the lifted up Son of man as that source. Reborn by the Spirit which is released to the world by the risen Lord, the believer, here and now, lives eternal life, God's life. No longer a remote possibility to come at the end of all things in the eschatological kingdom of God, life, John tells us, is now. The end of things can only confirm the present reality in Jesus.

The bond forged in the Johannine gospel between suffering and death and triumph and life draws us into the mission of the Word. If God submitted himself to flesh in Jesus Christ, it was, after all, our flesh as well, whose fate sentenced him to death as it does us.

If God vindicated flesh in Jesus Christ, our sentence of death too has been turned into a promise of glorification and a judgment of life. The Word spoken speaks what he is and does not return empty.

¹⁶For God so loved the world that he gave his only Son, that whoever believes in him should not perish but have eternal life. ¹⁷For God sent the Son into the world, not to condemn the world, but that the world might be saved through him. ¹⁸He who believes in him is not condemned; he who does not believe is condemned already, because he has not believed in the name of the only Son of God. ¹⁹And this is the judgment, that the light has come into the world, and men loved darkness rather than light, because their deeds were evil. ²⁰For every one who does evil hates the light, and does not come to the light, lest his deeds should be exposed. ²¹But he who does what is true comes to the light, that it may be clearly seen that his deeds have been wrought in God.

The discourse develops into a general summary of Johannine theology, merging in this small passage a multitude of characteristic words and concepts. Why is it that the Son of man must be lifted up in death? With what urgency does this press human existence? To what end?

This, one of the most famous passages in the gospel, begins with one of its most well-known sentences, "For God so loved the world. . . . " It would probably be impossible to determine whether more ink has been spilled (and more sermons preached) over this sentence or over Paul's hymn to love in 1 Corinthians 13. Certainly both run a tight race.

Each speaks from a different point of view, yet both share a common perspective: the mystery of love as it is comprehended in Christian belief. One might say that they are related as creative archetype to type. God's love is the condition and model for human love. An aspect of Paul's description may open a doorway of insight into the archetype. Emphasizing the daily responsibilities of love, Paul gives us a list of attributes—it is patient and kind, neither irritable nor jealous—that are overwhelmingly social. The context and direction of love is the other. Love, paradoxically, is a radical act of faith in the actuality and significance of all existence; at the same time, it may be a sign of hope to oneself and to others that individual human lives are not doomed to themselves.

God's love is in essence a social reality. He is love because he loves. That love is neither explicable nor motivated by the other. In verse 16 John uses a Greek verb, *agapein*, "to love," which is cognate to the noun, *agapē*. Throughout the New Testament, these generally express a technical Christian notion of love which may be sharply contrasted with the love expressed by *eros*. Erotic love springs from desire for an attractive object; agapic love imposes no conditions on the other. It is born not of desire but of God. At its source, it is God. Upon this love, then, the world can make absolutely no claim whatever. This is not because the world is hopelessly evil; this entire passage denies that. Nor is it because the world is in a state of estrangement from God and waiting for reconciliation. Simply, what comes from God is gift, not right.

Verse 16 encapsulates the answers to the three questions posed at the beginning of this section. Jesus must die not because the will of humans is irresistible but because God loved the world. The activity of love is giving and the nature of the gift defines the love. The Father gave the Son, uniquely his own, the Word spoken in flesh and to be lifted up on a cross. Through the gift of the Son, the world is called by the Word to decision and eternal life.

The mission of the Son to the world is to save, to offer a judgment of life, not a condemnation of death. Belief in Jesus who alone reveals the love of the Father is the single but absolutely human condition for the Father's love. It is a decision for or against Jesus which is effective now. In John's primary eschatological perspective, humankind is judged in the present by its reaction to the person of Christ. As it was throughout his ministry, so it is now.

The above strongly phrased dualism of this gospel passage should not lead us into thinking that there is an absolute predestination which both calls into question the quality of God's love and renders empty human responsibility for belief or unbelief. For John, it is true, humankind is divided into two irreconcilable classes, those who love the light and those who, hating the light, love darkness. Seemingly, people react to Jesus as they are already classified, and so saved or condemned by a destiny over which they have no control.

However, that stringent dualistic emphasis, in part, formulated John's focus on the absolute centrality of the person of Jesus. The urgency of his presence makes a total demand which allows no in between. Because he was sent to the world, that demand is universal. Through Jesus, all human existence is challenged to take a stand on the question of God—which is the question of the meaning of human existence itself. Shall it decide to live a lie or to live the truth? Shall it decide for darkness and death or for light and eternal life?

The Son is sent "not to condemn the world" but to save it; the Father's love is a judgment of life. But this love can become a force for destruction in the hands of those who reject Jesus and thus that love itself. Human beings condemn themselves by rejecting life. In an ultimate and completely perverse act of idolatry, they distort the love of the Father into an instrument of death and call down upon themselves the wrath of the god they have created.

Through the decision human beings must make, they are revealed to themselves as what they are. Deeds done in darkness no longer have the refuge of darkness, for the "light has come into the world" so that they "should be exposed." At the same time, they are condemned for having rejected the light. It is not that humans are sinners that is at issue here; this is axiomatic for all human beings. Rather, those who love darkness identify themselves with their evil actions and, by refusing to believe in Jesus, ratify all the evil actions of their lives. At the crossroads, they move into an even darker corner of the meaning built by their pasts. They move into themselves, not outward to the light.

On the contrary, to believe in Jesus is to find the meaning of one's existence in the present. No longer enclosed in the container of the past, in a life that has meaning only for itself, the believers' actions are found ratified in God. Those who do what is true, who keep faith in the incarnate Word, at once come to the light and are known by that light. At its crossroads, that human existence which has heard and answered the call beyond itself becomes both what it is and what it was. The meaning of its past is contained outside of itself in the present. And that present is Jesus. The urgency of decision placed upon us by Jesus is, in a sense, the actual choice that presses upon human existence to accept freedom from itself or slavery to itself. By responsible choice, we define ourselves and all our works in relation to the light. Not "in my beginning is my end" but "in my end is my beginning."

The Final Witness of the Baptist (3:22–36)

Chapter 3 concludes with a brief scene within which John the Baptist makes his last appearance in the gospel and a short discourse. Ostensibly a part of the Baptist's witness, verses 31-36 both continue and play a variation on the theme introduced in the Nicodemus episode and its consequent discourse (vv. 1-21). At the same time, they contribute something of a commentary on the Baptist's statement in verse 27: "No one can receive anything except what is given him from heaven."

The details of the narrative of verses 22-30 present the reader with many difficulties and inconsistencies. The scene opens with a journey of Jesus into the land of Judea. But the meeting with Nicodemus, which precedes this episode, takes place in Jerusalem which is in Judea. Both John and Jesus appear practicing parallel and rival baptismal ministries. Presumably, the baptism performed by Jesus was similar to John's eschatological water baptism of repentance for sin. Certainly no reference to Christian baptism by the Spirit could be intended because the gospel explicitly reminds us that the Spirit could not be sent until Jesus was glorified (7:39). Almost as a corrective to the information that Jesus also "baptizes," we are told later that Jesus' disciples baptized though he himself did not (4:2). Furthermore, according to the synoptics, Jesus' public ministry began only after the imprisonment of the Baptist (Mark 1:14). John's chronology pictures simultaneous ministries before the Baptist's imprisonment.

It is also somewhat confusing to note the reaction of the Baptist's disciples to Jesus' baptism. They seem perplexed and annoyed. Yet, they are disciples who heard the witness of John to Jesus recorded in chapter 1—a testimony, to say the least, hardly cryptic or vague. Jesus was saluted as the lamb of God; to make him known to Israel was itself the entire justification the Baptist gave to his own ministry.

It is probably useless to attempt to explain away these discrepancies. John's purpose in placing this bit of tradition about John the Baptist at this point of the gospel seems well enough served. The whole section leads up to and highlights the statement in verse 30 that the time has come for the Baptist's exit from the gospel scenario. Though no one greater may have been born of woman, "yet he who is least in the kingdom of heaven is greater than he." Once again, it may well be the intention of the fourth gospel to point up the inferiority of the Baptist to Jesus in the light of a sect of John's followers which rivalled the claims of early Christianity.

At the same time this section continues the baptismal motif introduced in the earlier Nicodemus scene.

²²*After this Jesus and his disciples went into the land of Judea; there he remained with them and baptized.* ²³*John also was baptizing at Aenon near Salim, because there was much water there; and people came and were baptized.* ²⁴*For John had not yet been put in prison.*

²⁵*Now a discussion arose between John's disciples and a Jew over purifying.* ²⁶*And they came to John and said to him, "Rabbi, he who was with you beyond the Jordan, to whom you bore witness, here he is, baptizing, and all are going to him."* ²⁷*John answered, "No one can receive anything except what is given him from heaven.* ²⁸*You yourselves bear me witness that I said, I am not the Christ, but I have been sent before him.* ²⁹*He who has the bride is the bridegroom; the friend of the bridegroom, who stands and hears him, rejoices greatly at the bridegroom's voice; therefore this joy of mine is now full.* ³⁰*He must increase, but I must decrease."*

The import of the Baptist's testimony is consistent and clear, in contrast to the attitude of his disciples. To them Jesus seems to present an unfair threat as a more successful "Johnny-come-lately" in the baptizing business. One can hear the resentment in their words, "here he is, baptizing, and all are going to him." John, however, has no qualms about Jesus. What success Jesus has, as well as what success John himself had, is given by God. It is the divine will that determines the result. John's role, itself heaven determined, was to reveal the Christ to Israel. His role, in fact, was like that of the best man to the bridegroom, whose function is to facilitate the marriage. Neither resentful nor regretful, John takes joy in his subsidiary role. He was a person who knew his place in relation to Jesus—a place he both celebrated and accepted. No finer tribute could be given to the greatness of the Baptist.

It is difficult to avoid finding an added significance in John's metaphor of the bride and bridegroom, especially if we recall the wedding symbolism in the Cana account of chapter 2. The wedding is a common metaphor to describe the relationship of God to Israel in the Old Testament. In Jeremiah, Yahweh remembers the early faith of Israel: " I remember the devotion of your youth, your love as a bride" (Jer. 2:2). Ezekiel, in an especially graphic way, describes the beginnings of Israel's election by God. Again it is Yahweh who speaks: "When I passed by you again and looked upon you, behold, you were at the age for love; and I spread my skirt over you, and covered your nakedness; yea, I plighted my troth to you and entered into a covenant with you, says the LORD GOD, and you became mine" (Ezek. 16:18). The usage of such imagery to express the intimacy of relationship continues into the New Testament transferred to Jesus and the Church. Paul's rather strained comparison between human husbands and wives and Christ and his body, the Church, are part of this metaphorical background. Husbands are enjoined to love their wives as "Christ loved the church and gave himself up for her, that he might sanctify her . . . that he might present the church to himself in splendor . . . " (Eph. 5:25ff.).

The Baptist, then, may well be referring to Jesus as the bridegroom of a new Israel. John's joy is all the more complete because he has been a special agent of the divine purpose in the preparations for this long-desired marriage. Yet, as offspring of the old covenant, the Baptist must stand on the sidelines and leave before the wedding-feast begins.

[31]*He who comes from above is above all; he who is of the earth belongs to the earth, and of the earth he speaks; he who comes from heaven is above all.* [32]*He bears witness to what he has seen and heard, yet no one receives his testimony;* [33]*he who receives his testimony sets his seal to this, that God is true.* [34]*For he whom God has sent utters the words of God, for it is not by measure that he gives the Spirit;* [35]*the Father loves the Son, and has given all things into his hand.* [36]*He who believes in the Son has eternal life; he who does not obey the Son shall not see life, but the wrath of God rests upon him.*

The discourse seems to begin with a contrast between Jesus and the Baptist in view of the Spirit and flesh contrast of the Nicodemus episode (the same word, *anōthen*, "from above," is repeated here). At the same time, the statement of the Baptist that "No one can receive anything except what is given him from heaven" (v. 22) takes on new meaning. The absolute superiority of Jesus to all humans is based upon his existence in the order of Spirit. Jesus' baptism, as the Church's after and through him, will be an outpouring of Spirit. John's is only that of water, a glimmer of the light. However, this is not a result of defect but of facticity. Like all humans and their works, John is of the earth, that is, he lives in and from the order of flesh. Born into natural existence, humanity was formed by God from the dust of the earth (Gen. 2:7). Ineffective of itself, humanity can only wait for rebirth from above, by the Spirit. The testimony of Jesus to himself, then, is a testimony born of the direct experience of his existence in God. The heavenly origin of Jesus is at once his Spirit-filled existence; to him alone the Spirit-power of God has been given without measure. What Jesus is God is; his words are God's words. The identity of the Father and the Son is an identity of power and purpose; and it is through the Son that the fidelity of the Father to his work of salvation is known. This work of salvation is itself identical to the mission of the Son. Human individuals are called to live in daily relationship to this mission. Acceptance of the Son results in eternal life, since salvation is identical with Jesus, rejection can only result in God's wrath resting upon the unbelievers who have excluded themselves from life. Faced by Jesus, humankind has but two choices: life or death, inclusion in or exclusion from God—not in some distant future, but now.

Among the Samaritans (4:1–42)

Because the Father so loved the world, he sent his Son. This premise which motivates the Johannine story of salvation receives dramatic form in the episode of Jesus in Samaria. The stage upon which the action of the gospel takes place is in reality a world-stage, its cast assembled by the love of the Father rather than the logic of ancient privilege.

There is a danger inherent in intimate human relationships that is true as well of the relationship between believers and their God. In both cases, the privilege of intimacy may become a pretext for exploitation and possession. Self-absorbed and self-congratulatory, one person may devour the freedom of another, even if unknowingly; in a similar way, a believer may attempt to constrain his God, enclosing him in the logic of a creed as closed as it is unimaginative. Speaking to Nicodemus, Jesus reminded us that the Spirit-power of God, like the wind, has no human master. In fact, it is supremely free and any human attempt to place limits or direction on it is delusion. The boundary between God and human beings as well as between one human person and another, once crossed in love, imposes upon us a new condition made possible only in freedom given and received.

The ancient privilege of the Jews as God's chosen people does not mean that they are God's only people. The story of Jesus and the Samaritan woman transports us beyond the frontiers of orthodox Judaism to clarify this relationship. Salvation may be of the Jews because they were specifically chosen to be the historic custodian of the divine promise; however, with the fulfillment of that promise in Jesus, their custodianship comes to an end. As acclaimed by the Samaritans, Jesus is the "Savior of the world."

Throughout Jesus' conversation with the woman at the well, themes which appeared previously in the gospel are reprised and renewed—rebirth, eternal life, the Spirit, Jesus himself, all mys-

47

teriously interrelated. Now, to the Samaritans, Jesus brings living water and the vision of an accomplished *eschaton*.

In the time of Christ the Samaritans inhabited a region west of the Jordan. The province of Judea was to the south and that of Galilee to the north. Though presenting themselves as worshipers of the one God, the Samaritans were outside the pale of orthodox Jewry. Rejecting the sacrality of both Jerusalem and its temple, they established their sacrificial cult on Mount Gerizim which for them was the true place of worship chosen by God and recorded in their Scriptures. Even after the destruction of their temple, Gerizim remained their center of cultus and, in fact, remains so to the present day.

The Samaritan scriptures are restricted to their own recension of the Pentateuch, the first five books of the Bible. These and these alone, they believed, were given by God to Moses along with the tables of the law on Sinai. No other part of the Bible is recognized. Consequently, the traditional messianic expectation of a royal anointed of David's line is absent from Samaritan belief. Rather, their eschatological hope is associated with the appearance of a figure more teacher and lawgiver than prince—foretold as the prophet like Moses in Deuteronomy 18:18.

Named originally from the old capital city of the northern kingdom of Israel, Samaria housed a mixed population: on the one hand, descendants of the native Israelites left behind during the forced deportations that followed the fall of the northern kingdom to Assyria in 721 B.C.; on the other hand, descendants of the various non-Israelites resettled in the land by the Assyrian conquerors. (Very modern in their fashion, the Assyrians seem to have been the first to play on a large scale the deport/import game with people.)

From the viewpoint of orthodox Judaism, the Samaritans were little more than outcasts. At best, their Yahwism was considered to be superficial; at worst, no more than a form of idolatry. In fact, according to the official Jewish version of Samaritan origins and history which is recorded in the Second Book of Kings (17:24f.), the Assyrian deportations emptied the land of the entire native Israelite population. Its subsequent inhabitants were then composed solely of foreigners resettled in the land. These peoples, the story goes, practiced a pragmatic worship of Yahweh as the god of the land; one among many gods, he too had to be placated along with service to "their own gods, after the manner of the nations from among whom they had been carried away" (2 Kings 17:33). For the Jews, then, the Samaritans were foreigners, one step above the Gentiles, but morally inferior and religiously debased.

In the New Testament, this official attitude is illustrated by the famous Lukan parable of the good Samaritan (10:25-37). The parable makes its point quite sharply by turning the tables on Judaism and reversing the expected roles of the actors. By all rights, the priest and the Levite, correct functionaries of the superior faith of Judaism, should have been motivated to come to the aid of the person beaten by robbers and left for dead. Yet they fail because their belief is translated into only one aspect of action, the concern to fulfill perfectly the ceremonial law. For this reason, they avoid the very danger of ritual impurity which any form of contact with a corpse would bring. The Samaritan, on the other hand, from whom one should expect a response in accord with his inferiority, performs the service of the good neighbor. Mercy and compassion, which should be at the heart and soul of Judaism, are here the qualities of a despised foreigner.

JESUS AND THE SAMARITAN WOMAN (4:1-30)

¹Now when the Lord knew that the Pharisees had heard that Jesus was making and baptizing more disciples than John ²(although Jesus himself did not baptize, but only his disciples), ³he left Judea and departed again to Galilee. ⁴He had to pass through Samaria. ⁵So he came to a city of Samaria, called Sychar, near the field that Jacob gave to his son Joseph. ⁶Jacob's well was there, and so Jesus, wearied as he was with his journey, sat down beside the well. It was about the sixth hour. ⁷There came a woman of Samaria to draw water. Jesus said to her, "Give me a drink." ⁸For his disciples had gone away into the city to bring food. ⁹The Samaritan woman said to him, "How is it that you a Jew, ask a drink of me, a woman of Samaria?" For Jews have no dealings with Samaritans.

A short transitional passage connects the scene to follow with the preceding section of the gospel. Previously, Jesus had appeared in Judea conducting a baptismal ministry alongside that of John's.

Jesus' success in this ministry brings him to the notice of the Pharisees. This, in turn, for some undisclosed reason, prompts Jesus to leave Judea and return to Galilee. For this purpose, Jesus travels the common time and distance saving route of pilgrims moving between Galilee and Judea, which led through Samaria.

Pausing on this journey, Jesus stops to rest at a site in Samaria which is known for its association with Jacob, the great ancestor of the Hebrew people. The well at this stopover is explicitly identified as Jacob's well.

The stories of most peoples are filled with popular traditions that connect places and things to special periods of their histories, especially to the periods of origin. Whether based on fact or not, such popular traditions are a source of local pride. They not only clothe the present with a sort of sacred lustre but also manufacture a kind of stability that derives from a feeling of historical continuity. In some way, the past is coerced to legitimate the present. More sophisticated modern societies may perhaps replace popular traditions with local historical societies and bronze placques detailing who slept where, but the effect is substantially the same.

In the Old Testament, Jacob is especially linked to the territory occupied by the northern tribes. He is directly associated with the vicinity of the town of Shechem—eventually passed on to Jacob's son Joseph and to his descendants (Gen. 33:19; 48:22; Josh. 24:32). More to the point is the prominence of Jacob as the father of the ancestor of the full twelve tribes of Israel. In the conversation that follows between Jesus and the Samaritan woman, it would have been difficult for the original reader of the gospel to ignore the contrast between Jesus and Jacob, between what Jesus offers and the Old Testament provides. Nor should the irony be lost that the bearer of living water has chosen to stop at Jacob's well.

Contemporary society offers few, if any, direct parallels to the framework of social interaction provided by the well in the ancient near Eastern world. Sociality organized around soda machines or office water coolers fall short of the mark and, certainly, there are few surprises in store for the one using the kitchen faucet. On the contrary, in the ancient near East, wells were good places for meeting people as well as animals and sometimes for significant encounters—at least between the people. Since it was customary for women to draw and carry water for the household, the well was an especially opportune place to meet women. The Book of Genesis gives us two excellent illustrations of such meetings (Gen. 24:10f.; 29:1f.), both to result in important consequences for the history of the Patriarchs and so for the future of Israel. The second of these, interesting from the point of view of the Jacob association of the Samaritan woman scene, describes the first meeting of Jacob with his future wife Rachel who was to become the mother of Joseph.

The very ordinariness of the setting in John's gospel of the scene at the well masks the significance of what is about to happen. One rarely expects to have one's life changed when going to the supermarket or laundromat. Yet that is what is going to happen to the woman who simply wants to get some water from a well. At this point the gospel may remind us through the discovery which the woman is to make that the ordinary does indeed cloak the extraordinary in all questions having to do with the incarnate Word. Once again in the gospel the line between appearance and reality is redrawn; what things seem to be they rarely are—neither travellers, nor water, nor even oneself.

Coming to the well at midday the Samaritan woman meets what appears to be a tired and thirsty traveller without any means of drawing water from the well. Jesus, as he usually does throughout the gospel, makes the first move—this time with a request that seems to rise from his immediate physical need: "Give me a drink." Startled and perhaps somewhat put off, the reply of the woman addresses itself to the quarrel between the Jews and the Samaritans, a context whose significance is already passé for Jesus. As she categorizes Jesus, she sees only a Jew whose need has prompted him to break the religious proprieties by entering into contact with someone considered ritually unclean.

From the beginning then, this meeting revolves around a thorough misunderstanding, one based upon the primary Johannine opposition of heavenly and earthly, Spirit and flesh. For those of earth, appearance is mistaken for reality.

[10]*Jesus answered her, "If you knew the gift of God, and who it is that is saying to you, 'Give me a drink,' you would have asked him, and he would have given you living water."*[11]*The woman said to him, "Sir, you have nothing to draw with, and the well is deep; where do you get that living water?* [12]*Are you greater than our*

father Jacob, who gave us the well, and drank from it himself, and his sons, and his cattle?" [13]Jesus said to her, "Everyone who drinks of this water will thirst again, [14]but whoever drinks of the water that I shall give him will never thirst; the water that I shall give him shall become in him a spring of water welling up to eternal life." [15]The woman said to him, "Sir, give me this water that I may not thirst, nor come here to draw."

As we have already seen, the water of John's baptism as well as the ritual waters of Jewish purificatory washings become empty signs with the appearance of Jesus. His presence is the eschatological consummation which brings rebirth through water and Spirit. With Jesus' reply to the woman in verse 10 we are reintroduced to the symbolism of water in the fourth gospel.

The effectiveness of this symbol, as of all symbols, for communication does not simply rest upon an explanation of intellectual content, as if a symbol were a colorful mask worn by abstract thought. Any symbol is usually more than that since it possesses its own reality as a thing apart from what it points to or represents— and the most powerful symbols in our lives, cultural and personal, are certainly more than that. Something elusive about such a symbol, some almost mystical connection between itself and understanding, remains as testimony to its inexhaustibility, even when it has been rationalized and interpreted. In the last analysis, the symbol tenaciously survives interpretation, is itself renewed in strength, and forces itself even more compellingly upon the emotional and intellectual experience of the one to whom it is addressed. If the history of interpretation throughout Western civilization has shown us anything, it is that literature and art usually manage to survive their commentators, as well as religion its theologians.

The direct dependence of all forms of life upon water lends to its symbolic usage and uniquely expressive force. At the same time, in the biblical world this necessary natural connection between water and physical life is contained in a situation of water's relative scarcity. There was never enough to waste or wantonly pollute. Nor, presumably, did one throw one's garbage into the water supply. As contemporary Western society might dream of a future golden age in terms of endless rows of inexhaustible gasoline pumps, Israel often did dream of superabundant supplies of fresh running water—living water.

Jesus' reply to the woman sets the record straight about himself and the reason for his request: "If you knew the gift of God, and who it is that is saying to you, 'Give me a drink,' you would have asked him, and he would have given you living water." The woman has completely misunderstood his request for water—a request made with view to her spiritual need rather than to Jesus' physical need. If anything, her stance vis-à-vis Jesus is an all-too-human smokescreen sent up to cover inner dissatisfaction and spiritual restlessness. Nor is Jesus interested in being sidetracked by the religious conflict between Jews and Samaritans—a conflict now devoid of substance. To this Jesus will explicitly address himself in verses 21-24 when he speaks of the reestablishment of the bases of worship in Spirit and in truth, and therefore the dissolution of the traditional boundaries and divisions among peoples. First, however, nothing must distract from the reason for it all—the reconstitution of the basis of life itself by the one sent to offer humankind the living water. *N B*

To this purpose, Jesus confronts the woman in verse 10 with a simple emphatic statement of his superiority which, in effect, turns her answer against her. If she had been able to see through his apparent request and to recognize the truth about Jesus who bears the gift of God, she would have sought from him living water. In Rabbinic writings the Torah is spoken of as the chief gift of God; and like water Torah is life-giving to those who drink of it. Once again the fourth gospel continues the theme laid out in the prologue: the law came through Moses, grace and truth through Jesus Christ (1:17). Torah, the cornerstone of the old dispensation, is replaced by Jesus, the living revelation of God.

As yet unchanged, the understanding of the woman puzzles over the appearances of things: "Sir, you have nothing to draw with, and the well is deep; where do you get that living water?" As the dialogue develops she will, in contrast to Nicodemus, show herself receptive to the startling words of Jesus and, in some measure, embrace them. However, at this point, she only compounds her misunderstanding. Forcing herself upon the words of Jesus, she has altered their context—her life, her world, not his. In that sense, her reply is less a response to Jesus than an echo of her own existence. Thus, for her, the water that Jesus offers is material substance, water and nothing more. In fact, Jesus seems to be offering something to her that is an impossibility. Even if he had the wherewithal to draw water from the well, how could it be superior to the water of Jacob's well? Almost naively, she asks, "are you greater than our father Jacob?"

Unraveling the irony of her question, Jesus clarifies his assertion of superiority made in verse 10. What he has come to give is not water to quench the thirst that arises from physical life. Jacob did that and was unable to do more. On the contrary, Jesus, who dispenses the gift of God and is himself the Father's supreme gift, offers heavenly water. In the believer that water will slake humanity's thirst for God and become a "spring . . . welling up to eternal life"—fountains of living water quenching the human desert, creating a civilization of the Spirit.

Still unable to reach the level of understanding that Jesus' words demand, the woman however begins to hear something more than before, if only that it is her need that is in question not Jesus': "Sir, give me this water, that I may not thirst, nor come here to draw."

Under the symbol of the living water the gospel presents a complex of associations. Built out of a background imagery of Old Testament expectations of the eschatological age, water and the Spirit were joined as agents of heavenly rebirth in the Nicodemus episode (3:5). In chapter 7 of the gospel, Jesus, speaking not of a gift he brings but of himself, invites those who thirst to come to him and drink. From those who do drink, who believe in Jesus, there "shall flow rivers of living water" which John explicitly identifies as the Spirit (7:38-39). If the Spirit is living water which Jesus gives to those who come to him, so also are the words of Jesus. In the writings of the Old Testament and of Judaism, both wisdom and Torah were described under the symbolism of water, from whose teachings people drink. For John, Jesus replaces both wisdom and Torah; from him and him alone come the words which bring eternal life to those who listen. Understood as both the Spirit which Jesus sends and the revelation which Jesus speaks, the symbol of living water ends for us as it began, offering us pieces of an inexhaustible mystery both revealed and hidden in the symbol. In the end result, it is the hidden reality which animates the symbol that must touch our being.

16Jesus said to her, "Go call your husband, and come here." 17The woman answered him, "I have no husband." Jesus said to her, "You are right in saying, 'I have no husband'; 18for you have had five husbands and he whom you now have is not your husband; this you said truly." 19The woman said to him, "Sir, I perceive that you are a prophet. 20Our fathers worshiped on this mountain; and you say that in Jerusalem is the place where men ought to worship." 21Jesus said to her, "Woman, believe me, the hour is coming when neither on this mountain nor in Jerusalem will you worship the Father. 22You worship what you do not know; we worship what we know, for salvation is from the Jews. 23But the hour is coming, and now is, when the true worshipers will worship the Father in spirit and truth, for such the Father seeks to worship him. 24God is spirit, and those who worship him must worship him in spirit and truth."

Not all misunderstandings of Jesus are final. They may themselves be part of a process which must be endured in the struggle to see the light. What is necessary is to follow where Jesus leads. In conversation with Nicodemus Jesus led to rebirth by the Spirit; Nicodemus chooses an incomprehension that finished the conversation: "How can this be?" (3:9). Seemingly, Jesus had nothing to say to him that he wanted to hear. In contrast, the woman at the well, though she does not yet understand, sees something of Jesus' fullness and something of her emptiness. Because she knows that Jesus has something she needs, she holds open the lines of communication and the conversation continues. "Sir, give me this water. . . ."

To speak with Jesus is always risky; topics discussed tend to get quite personal. One's sense of privacy suffers and countless self-evasions may be called into question. In such conversations, while one finds out things about Jesus, one also finds out things about oneself. Then, uncomfortably, one may have to make a decision by which one stands or falls. The fourth gospel has already spoken of this as the judgment: " . . . the light has come into the world, and men loved darkness rather than the light, because their deeds were evil. For every one who does evil hates the light, and does not come to the light, lest his deeds should be exposed. But he who does what is true comes to the light, that it may be seen that his deeds have been wrought in God" (3:19-21).

If she will take it, Jesus gives to the woman a further chance both

55

to recognize him and to make a decision for the light. With that more than human knowledge characteristic of Jesus in John's gospel, he exposes the immorality of her personal life: "You are right in saying, 'I have no husband'; for you have had five husbands, and he whom you now have is not your husband." The statement is matter-of-fact and, by certain standards, tactless. (Is this any way to start a religion?) The woman, however, is jarred into insight. Instead of driving the woman away into the temporary hiding place of the darkness, Jesus' knowledge of her leads to her confession of him as a prophet, someone inspired, whose range of power and perception exceeds that of ordinary people whose authority must be recognized. Faced with an uncomfortable truth, she does not turn away but continues the conversation with an increased awareness of to whom she is talking. Little by little the appearances through which she had been interpreting this meeting at the well are leading to reality.

This same interplay between appearance and reality may underlie the three addresses of the woman to Jesus in verses 11, 15, and 19, which the RSV translates as "Sir." The same Greek word, *kyrios*, may be used as a normal form of polite address ("sir") or it may be an elevated title, "Lord." In the early Church, the risen Jesus was confessed as *kyrios*, "the name which is above every name" at which "every knee should bend, in heaven and on earth and under the earth" (Phil. 2:9-10). He whom the Samaritan woman met at the well is the risen *kyrios* encountered by the reader of the gospel.

Verse 20 shifts the focus of Jesus' discourse to the question of true worship. Returning to the topic she introduced in verse 9 (then ignored by Jesus), the woman restates the Samaritan/Jew opposition in terms of the divinely appointed place of worship—for the Samaritans, Mount Gerizim rather than Jerusalem.

For Jesus this question of place of worship is fundamentally as irrelevant as those regulations of ritual purity which he violated in his meeting with the woman. He does indeed affirm the crucial role of Israel in the scheme of salvation: "Salvation is from the Jews," as the specific people elected by God to be the instrument through which his saving activity would be channelled to the world. As the bearer of his revelation and his promises, Israel was entrusted with service of a God who made his purpose known only to them. As a kingdom of priests, a holy nation, they were unique human instruments of divine worship. All these things, the Samaritans, cut off from the mainstream of revelation, were not. However, the authority of Israel's privileged position within the divine plan has passed; what it was it is no longer. Despite its special position, Israel itself, with all its institutions, comes under judgment of the absolute dualism between flesh and Spirit: "The hour is coming, and now is, when the true worshipers will worship the Father in Spirit and truth." The mystery of the rebirth of the world through the Spirit is now the mystery of the revealer and his revelation. Both Spirit and revelation are contained under the image of the living water, the eschatological gift of God which Jesus dispenses for eternal life. If Jesus himself was to be the living temple of the *eschaton* in place of the legitimate cult of Israel, the nature of worship itself was to be fundamentally changed—its basis no longer in the ineffectual order of flesh but in Spirit and truth.

Jesus is not rejecting one form of worship in favor of another. Worship in Spirit and truth is not a plea for a completely interiorized religion of the heart stripped of external observance and ceremony. Any rejection of religious ritual as such would be foreign to Jesus and to the early Church and waits for more Manichean times. Nor is it even a call for the reform of religious practices grown either too mechanical or too lush. The religion of Israel knew many such voices which were raised against the performance of empty rites, ceremony divorced from piety and love.

The order of worship that Jesus announces is a total eschatological reality made possible only by the power of God. Its entrance into the world coincides with the hour of Jesus' death, resurrection, and ascension and now is anticipated in his ministry. Spirit, as verse 24 makes clear, is no rarefied human distillation but the dynamic Spirit of God. God is Spirit not as he is defined in his essence but as he represents himself to humanity. This is the Spirit poured out in the messianic age that renews humankind from above. As Spirit-reborn children of God, those sought out by the Father are empowered to approach him in worship.

Nor is Spirit understood apart from truth. In the Gospel we have already seen a notion of truth which emphasizes its active ethical character. Drawn from a Hebrew background, truth, in this sense, is faithfulness; it is absolutely asserted of God whose fidelity to his promises is unquestioned. However, John's usage of the Greek noun *alētheia* (truth) here and at other places throughout the gospel seems closer to a concept of truth in the Hellenistic world. There truth was identified with ultimate reality in contrast to the world of appearance. In a similar way, this notion occurs in apocalyptic and sapiential writings where truth is equated both with the divine mystery of salvation and with wisdom.

Worship in Spirit and truth, then, are sides of a coin—a heavenly reality inextricably linked to the work of Jesus. As Jesus sends the Spirit, so he reveals the Father's truth to the world. The living water he offers is at one and the same time the drink that confers eternal life and the source from which springs all true worship of the Father. What the believer receives as well as gives is made possible only by the power of God—for such the Father seeks to worship him.

Jesus, his relevation, the Spirit—these are strands interwoven into one tapestry by the Johannine gospel. As the revealer of the Father, Jesus himself is the truth (14:6). The Spirit is the spirit of truth who will come to bear witness to Jesus. This same Spirit is at once the Spirit of God and the Spirit of Jesus, his to send into the world (15:26-27). At the center of the tapestry is the glorified Lord who releases God's power and who looses human powerlessness, the same whom the woman met at the well.

²⁵*The woman said to him, "I know that Messiah is coming (he who is called Christ); when he comes, he will show us all things." ²⁶Jesus said to her, "I who speak to you am he."*

Aided by Jesus, the woman reaches a certain level of understanding which again allows the conversation to continue. She knows that Jesus is speaking of the eschatological event, though she does not yet realize the relation of Jesus to that event. What he has been speaking of awaits the coming of the Messiah who will announce (RSV, "will show") all things. Her reply is voiced in terms of Jewish eschatological expectation rather than Samaritan. For the Samaritans, the one to come was the *Taheb*, more a Mosaic prophet and teacher than an anointed royal prince. It is, in fact, in this fashion that Jesus is represented to her throughout the dialogue—as a prophet with knowledge of human affairs who has instructed her in the meaning of the living water and in the meaning of true worship.

Clearly and simply, Jesus leaves no doubt that he is the one of

58

whom she is speaking: "I am he." Through the use of these words, which also evoke the divine name revealed to Moses in Exodus 3:14-15, Jesus, at one and the same time, may be revealing himself as Messiah and claiming divine status. (On this point, see commentary on 6:20.)

27Just then his disciples came. They marveled that he was talking with a woman, but none said, "What do you wish?" or, "Why are you talking with her?" 28So the woman left her water jar, and went away into the city, and said to the people, 29"Come, see a man who told me all that I ever did. Can this be the Christ?" 30They went out of the city and were coming to him.

These few verses serve both to conclude the dialogue with the woman and to introduce the two final scenes of this Samaritan episode, Jesus' conversation with his disciples and the approach of the townspeople to Jesus in faith. With the conversion of the townspeople, the entire episode receives its almost natural conclusion, the Samaritans appearing as a kind of microcosmic reflection of the world to which Jesus is sent. For to whom should humankind go in their efforts to know reality and to satisfy life's thirst if not to the one who brings living water, who ends our search in Spirit and truth?

With verse 27 the disciples, who had previously left Jesus in order to find food in the town, appear on the scene. Their immediate reaction is interesting. They are surprised, perhaps more shocked than surprised, to find Jesus in conversation with a woman! The fact that she is a Samaritan seems to hold no special interest for them. In this, they merely reflect Jesus' attitude. But they are astonished to find him talking with a woman. However, read against the background of first-century Judaism, the reaction of the disciples is not unusual. By a curious reversal, it is Jesus who is acting abnormally. The teachings of the Rabbis frequently warned of the dangers which women present to men (not to mention, especially to Rabbis), and advised of precautionary measures which could be taken to ward off lustful ensnarements. Among others, one avoided walking behind women as well as looking at them for any length of time and, specifically, one shunned any form of extended conversation with them.

Though such precautions may now seem to us exaggerated, mirroring the morality of another time and another way of life, they are perhaps not as foreign as they appear at first sight. They may, in fact, not be far removed from a negativity toward women which is found in most societies and which exists alongside other positive evaluations. Perhaps voicing sexual threat to the integrity and dominance of the male principle in society, this negativity portrays fears and suspicions buried deep in the dark fantasy life of most peoples, surfacing again and again throughout the various cultural codes through which societies embody themselves.

An instance of only one, though major, cultural tradition among many, the Rabbinical teachings themselves are not unfaithful to a certain strain in biblical thought which evidences this negativity. The story of the fall in Genesis pointedly makes it clear that, if Adam is to bear prime responsibility for the disastrous first sin, it is still the woman who was the first transgressor. It is she who first succumbs to the serpent and actually becomes the accomplice of the serpent in causing Adam to sin. The story of Genesis certainly contains the basis for the later attitude expressed in Sirach which is quite explicit in placing blame: "From a woman sin had its beginning, and because of her we all die" (Sir. 25:24). Nor is this line of thought completely unknown to the New Testament (e.g., 1 Tim. 2:14-15). As we look back from sadder and supposedly wiser times, we may be tempted to congratulate ourselves on our liberation from the unenlightened beliefs of our heritage's childhood. However, even secularized Judaeo-Christian consciousness has thinly disguised many of the ancient myths. Concerning the character of women, Sirach had nothing on Freud for whom women seemed deficient men. As he writes, "I cannot escape the notion (though I hesitate to give it expression) that for woman the level of what is ethically normal is different from what it is in men. . . . We must not allow ourselves to be deflected from such conclusions by the denials of the feminists, who are anxious to force us to regard the two sexes as completely equal in position and worth."

It may be interesting and not completely unwarranted to contrast the disciples' reaction to Jesus' action in terms of the contrast of flesh to Spirit in the gospel. There is no difficulty in accepting the reaction of the disciples. On its own terms, it is a cogent expression of their understanding and the understanding of their world. But this is as far as it goes. It remains part of the self-serving realm of appearance whose conventions are themselves under judgment. Jesus is performing a reality of self-giving. He constitutes the paradigm of performance and understanding. He speaks to whom he wishes, when he wishes, and for what purposes he wishes; that he is not to be questioned about his actions, that much at least his disciples know. As to who or what one is, it is Jesus who decides not man. Presumably, the community of the *eschaton* called together by the Christ dissolves the force of certain distinctions or at least makes them highly irrelevant. At the risk of one more repetition anesthetizing us to their impact, it is not inappropriate to recall Paul's words: "For as many of you as were baptized into Christ have put on Christ. There is neither Jew nor Greek, there is neither slave nor free, there is neither male nor female; for you are all one in Christ Jesus" (Gal. 3:27-28). In good faith, it seems necessary to read this statement of Paul as more than a piece of sociological and biological naiveté; in good faith, it also seems necessary to reunderstand it in the changing circumstances of history—as far as our insight will inform us and our courage will allow us.

THE MESSENGERS OF REVELATION (4:31–42)

[31]*Meanwhile the disciples besought him, saying "Rabbi, eat."* [32]*But he said to them, "I have food to eat of which you do not know."* [33]*So the disciples said to one another, "Has anyone brought him food?"* [34]*Jesus said to them, "My food is to do the will of him who sent me, and to accomplish his work.* [35]*Do you not say, 'There are yet four months, then comes the harvest'? I tell you, lift up your eyes, and see how the fields are already white for harvest.* [36]*He who reaps receives wages, and gathers fruit for eternal life, so that sower and reaper may rejoice together.* [37]*For here the saying holds true, 'One sows and another reaps.'* [38]*I sent you to reap that for which you did not labor; others have labored, and you have entered into their labor."*

The synoptic gospels do not report a ministry of Jesus in Samaria. To all appearances, the history of the evangelization of Samaria contained in the Acts of the Apostles would indicate that any Samaritan mission at all was entirely the work of the post-resurrectional church (8:1-25). Through John's account of Jesus' successful if limited activity in Samaria, the Church's later ministry to the Samaritans is grounded in an incident in the earthly ministry of Jesus. John's repeated emphasis on the continuity between the earthly visible Jesus and the risen Lord who lives invisibly in his Church makes it plain that Christian faith is the result of a direct encounter with the revealer of the Father, not the result of human effort.

Verses 28-30 have prepared us for an immediate response on the part of the Samaritans to Jesus' revelation to the woman. At the arrival of the disciples, she leaves to announce Jesus to the townspeople: " 'Come, see a man. . . . Can this be the Christ?' " They, in turn, go out to meet Jesus. It is against this backdrop that the scene with the disciples is played.

The scene begins with a misunderstanding similar to that between Jesus and the woman. Nor is the point of view that brings this understanding into being really distinct from hers. Both address themselves first and foremost to physical need; both inhabit a world in which things are as they appear. In such a world, literalistic to the point of banality, the symbol always has a precarious existence. Though their faith in Jesus is unquestioned, the full understanding of the disciples, perhaps one could say their religious imagination, still awaits the post-resurrectional gift of the Spirit. They too, during the ministry, are caught in the dichotomy of flesh and Spirit.

The disciples have brought Jesus food for which he has no need: "I have food to eat of which you do not know." The confusion of the disciples ("Has anyone brought him food?") prompts Jesus' explanation. The food which sustains him is a heavenly reality—that of the ministry of the Son who is one with the Father because he obeys perfectly the Father's will. Through Jesus the work of the Father is performed in the world. Through the oneness of purpose Jesus draws nourishment—nourishment, in turn, for the completion of the Father's purpose. Jesus' words here recall the scene in the gospel of Matthew (4:1f.). Hungry from his long fast in the desert and tempted by the devil, Jesus rejects the temptation with a citation from the Book of Deuteronomy: "Man shall not live by bread alone, but by every word that proceeds from the mouth of God" (Deut. 8:3/Matt. 4:4).

The rich development of Johannine food symbolism, paralleling that of water, awaits the bread of life discourse in chapter 6. For

now, Jesus introduces the metaphor of the harvest to speak of his
mission among the Samaritans—a mission which is simply one con-
crete accomplishment in Jesus' ministry of the nature of this work
of the Father. In the synoptics, the parables of Jesus frequently
employ images drawn from daily agricultural life—the sowing of
seed, the reaping of grain—to speak of the kingdom of God (e.g.,
Matt. 9:37; 13:7f.). Jesus employs similar imagery here set in relation
to two proverbs. The first of these cited in verse 35 is predicated
on the necessary natural order: "'There are yet four months, then
comes the harvest.'" Between sowing and reaping, nature has established an interval of four months, during which people must
patiently and inevitably await the fruit of their labors. This is nature's
wisdom. In contrast, the eschatological order established by Jesus
is of a wholly other kind where the usual interval between sowing
and reaping is abolished by the urgent nature of Jesus' mission. The
eschatological harvest, in its abundance, does not await the future
"when the plowman shall overtake the reaper/and the treader of
grapes him who sows the seed" (Amos. 9:13). Rather, it is present
through the work of Jesus and his disciples. So the Samaritans who
who are coming out to Jesus—"lift up your eyes, and see how the
fields are already white for harvest"—are already the fruit of the
revelation to the woman. This harvest brings joy to sower and reaper
alike, both of whom have their assigned and mutual functions in
gathering believers into eternal life. If as the second proverb main-
tains—"One sows, and another reaps"—their labors differ, still their
common joy remains true: They both share in the work of the harvest.

Verses 34-36 may be understood to apply to the specific context
of John's account of Jesus' activity in Samaria. What he has sown
is about to be reaped in the harvest of the townspeople coming out
to him in faith. At the same time, verses 37-38, especially, seem to
look to another context for explanation, one that more adequately
accounts for the division between sowers and reapers and yet the
unity of their labors. In verse 38 Jesus speaks in the past tense of
a mission of reaping upon which he sent his disciples. However,
this mission was to be part of the mission of others who, by their
labors, had already sown the word of Christ.

Seen against the background of the Samaritan mission in the post-
resurrectional Church, these words of Jesus take on new clarity as
John connects the later mission with Jesus' own mission among the

63

Samaritans. Once again, the fourth gospel is graphically demonstrating the unity of all the work of Jesus in behalf of the Father. That Jesus of the earthly ministry is the glorified Jesus who lives in his Church through the Spirit, that same Jesus whose present ministry is identical with that of his disciples: "As the Father sent me, I also send you" (20:21).

The Book of Acts records the early Church's successful evangelization of the Samaritans, begun by Philip who first "proclaimed to them the Christ"; and later confirmed by Peter and John through the imposition of hands and the conferral of the Holy Spirit (Acts 8:1-25). The Samaritan mission was then a joint enterprise of Hellenistic Christianity represented by Philip, and the more traditional Jewish Christianity of the apostolic Church at Jerusalem represented by Peter and John. If the Hellenistic Christians sowed the harvest, the apostles reaped it. In both cases, John reminds his readers, Jesus empowered it. Jesus is the reality of the harvest and the unity of the enterprise.

[39]*Many Samaritans of that city believed in him because of the woman's testimony, "He told me all that I ever did."* [40]*So when the Samaritans came to him, they asked him to stay with them; and he stayed there two days.* [41]*And many more believed because of his word.* [42]*They said to the woman, "It is no longer because of your words that we believe, for we have heard for ourselves, and we know that this is indeed the Savior of the world."*

Even partial faith can serve as testimony and can lead others to Jesus. The importance of the woman is not found in her own conversion which still leaves room for doubt ("Can this be the Christ?") and, therefore, in the integrity of her witness to Jesus. Rather, as an intermediary of the Word, she is a channel of communication between Jesus and others. In the end result, all intermediaries, all human witnesses, are simply preparation for the witness of Jesus to himself. The believer finally believes no one but Jesus. Brought to Jesus by the words of the woman, the Samaritans ask Jesus to stay (again, the word *menein*) with them. However briefly, the presence of the Word may touch human existence, it changes lives. After the two disciples of the Baptist stay with Jesus, they know that they have found the Messiah (1:35f.). So the Samaritans in the presence of the Word become believers of his word and know that they have found the savior of the world.

John's sense of the absurd is at play here. The Jews in Jerusalem who came to believe in Jesus did so because of his miraculous works; nor was this belief trustworthy (2:23-25). Nicodemus, a teacher of Israel, could accept no part of Jesus' teaching. Yet, the impure Samaritans confess Jesus, on the basis of his words, as savior of the world, a title which is virtually a paraphrase of the essence of Jesus' mission: "God sent the Son into the world, not to condemn the world, but that the world might be saved through him" (3:17).

Savior was a common title for the risen Jesus in the early Church. So Peter in Acts confesses that God exalted Jesus "at his right hand as Leader and Savior, to give repentance to Israel and forgiveness of sins" (5:31). As a christological title, it is probably a reapplication to Jesus of its religious usage in the Hellenistic world; there both gods and humans were called saviors, especially the gods of the mystery religions and the Roman emperors as the center of the imperial ruler cult. Reapplied to Jesus it further conjures up an extensive Old Testament background. Never a title for the Old Testament Messiah, savior could be applied to individual persons only because Yahweh raised them up to accomplish his salvation. He was *the* Savior who repeatedly performed his mighty actions on behalf of the redemption of Israel and who, in the final days, would declare himself decisively to the world. For Israel then, Yahweh can declare, "I, I am the LORD/and besides me there is no savior" (Isa. 43:11). As savior, Yahweh is also creator (Isa. 43:14f.). His ultimate act of salvation is, at the same time, the recreation of the world (Isa. 66:18f.). These two interwoven Old Testament images of salvation and creation become enfleshed in the mission of the Son: "that whoever believes in him should not perish but have eternal life" (3:16).

The Official's Son (4:43–54)

The second of the signs reported by John, the healing of the official's son, parallels the story of the healing of the centurion's slave in the gospels of Matthew (8:5-13) and Luke (7:1-10). To identify the centurion's son, Matthew uses throughout his narrative the Greek word *pais* which can mean either child or servant; only in Luke is the sick person unequivocally a *doulos*, a slave of the centurion.

All three stories of the healing speak of faith. In Matthew and Luke Jesus explicitly contrasts the superior faith of the Gentile centurion with the inferior faith of Israel. The universal embrace of the Gospel and the displacement of Israel implicit in Jesus' dealings with the Gentile centurion find explicit formulation in Matthew. There Jesus speaks both of the entrance of the Gentiles into the kingdom and Judaism's rejection of the Gospel: "I tell you, many will come from the east and west and sit at table with Abraham, Isaac, and Jacob in the kingdom of heaven, while the sons of the kingdom will be thrown into the outer darkness" (8:11-12).

In John's account, this theme of faith takes a different direction, closely related to his notion of the sign-value of Jesus' miracles and to the entire section of his gospel which began with the first miracle at Cana. In the scene with Nicodemus, Jesus has promised eternal life to those who come to him in faith. Into this life (or, if we may combine two images), into the kingdom of life the believer is reborn by the power of the Spirit. As the bearer of living water, Jesus made himself known to the Samaritan woman. Now, to the official, Jesus makes himself known as the bearer of life itself.

The response of the official is one of complete and absolute faith in Jesus. This second sign at Cana stands in direct relation to the first. There the disciples believed not in Jesus the wonder-worker but in Jesus the *eschaton*-bearer, as manifested through the meaning of the sign. It is to this same Jesus understood through the healing of his child that the official submits in faith. From Cana to Cana, the journey of Christian faith has a single clear destination in the fastness of the incarnate Word—to reveal this miracle all the signs are transparent windows.

⁴³After two days he departed to Galilee. ⁴⁴For Jesus himself testified that a prophet has no honor in his own country. ⁴⁵So when he came to Galilee, the Galileans welcomed him, having seen all that he had done in Jerusalem at the feast, for they too had gone to the feast.

Verses 43-45 form a brief transitional passage between the Samaritan episode and the narrative that is to follow. Continuing the journey that originally brought him into Samaria (4:1), Jesus arrives back in his home country of Galilee. Upon arriving, he is greeted by the Galileans on the basis of the miracles he had performed in Jerusalem while he was there for the feast.

The Galileans, like the Jerusalemites, acclaim Jesus for the wrong reasons and are accomplices in that superficial faith which Jesus finds untrustworthy (2:23)—a faith which certainly does not survive the events of his ministry.

Verse 44 is introduced as a parenthesis by the evangelist, which encapsulates a saying of Jesus also known from the synoptic tradition: "A prophet is not without honor, except in his own country, and among his own kin, and in his own house" (Mark 6:4). Rather than breaking the sequence of verses 43 and 45 (as the RSV suggests), verse 44 makes clear Jesus' attitude to his Galilean reception and to the true basis of Christian faith. This saying of Jesus is now to be fulfilled in what follows. With poignance, the gospel may well be recalling his acceptance among the Samaritans. In Samaria, foreigners and schismatics acknowledged him as a prophet, and believed him on the basis of his words. Now among Israelites, and Israelites of his own birthplace and home, he is not recognized as the revealer of the Father but only as the maker of miracles.

⁴⁶So he came again to Cana in Galilee, where he had made the water wine. And at Capernaum there was an official whose son was ill. ⁴⁷When he heard that Jesus had come from Judea to Galilee, he went and begged him to come down and heal his son, for he was at the point of death. ⁴⁸Jesus therefore said to him, "Unless you see signs and wonders, you will not believe." ⁴⁹The official said to him, "Sir, come down before my child dies." ⁵⁰Jesus said to him, "Go, your son will live." The man believed the word that Jesus spoke to him and went his way. ⁵¹*As he was going down, his servants met him and told him that his son was living.* ⁵²*So he asked them the hour when he began to mend, and they said to him, "Yesterday at the seventh hour the fever left him."* ⁵³*The father knew that that was the hour when Jesus had said to him, "Your son will live"; and he himself believed, and all his household.* ⁵⁴*This was now the second sign that Jesus did when he had come from Judea to Galilee.*

Jesus' journey to Galilee brings him to Cana. It is at the scene of the first of his signs that the gospel has set the story of the healing. In Matthew and Luke the miracle takes place at Capernaum. For John, as we have seen, the Cana setting intentionally recalls the first sign. Both Cana miracles, in fact, come about in a similar manner. As Jesus at first refused the request of his mother and then unexpectedly assented to it, so too he rejects the petition of the official and then unexpectedly grants it. Nor is there, in either case, any indication of how the miracle comes about. The power of Jesus' word is, for John, sufficient explanation. In the story of the healing this is even more emphasized by increasing the physical distance at which the healing takes place—from Cana to Capernaum rather than at capernaum itself (Matt. 8:5/Luke 7:1).

Hearing of Jesus' presence in Galilee, he is approached by a *basilikos*, a royal official, presumably of the court of Herod Antipas, who held the position of tetrarch or ruler of Galilee under Roman overlordship. As Jesus' reply in verse 48 seems to make clear, the official is a Jew who shares the belief of the Galileans in the miraculous power of Jesus. Because of this he begs Jesus to come down to Capernaum to cure his small son, sick to the point of death.

Jesus replies with a pointed refusal, which is a rebuke both to the official and more generally to the Galileans whom he represents: "Unless you see signs and wonders, you will not believe." Neither arbitrary nor unfeeling, the refusal is directed to the actual heart of the official's request, the superficial nature of such faith based on signs and wonders. Such faith dishonors the mission of the word. Perhaps recalling Yahweh's words in Exodus 7:3-4, Jesus' reply may be underscoring, with some sadness, the emptiness underlying such faith. Though Yahweh would multiply signs and wonders in Egypt, Pharoah still would not listen to Moses; if Jesus proved himself by miracles, whatever faith they produced would ultimately lead to nothing.

Responding to Jesus' rebuke, the official, as an anxious father, can only repeat his request: "Sir, come down before my child dies." With no added motivation, Jesus now responds with a sign. The physical miracle is given but only as a part of a greater miracle—the presence of Jesus who confronts the official as the giver of life. It is to the revealer of the Father manifested through the sign as well as through his words that the royal official is called to a decision of faith. Significantly, it is a word that accomplishes the sign: "Go, your son will live." In biblical thought, sickness was a kind of death. The sick person was already in the power of death and so the psalmist, in his affliction, could cry out that he was "like one forsaken among the dead, like the slain that lie in the grave" (Ps. 88:5). To the boy, then, Jesus sends a word restoring life.

For the official Jesus' word is sufficient. Like the Samaritans before him, his faith has been changed by the presence of Jesus. Faith based on the reports of others, the Galileans, has become faith in the words of Jesus himself. Faith misplaced in the miracles of Jesus has now turned to Jesus himself. That faith becomes absolute as Christian faith at the moment that Jesus becomes for him fully revealed through the sign. "'Yesterday at the seventh hour the fever left him.' The father knew that that was the hour when Jesus had said to him, 'Your son will live.'" Understanding that the word of life spoken by Jesus and the life of the boy are one in the lifebringer, "he himself believed, and all his household."

Jesus and the Sabbath (5:1–47)

The healing of the sick man by the pool of Bethzatha is the third of the miracles performed by Jesus recorded by John. Like the first two, this miracle is also a sign, which goes beyond appearances, an event which reveals something about the person of Jesus. Jesus' healing of this man reveals Jesus as the giver of life and as the one who has the authority to execute judgment in the world. At the same time, the very context within which Jesus performs the miracle, the situation of conflict which arises from Jesus' deliberate violation of the Sabbath, becomes the occasion for the revelation of the special relationship existing between Jesus and the Father. Finally, the angry confrontation between Jesus and the Jewish leaders culminates in the exposure of the leaders' attitude which underlies their reaction to him, an attitude of deliberate disbelief.

CURE ON THE SABBATH (5:1–15)

¹After this there was a feast of the Jews, and Jesus went up to Jerusalem. ²Now there is in Jerusalem by the Sheep Gate a pool, in Hebrew called Bethzatha, which has five porticoes. ³In these lay a multitude of invalids, blind, lame, paralyzed. ⁵One man was there, who had been ill for thirty-eight years. ⁶When Jesus saw him and knew that he had been lying there a long time, he said to him, "Do you want to be healed?" ⁷The sick man answered him, "Sir, I have no man to put me into the pool when the water is troubled, and while I am going another steps down before me." ⁸Jesus said to him, "Rise, take up your pallet, and walk." ⁹And at once the man was healed, and he took up his pallet and walked.

Now that day was the sabbath. ¹⁰So the Jews said to the man who was cured, "It is the sabbath, it is not lawful for you to carry your pallet." ¹¹But he answered them, "The man who healed me said to me, 'Take up your pallet, and walk,' " ¹²They asked him, "Who is

the man who said to you, 'Take up your pallet, and walk'?" [13]*Now
the man who had been healed did not know who it was, for Jesus
had withdrawn, as there was a crowd in the place.* [14]*Afterward
Jesus found him in the temple, and said to him, "See, you are well!
Sin no more, that nothing worse befall you."* [15]*The man went away
and told the Jews that it was Jesus who had healed him.*

Jesus travels to Jerusalem during one of the feasts on which all Jews
are obliged to travel to Jerusalem. Scholars are unable to agree on
the identity of the feast. However, whether it was Pentecost, the
feast of Tabernacles or of Passover, they all agree that the factor
which is relevant and central to this miracle is that the event occurs
on the sabbath. The place where the healing occurs is a pool located
near the Sheep Gate, in the northeast area of the temple, where
the sheep were brought to Jerusalem for sacrifice. The pool, trap-
ezoidal in shape, was divided by a central partition. It had colon-
nades on the four sides and on the partition (the five porticoes
described by John), and stairways in the corners by which people
could descend to the pool. The pool described here can now be
seen on the property of the White Fathers near St. Anne's Church
in Jerusalem.

The accepted text (vv. 1-32) merely indicates that the porticoes
were crowded with invalids, the blind, the lame, and the paralyzed.
However, other texts (vv. 3b-4) add that they were "waiting for the
moving of the water; for an angel of the Lord went down at certain
seasons into the pool, and troubled the water; whoever stepped in
first after the troubling of the water was healed of whatever disease
he had." Although this is a later addition to the authentic text, it
may reflect a popular tradition about the pool. The Jews believed
that the pool had curative powers, and that these powers were most
potent when the water bubbled, when the underground spring that
fed the pool became more active.

Jesus comes upon the scene and encounters a man whom the
fourth gospel notes had been ill for thirty-eight years. The length
of the illness is underlined by John as it is also emphasized in other
healing narratives by the synoptics (Mark. 5:25/Luke 13:11), probably to stress the hopelessness of the situation. Upon Jesus' command, the man is healed "at once." The immediate effect of Jesus'
simple healing word, evidence of his power, is present in numerous

other healing narratives of the synoptics as well (Matt. 8:3; 15:28; Mark 5:29).

The sick man leaves the pool area, carrying his pallet or mattress, and is immediately observed by the Jewish leaders. They admonish him for his violation of the sabbath, for the carrying of an empty bed on the sabbath is specifically forbidden by a rabbinical law. When the man explains that he was merely following the directions of the man who healed him, the Jews demand to know the identity of the healer. It is obvious that their interest lies primarily in finding the culprit who has led this individual to violate the sabbath, and that they are not awed in the least by the cure of a man who had been sick for thirty-eight years. Initially unable to identify Jesus for them, the man returns to the temple, where he again meets Jesus, and somehow learns who it was who healed him. When Jesus sees the man, he sternly warns him that unless he refrains from further sin, something worse may befall him. This remark, in which Jesus appears to accept a cause-effect relationship between sin and suffering, is something of a puzzle, particularly in view of the fact that elsewhere Jesus specifically denies this connection (9:3; Luke 13:1-5). The denial in other texts, however, is primarily a rejection of the Old Testament tendency to connect one's *specific* sickness with personal guilt. Jesus did, in fact, consider the phenomenon of sickness in the world as one significant manifestation of the reign of evil and the power of Satan in the world. Jesus explicitly, for example, points to the woman "who was bent over and could not fully straighten herself" as "a daughter of Abraham whom Satan bound for eighteen years." (Luke 13:11-16). The exorcisms of Jesus, which frequently take the form of cures (e.g., Matt. 9:32-34); 17:14-18) assume that the illnesses which afflict human beings are a sign of Satan's domination in the world. By his healing and by his exorcisms, Jesus destroys that power. In another healing-exorcism, this one of the blind and dumb demoniac, Jesus pictures the world of sickness and suffering as "the strong man's house," that is, as the castle ruled over by Satan. Through his healings, Jesus "plunders the house" of the strong, that is, he frees human beings from Satan's power. Jesus is capable of plundering since he first "binds the strong man" (Matt. 12:22-29). Time and again, the backdrop against which Jesus heals is a world in which the rule of Satan and evil, manifested in human illness and suffering, is broken by the power of the one who eliminates sickness. The other significant manifestation of the presence of evil in the world is, of course, sin. As John's narrative of the resulting confrontation between the Jewish leaders and Jesus continues, we see more clearly that Jesus' power to heal is an awesome symbol of his power to give eternal life.

THE WORKS OF THE SON (5:16–30)

[6]*And this was why the Jews persecuted Jesus, because he did this on the sabbath.* [17]*But Jesus answered them, "My Father is working still, and I am working."* [18]*This was why the Jews sought all the more to kill him, because he not only broke the sabbath but also called God his Father making himself equal with God.*

[19]*Jesus said to them, "Truly, truly, I say to you, the Son can do nothing of his own accord, but only what he sees the Father doing; for whatever he does, that the Son does likewise.* [20]*For the Father loves the Son, and shows him all that he himself is doing; and greater works than these will he show him, that you may marvel.* [21]*For as the Father raises the dead and gives them life, so also the Son gives life to whom he will.* [22]*The Father judges no one, but has given all judgment to the Son,* [23]*that all may honor the Son, even as they honor the Father. He who does not honor the Son does not honor the Father who sent him.* [24]*Truly, truly, I say to you, he who hears my word and believes him who sent me, has eternal life; he does not come into judgment, but has passed from death to life.*

[25]*"Truly, truly, I say to you, the hour is coming, and now is, when the dead will hear the voice of the Son of God, and those who hear will live.* [26]*For as the Father has life in himself, so he has granted the Son also to have life in himself,* [27]*and has given him authority to execute judgment, because he is the Son of man.* [28]*Do not marvel at this; for the hour is coming when all who are in the tombs will hear his voice* [29]*and come forth, those who have done good, to the resurrection of life, and those who have done evil, to the resurrection of judgment.*

[30]*"I can do nothing on my own authority; as I hear, I judge; and my judgment is just, because I seek not my own will but the will of him who sent me."*

John points to this healing and the ensuing discussions between Jesus and the Jewish leaders as the beginning of the campaign of persecution against Jesus. Lest we underestimate the seriousness of Jesus' action, it is useful to recall the significance and sacredness of the sabbath observance for the Jewish people. The sabbath was not merely a holiday of rest for the Israelites, but at a deeper level, it was bound up with the covenant God had made with his people. It was to be a day consecrated to him in a special way. While both schools of thought, one stressing the humanitarian aspects of the sabbath as a day of rest (Deut. 5:14b-15), the other stressing the religious aspect, (Gen. 2:2-3; Exod. 31:12-17) focused on God, it was the religious perspective which prevailed at the time of Jesus (Lev. 23:3, 28; Exod. 20:11). The observance of the sabbath had also developed through the years from a joyful and relaxed holiday to an observance that was characterized by meticulous restrictions, such as the one which was broken by the man in this narrative who carried an empty bed from one place to another. However, although we may find this regulation rigid to the point of absurdity, the overriding factor is that in violating the sabbath in any way, Jesus was seen as a person who showed disrespect for the sacredness of a day which commemorated the covenant with Israel's God.

Only in this light can the indignation of the Jewish leaders be appreciated. They persecuted him because he had violated something sacred by healing on the sabbath. It seems clear that Jesus' violation of the sabbath was a deliberate act. Rabbinical opinion generally permitted the practice of healing on the sabbath if there were danger of death, but not if the healing could be postponed until the following day. If the man had waited for thirty-eight years, what difference would one day make? It is clear also from Jesus' response to the hostility of the Jews that his decision to heal on the sabbath is deliberate and is intended to reveal his role in the world as life giver and judge.

Jesus' justification of his work of healing on the sabbath is not humanitarian, as in the synoptic tradition (Luke 13:15, 14:5), but theological: "My Father is working still, and I am working." Notwithstanding the connection made by Exodus 20:11 between the sabbath rest and the rest of God on the seventh day, Jewish theologians did not believe that God ceased working completely on the sabbath. Rabbis reasoned that without God's continued activity, the world would cease to exist (Ps. 104). In particular, without the active intervention of God in the human realm, it would be impossible for human beings to be born or to die on the sabbath. God was the source of human life (Ps. 139:13-16; Ec. 11:5; 2 Macc. 7:22-23) and the judge of all at their deaths (Wisd. of Sol. 3; Dan. 12:2-3; Ezek. 37:13). By claiming that he could work on the sabbath just as the Father did, Jesus was claiming a divine prerogative. The Jews, therefore, considered his statement blasphemy, deserving of death. In fact, Jesus was finally condemned to death by the Sanhedrin for the sin of blasphemy since he had laid claim to divine prerogatives (Matt. 26:65).

In response to the Jewish accusations of prideful arrogance and blasphemy, Jesus insists that he never acts independently of the Father, and emphasizes the absolute harmony existing between him and the Father. He does nothing on his own, only what he sees the Father doing. In fact, Jesus insists that the very *raison-d'etre* of his existence is to do the will of his Father, to accomplish his work (e.g., 4:34, 5:30, 6:38). Among the works which Jesus sees his Father accomplish and which he imitates, Jesus focusses on the works of giving life and of passing judgment, which the rabbinical teaching proposes are works done by the Father on the sabbath.

Jesus, once again passing from one level of perception to a deeper level, once again passing beyond the symbol to the reality that is symbolized, points out that the healing he has accomplished is to be surpassed by the work which this healing signifies, the giving of eternal life. Together with his Father, who gives life to those who have died, Jesus gives eternal life to those who believe.

Some authors believe that verses 21-24 on the one hand, and verses 26-30 on the other, are two different versions of Jesus' statement concerning his activities of giving life and of judging. The first version (vv. 21-24) is set within the context of the belief that the bestowing of life and the passing of judgment are not actions which are to take place at some future date, but are actions which occur here and now. The life (*zoe*) which Jesus gives is qualitatively different from natural life (*psyche*): it is the life by which God himself lives, and which the Son possesses from the Father (5:26; 6:57). This life consists in the knowledge of the only true God (17:3), a knowledge which, however, is not merely speculative, but a practical knowledge culminating in love. Through this life, this loving knowledge of God, the human person becomes like God. Later theology describes this relationship as grace, or as gift, the foundation of the

75

human ability to believe in, trust in and to love God, that is, the theological virtues of faith, hope and charity.

The other activity in the first version attributed to the Father on the sabbath by rabbinical teaching is the work of judgment, which Jesus himself is commissioned by the Father to carry out. The Greek verb, *krinein*, can be translated either as judging or condemning, depending upon the context. Some statements in John suggest that Jesus did not come to condemn (*krinein*): "For God sent the Son into the world, not to condemn the world, but that the world might be saved through him" (3:17); "If any one hears my sayings and does not keep them, I do not judge (condemn) him; for I did not come to judge (condemn) the world but to save the world" (12:47). Other texts, however, indicate that Jesus did come into the world to judge: "The Father judges no one, but has given all judgment to the Son . . . " (5:22); Jesus said, "For judgment I came into this world . . ." (9:39). Jesus is the judge in the same sense in which God is seen as judge in the Old Testament. God intervenes to punish those who do evil (Ps. 7:9, 26:1, 35:24, 43:1); his judgment is also a justification of the good (Judg. 11:27, 1 Sam. 24:13, 15; 2 Sam. 18:19). Jesus is not a judge in the sense that he labels actions which he observes as good or evil. He is judge in the sense that he created the milieu and the occasion which provokes the human person to behavior which will be either salvific or destructive. The individual who hears Jesus' word and believes passes from death to life. On the other hand, the person who hears but refuses to believe brings eternal condemnation upon himself.

The second version of Jesus' statement about his role of giving lifetime of the early Church in the form of the second coming of Christ and the end of the world. This interpretation appears justified by the use of the title Son of man, which recalls Daniel 7:13, where the Son of man appears in the context of the final judgment. The by the use of the title, Son of man. which recalls Daniel 7:13, where the Son of man appears in the context of the final judgment. The reference to the dead rising from their tombs brings to mind the resurrection of the physically dead. On the day of the resurrection, both the good and the evil will experience the consequences of their actions. Jesus' description of the giving of life and the passing of judgment appears to be inspired by Daniel 12:2.

The closing verse of the second version is completely parallel with the opening verse of the first version in which Jesus emphasizes the absolute harmony that exists between him and his Father. Thus, in both versions, while there are the differences cited above, the one constant is Jesus performing the will of his Father.

WITNESSES TO JESUS (5:31–47)

[31]If I bear witness to myself, my testimony is not true; [32]there is another who bears witness to me, and I know that the testimony which he bears to me is true. [33]You sent to John, and he has borne witness to the truth. [34]Not that the testimony which I receive is from man; but I say this that you may be saved. [35]He was a burning and shining lamp, and you were willing to rejoice for a while in his light. [36]But the testimony which I have is greater than that of John; for the works which the Father has granted me to accomplish, these very works which I am doing, bear me witness that the Father has sent me. [37]And the Father who sent me has himself borne witness to me. His voice you have never heard, his form you have never seen; [38]and you do not have his word abiding in you, for you do not believe him whom he has sent. [39]You search the scriptures, because you think that in them you have eternal life; and it is they that bear witness to me; [40]yet you refuse to come to me that you may have life. [41]I do not receive glory from men. [42]But I know that you have not the love of God within you. [43]I have come in my Father's name, and you do not receive me; if another comes in his own name, him you will receive. [44]How can you believe, who receive glory from one another and do not seek the glory that comes from the only God? [45]Do not think that I shall accuse you to the Father; it is Moses who accuses you, on whom you set your hope. [46]If you believed Moses, you would believe me, for he wrote of me. [47]But if you do not believe his writings, how will you believe my words?"

After clearly laying claim to the divine prerogatives of giving life and judging, Jesus anticipates the objection of the Jewish leaders that his claim is purely gratuitous. He admits that unless he has the support of another's testimony, his own assertions cannot be accepted as true. Jesus repeats this legal principle in 8:17, referring to the law (Deut. 19:15). While this Old Testament principle refers to the necessity of more than one witness when a person is accused

77

of a crime, Jesus expands the principle as rabbinic documents had done.

Jesus in the fourth gospel points to four witnesses which ought to have moved the Jewish leaders to belief. These witnesses can be considered four different aspects of "another, who bears witness to me . . . " the "another" in reality being the Father. The first of those witnesses is John the Baptist, whose authority was accepted by the Jews without question. John identifies Jesus as the Son of God, who will baptize with the Holy Spirit (1:19-34).

The second witness of the validity of Jesus' claims are the works which the Father enables Jesus to accomplish. The word Jesus uses to refer to his miracles, "works," (erga), is a term which refers to the activity of God in the Old Testament on behalf of his people, beginning with creation and continuing through the entire history of their salvation. In using this same expression, Jesus points to the continuity between his work and the work of his Father. Although the works of Jesus refers to his ministry as a whole and even to his words (17:4), miracles are prominent among the works which Jesus is enabled to accomplish by his Father. These miracles reveal the truth of Jesus' claims not only because they are made possible solely by the power of the Father but because the miracles themselves are salvific and life-giving, a reflection of the works of the Father.

The third witness to Jesus is an interior witness of the Father. Although the fourth gospel possibly refers to some external self-disclosure of the Father, such as at Sinai (Exod. 19:9,11), it is more likely that John is referring to some inner testimony of the Father within the hearts of people. This seems especially true when Jesus says that "you do not have his word abiding in you, for you do not believe him whom he has sent," suggesting that the opposite would be true, that those who believe have the word of God in their hearts.

The fourth and final witness to the authenticity of Jesus' claims are the Scriptures, which clearly come from God and which the Jewish leaders accept as the source of life (e.g., Deut. 4:1; 30:15-20). On numerous occasions Jesus states very clearly that his life and ministry are a fulfillment of the Old Testament, and refers to specific texts which predict his coming and the nature of his mission and final destiny (Matt. 5:17; 11:2-6; 26:24; Luke 4:16-21; 24:25-27).

Notwithstanding the impeccability of the witnesses which clearly support Jesus' claims, he is rejected by the Jewish leaders. They will not accept him as the source of life and as one who has been sent by the Father. The faith which Jesus demands involves more than trusting in him; Jesus rightfully expects them to dedicate themselves to him and to commit themselves to a way of life to which he calls them. Their resistance to him, that is, their disbelief, is rooted in the absence of God's word and in the absence of the power of God's love in their hearts. Jesus views their present attitude towards him as the reflection of, the culmination of, a lifetime of infidelity to the covenant and to the Father, which has driven God's word and God's love from their inner selves. Their decision to reject Jesus exposes them for the unfaithful disciples of the Father they really are. In another confrontation with the Jews, Jesus denies that they are children of Abraham or of the Father, and goes so far as to claim that their true father is the devil (8:39-44). Jesus interprets their rejection of him as a rejection of the Father. He thus accuses them of being more interested in honoring each other than with glorifying the Father.

Jesus shatters the false security which is rooted in their belief that they are genuine disciples of Moses (9:28) by claiming that even Moses will reject them. If the law and the prophets witness to the validity of Jesus' claims, then the Jewish leaders find themselves deprived of all hope and security, since they are implicitly rejected by the founders of their own tradition. The hatred for Jesus on the part of the Jews intensifies once they realize that Jesus asserts that they have placed themselves outside the pale of salvation (Luke 13:28).

The Feeding of the Five Thousand;
Discourse on the Bread of Life (6:1–71)

Following the miraculous feeding of the five thousand at the Sea of Galilee, Jesus challenges the crowd and his disciples to move beyond the reality of bread, physical nourishment and natural life, to the higher level of spiritual nourishment and eternal life. Just as he has identified himself in chapter 5 as the healer who "gives life to whom he will" (v. 21), so here he identifies himself as the "bread of God" which "gives life to the world." As we shall see, Jesus nourishes and gives life not only as the revelation of God which is to be believed but also as the one who is present in the Christian Eucharist to be eaten and drunk with faith. The tragic rejection which he experienced with the Jewish leaders in Jerusalem following the miraculous healing at the pool of Bethzatha is repeated in the province of Galilee. Even more tragic is the fact that he is now not only rejected by the Jewish leaders, and the crowds in Galilee, but also by many of his own disciples.

THE FEEDING OF THE FIVE THOUSAND (6:1–15)

¹After this Jesus went to the other side of the Sea of Galilee, which is the Sea of Tiberias. ²And a multitude followed him, because they saw the signs which he did on those who were diseased. ³Jesus went up into the hills, and there sat down with his disciples. ⁴Now the Passover, the feast of the Jews, was at hand. ⁵Lifting up his eyes, then, and seeing that a multitude was coming to him, Jesus said to Philip, "How are we to buy bread, so that these people may eat?" ⁶This he said to test him, for he himself knew what he would do. ⁷Philip answered him, "Two hundred denarii would not buy enough bread for each of them to get a little." ⁸One of his disciples, Andrew, Simon Peter's brother, said to him, ⁹"There is a lad here who has

five barley loaves and two fish; but what are they among so many?"
¹⁰Jesus said, "Make the people sit down." Now there was much grass in the place; so the men sat down, in number about five thousand. ¹¹Jesus then took the loaves, and when he had given thanks, he distributed them to those who were seated; so also the fish, as much as they wanted. ¹²And when they had eaten their fill, he told his disciples, "Gather up the fragments left over, that nothing may be lost." ¹³So they gathered them up and filled twelve baskets with fragments from the five barley loaves, left by those who had eaten. ¹⁴When the people saw the sign which he had done, they said, "This is indeed the prophet who is to come into the world!"

¹⁵Perceiving then that they were about to come and take him by force to make him king, Jesus withdrew again to the hills by himself.

The miraculous feeding of the five thousand takes place on the southwest shore of the Galilean lake which came to be known as the Sea of Tiberias, after the city of Tiberias (named after the Emperor) established by Herod Antipas in A.D. 20. Jesus notices that he has been followed there by the crowds who were attracted to him due to the miraculous healings he had performed. The reference to signs, which would normally imply a larger number than the two which had been recorded in the fourth gospel (chaps. 4 and 5), is somewhat puzzling. In fact, only one of these, the healing of the official's son at Capernaum, was performed in Galilee. However, it should be pointed out that the miracles which John's gospel narrates are probably only a very limited selection from a collection of miracle-stories contained in material which had been edited for use in the fourth gospel.

The crowd which follows him has been moved to an incipient belief, an imperfect acceptance of Jesus with which Jesus is dissatisfied. Jesus' expectation is that the people will see his signs as something more than evidence of a supernatural power; he will be satisfied only when those who observe his signs become capable of perceiving beyond the external reality to the higher reality which is symbolized.

The miracle that now follows is the only miracle which is narrated in all four gospels. Matthew (14:13-21; 15:29-38) and Mark (6:31-44; 8:1-10) have two accounts of the same incident, while Luke has one account (9:10-17). The fourth gospel emphasizes that the miracle takes place around the feast of Passover. The importance of this time frame will be better appreciated as the discourse unfolds.

When Jesus goes up into the hills (some translators point to the definite article that accompanies the Greek word for mountain, *to oros*, and translate *the* mountain), he sits with the disciples. *The mountain calls to mind Sinai*, the mountain of Moses, who is compared to Jesus in this chapter of the fourth gospel. Jesus sits as if to teach, although John does not explicitly refer to any teaching at this time as Mark does in his account of the miracle, at 6:34. Jesus prepares the stage for the sign he is about to perform by asking Philip where enough bread can be purchased for this number of people. Jesus' question to Philip is similar to the question which Moses asks of the Lord when he had to face the people of Israel in the wilderness (Num. 11:13). The magnitude of the task facing Jesus and the disciples is underlined by Philip's response that not even 200 denarii, the wages earned by one person working for 200 days, would suffice to satisfy this crowd. The power of Jesus enables him to feed a crowd consisting not merely of five thousand men but also, as Matthew's narrative makes clear, the women and children accompanying them (Matt. 14:21).

Jesus takes the bread obtained from the young boy, and gives thanks. While John uses the word *eucharistein,* which in classic and Koine Greek signifies giving thanks, the synoptics in their account of the feeding of the five thousand use the word *eulogein.* *Eulogein* translates the Hebrew word *barak*, meaning to bless, which has a broader meaning than giving thanks. In the Old Testament, to bless God means to recognize and honor God's power, sublimity, and holiness, and to express that recognition in prayers of praise (Gen. 24:48; Deut. 8:10; Judg. 5:2,9). As he held the bread, Jesus may have spoken a simple Jewish prayer of praise. John has Jesus distributing the bread while the synoptics, more realistically, state that the disciples carried out this task among such a large crowd. By having Jesus distribute the bread directly, as the synoptics have him do in their account of the last supper, it appears that at this point John already makes allusion to his narrative of Jesus' institution of the Eucharist which is contained later in this chapter (vv. 51-58).

The people, aware of what has happened, interpret the event as evidence of a power which can deliver them from their political bondage, and hail Jesus as "the prophet who is to come into the world." Whether this is a general reference to any prophet (as in 9:17), to Moses (relating to the allusion to the manna in v. 31), or to Elijah (1:24-28), it is clear that they see him as a political Messiah, someone who could repeat the wonders of the exodus. Jesus, realizing that they will attempt to force him into taking a political role, moves farther up the mountain.

THE STILLING OF THE STORM (6:16–20)

[16]*When evening came, his disciples went down to the sea, [17]got into a boat and started across the sea to Capernaum. It was now dark, and Jesus had not yet come to them. [18]The sea rose because a strong wind was blowing. [19]When they had rowed about three or four miles, they saw Jesus walking on the sea and drawing near to the boat. They were frightened, [20]but he said to them, "It is I; do not be afraid." [21]Then they were glad to take him into the boat, and immediately the boat was at the land to which they were going.*

In the fourth gospel, as in Matthew and Mark, the feeding of the crowd is followed by the description of Jesus' miraculous walk on the lake during a sudden storm (Matt. 14:22-27; Mark 6:45-51). In Mark and Matthew, great stress is laid upon the fury of the storm and upon the ability of Jesus to silence this wild force of nature. They also underline the fact that Jesus rescued the disciples from danger. The fourth gospel, however, has a different focus. The narrative may be considered a corrective to what Jesus considered the crowd's superficial interpretation of the multiplication of the loaves and fishes. While they see Jesus as another Moses, Elijah, or one of the prophets, he wishes to make it clear that he belongs to the realm of the divine.

The key words in this scene are Jesus' response to the disciples in his attempt to reassure them in their fright: "It is I; do not be afraid." Throughout the fourth gospel, the expression *ego eimi* (it is I) is a clear indication of the divinity and transcendence of Christ (see also the commentary on 7:33). Furthermore, the reassuring words *me phobeisthe* (do not fear) occur frequently in the Old Testament within the context of a theophany (Gen. 15:1; 26:24; Josh. 1:9; Isa. 41:14).

John's narrative of the miraculous walking on the water may also be seen as reminiscent of the first Passover during which the people of Israel escaped the bondage of Egypt. This interpretation becomes all the more persuasive if we recall that John makes explicit mention of the feast of the Passover as the time frame for this occurence, and if we also consider the other Passover elements in this chapter (vv. 31-32, 49). Through this miracle, Jesus reminds us of the one whose control over the sea enabled Israel to make its escape (Exod. 14:19 ff.; 15:1-21; Ps. 77:17-21). Furthermore, the Passover significance of Jesus' display of his power over the sea within the framework of this chapter may also be seen in Psalms 78 and 107, which celebrate in close proximity the spectacle of the crossing of the Red Sea and the gift of manna, the grain of heaven. Finally, aside from the specific references to the power of God over the waters during the event of the exodus, the Old Testament has always considered domination over the seas as a divine prerogative (Gen. 1:2, 6ff; Ps. 74:12-15; 93:3f.).

JESUS THE BREAD OF LIFE (6:22-71)

²²On the next day the people who remained on the other side of the sea saw that there had been only one boat there, and that Jesus had not entered the boat with his disciples, but that his disciples had gone away alone. ²³However, boats from Tiberias came near the place where they ate the bread after the Lord had given thanks. ²⁴So when the people saw that Jesus was not there, nor his disciples, they themselves got into the boats and went to Capernaum, seeking Jesus.

²⁵When they found him on the other side of the sea, they said to him, "Rabbi, when did you come here?" ²⁶Jesus answered them, "Truly, truly, I say to you, you seek me, not because you saw signs, but because you ate your fill of the loaves. ²⁷Do not labor for the food which perishes, but for the food which endures to eternal life, which the Son of man will give you; for on him has God the Father set his seal." ²⁸Then they said to him, "What must we do, to be doing the work of God?" ²⁹Jesus answered them, "This is the work of God,

*that you believe in him whom he has sent." *[30]*So they said to him, "Then what sign do you do, that we may see, and believe you? What work do you perform? *[31]*Our fathers ate the manna in the wilderness; as it is written, 'He gave them bread from heaven to eat.' " *[32]*Jesus then said to them, "Truly, truly, I say to you, it was not Moses who gave you the bread from heaven; my Father gives you the true bread from heaven. *[33]*For the bread of God is that which comes down from heaven, and gives life to the world." *[34]*They said to him, "Lord, give us this bread always."*

Some of the crowd which had attempted to force Jesus to become their political Messiah refused to give up, and searched for him after his disappearance. After failing to locate him in the area where they had witnessed the miraculous feeding, they went on to Capernaum. Finding him there, they express their puzzlement and question him concerning his arrival there. Jesus does not respond directly to their question by disclosing to them the manner by which he had arrived. Rather, he raises their question to a higher level and speaks of his origins within a theological context by his reference to the Son of man and to the "bread from heaven."

Jesus confronts the crowd with their failure to see beyond the material reality of the sign to the higher reality still hidden from them. He challenges them to work not for the bread which perishes (and which allows them to perish) but to work for a food which endures for eternal life (which brings that life to them). Jesus' conversation with the crowd is reminiscent of his dialogue with the Samaritan woman. When Jesus spoke to her of the "living water" (4:10f.), she could not see beyond the material water in the well. Referring to himself as the Son of man, in anticipation of his future glory after his death and resurrection, Jesus promises that it is he who will give them the food through which they will possess eternal life, the life of God himself. In response to their query as to what they must do, Jesus responds simply that there is nothing they can do to earn that life. All that is required of them is that they "believe in him whom he has sent." Jesus makes the same uncompromising demand here which he made in his discussion with the Jewish leaders at the pool of Bethzatha. Eternal life will be granted only to those who believe in him.

We can understand the nature of the faith which Jesus demands if we take note of the fact that the fourth gospel never uses *pistis* (faith), a noun, when the issue of faith arises. John considers faith an *active* commitment, and not merely a static disposition. To express that sense of action, John uses the verb, *pisteuin* (to believe). Furthermore, to underline even more the sense of action and movement, he always uses the preposition *eis* (into), with the verb *pisteuin*. Having faith in (into) Jesus implies an active acceptance of his words, which inevitably leads to action.

The Jews respond to Jesus' demand for faith by challenging him to perform a sign, implying that they can place their belief in him only if he proves himself and performs, for example, a miracle such as Moses performed in producing the manna in the desert, considered to be his greatest miracle (Exod. 16; Num. 11). The crowds expect something similar from Jesus since they consider him a prophet like Moses (v. 14). On the other hand, this demand for a sign at first appears puzzling, since the crowd had already witnessed the miraculous feeding on the previous day. However, it may very well be that there were some in the crowd at Capernaum who were not present at that occurrence.

The sign insisted upon by the crowd is not a sign *(semeion)*, in the normal usage of the fourth gospel. In the mind of the crowd, the sign they desire is an outward miraculous deed which will prove to them that Jesus has the authority to demand faith (Matt. 12:38-39; Luke: 11,29; 23:8). On the contrary, in the sign of John's gospel, the material phenomenon is secondary and is not intended to authenticate Jesus' claims. The primary value of the sign in the fourth gospel is its value as a symbol, insofar as it points beyond itself to the spiritual results of God's action upon his people. When Jesus heals the man at the pool of Bethzatha (chap. 5), his primary interest is not in the external deed of healing or in revealing himself as the healer of bodies, but in manifesting himself as the one who possesses the ability to destroy Satan's domination over the world, and to bring eternal life to Satan's prisoners.

Rather than becoming entangled in an argument over the crowd's lack of perception, Jesus seizes upon the Old Testament text which they quoted when they referred to Moses' miracle of the manna: "He gave them bread from heaven to eat." This citation may refer to several Old Testament texts which refer to the bread given from heaven (Exod. 16:4; Neh. 9:15; Ps. 78; 105:40). Jesus corrects their interpretation, stating that his Father, and not Moses is the source of the bread from heaven. At the same time, the bread, the true bread from heaven was not given in the past, but is given now by the Father. Jesus tells them that the bread of God is that which comes down from heaven and gives life to the world. Just as the Samaritan woman failed to perceive the reality beyond the material water (4:15), so the crowd continues to ask Jesus for material bread. It is this persistent lack of understanding which leads Jesus into the long discourse on the bread of life and which compels him to point to himself as the source of eternal life.

[35]*Jesus said to them, "I am the bread of life; he who comes to me shall not hunger, and he who believes in me shall never thirst.* [36]*But I said to you that you have seen me and yet do not believe.* [37]*All that the Father gives me will come to me; and him who comes to me I will not cast out.* [38]*For I have come down from heaven, not to do my own will, but the will of him who sent me;* [39]*and this the will of him who sent me, that I should lose nothing of all that he has given me, but raise it up at the last day.* [40]*For this is the will of my Father, that every one who sees the Son and believes in him should have eternal life; and I will raise him up at the last day.*

[41]*The Jews then murmured at him, because he said, "I am the bread which came down from heaven."* [42]*They said, "Is not this Jesus, the son of Joseph, whose father and mother we know? How does he now say, 'I have come down from heaven'?"* [43]*Jesus answered them, "Do not murmur among yourselves.* [44]*No one can come to me unless the Father who sent me draws him; and I will raise him up at the last day.* [45]*It is written in the prophets, 'And they shall all be taught by God.' Every one who has heard and learned from the Father comes to me.* [46]*Not that any one has seen the Father except him who is from God; he has seen the Father.* [47]*Truly, truly, I say to you, he who believes has eternal life.* [48]*I am the bread of life.* [49]*Your fathers ate the manna in the wilderness, and they died.* [50]*This is the bread which comes down from heaven, that a man may eat of it and not die."*

Jesus now makes it very clear to the crowd that the bread with which he nourished them on the previous day was a sign pointing to himself: "I am the bread of life." He is the source of spiritual life and nourishment. *Ego eimi* (I am) stresses not Jesus' identity in himself, but who and what he is for others. He is bread *for them*. He predicts that the person who believes in him shall not thirst. Jesus' statement brings to mind the words which personified wisdom speaks of herself in 24:21 of the Book of Sirach: "Those who eat me will hunger for more, and those who drink me will thirst for more." Just as the person who approaches wisdom can never be satisfied and cannot be brought to leave the banquet of wisdom, so the person who believes in Jesus will hunger and thirst for the nourishment and life which flow from him, and care for nothing else. The relationship between wisdom and nourishment in the Old Testament, an antecedent to Jesus' discourse, will be discussed later.

In what sense does Jesus see himself as bread, as nourishment, as the source of eternal life? A study of the text of the discourse on the bread of life shows that it is divided into two sections, one comprising verses 35–50, the second, verses 51–58. In the first section, Jesus points to himself primarily as the bearer of divine revelation, while in the second section, he speaks primarily of his presence in the Eucharistic bread. As will be noted below, the second section appears out of place when inserted into this period of Jesus' ministry, and fits better with the account of the last supper.

In the first section it is clear from the type of reaction which he expects from the crowd, that Jesus considers himself to be the source of nourishment and life inasmuch as he is the bearer of divine revelation. He demands and expects that the crowd will believe in him or come to him, which is synonymous with believing in him. The connection Jesus makes between revelation and nourishment is rooted in the Old Testament, where the divine word and wisdom are often described as nourishment and the source of life. Wisdom, which is a very complex concept in the Old Testament, is frequently seen as the experiential knowledge which enables the human person to be virtuous. In the Book of Proverbs, for example, wisdom, which is a gift from the Lord, will enter the heart of the human person, "delivering you from the way of evil, from men of perverted speech . . . men whose paths are crooked, and who are devious in their ways" (2:12, 15). The one who receives this gift "will walk in the way of good men and keep to the paths of the righteous" (Prov. 2:20). The wise person inevitably receives the rewards of happiness and life (Prov. 8:32-36). Time and again, the reward promised to those who follow wisdom is expressed in terms of life (e.g., Prov. 12:28; 11:30; 13:12; 15:4). Wisdom is identified with the law of Moses (Sir. 24:22-29): the one who obeys the law will live (Deut. 5:33); obedience to the law means life, disobedience means death (Deut. 30:15-20). Wisdom is the source of nourishment and life: "Come to me, you who desire me, and eat your fill of my produce. . . . Those who eat me will hunger for more, and those who drink me will thirst for more" (Sir. 24:19, 21-22). Wisdom invites us to her table (Prov. 9:1, 2, 5): "Wisdom . . . has slaughtered her beasts, she has mixed her wine, she has also set her table. . . . Come, eat of my bread, and drink of the wine I have mixed." Of course, the life promised in the Old Testament to those who follow wisdom and obey the law consists of longevity, riches, success, prestige. The life which Jesus promises to those who believe in his word and obey him infinitely surpasses that life, just as the life of the creator infinitely surpasses the life of the creature.

Jesus makes it clear, as if responding indirectly to the crowd's previous question concerning the type of work they must accomplish if they are to gain eternal life, that the capacity to believe in Jesus is a *gift* of the Father, and therefore that he expects openness on their part. Believers are given by the Father to Jesus. Since Jesus has come down from heaven to do the will of his Father, those who are given the power to believe have a divine guarantee, and they cannot be rejected by Jesus. The intermingling of the two traditions of realized eschatology (life here and now) and of final eschatology (life hereafter at the end of the world), which we saw in chapter 5, occurs again in this chapter. In verses 35–38 belief in Jesus implies life here and now, acceptance by Jesus here and now. In verses 39–40, Jesus promises to those who believe in him that he will raise them up on the last day.

The crowd murmurs against Jesus, as their ancestors had murmured against Moses and Aaron in the wilderness (Exod. 16:2, 7, 8). If Jesus' earthly origins are known to them, how can he be the Son of man and the bread of life which has come down from heaven? Jesus ignores their question, and commands them to leave their complaining and their criticism and to open their hearts to the movement of the Father, who can draw them to believe in him. This, Jesus claims, is the age of the new Zion, foretold by Isaiah 54:13, in which the people will be taught directly by God. Jesus repeats his claim to be the bread of life, and, referring back to the Jews' introduction of the miracle of the manna, underlines his superiority to the bread which Moses produced in the desert. Whereas their ancestors have all died (physically), they will live forever if they believe in him.

[51]"*I am the living bread which came down from heaven; if any one eats of this bread, he will live for ever; and the bread which I shall give for the life of the world is my flesh."*

[52]*The Jews then disputed among themselves, saying, "How can this man give us his flesh to eat?"* [53]*So Jesus said to them, "Truly, truly, I say to you, unless you eat the flesh of the Son of man and drink his blood, you have no life in you;* [54]*he who eats my flesh and drinks my blood has eternal life, and I will raise him up at the last day.* [55]*For my flesh is food indeed, and my blood is drink indeed.* [56]*He who eats my flesh and drinks my blood abides in me, and I in him.* [57]*As the living Father sent me, and I live because of the Father, so he who eats me will live because of me.* [58]*This is the bread which came down from heaven, not such as the fathers ate and died; he who eats this bread will live for ever."* [59]*This he said in the synagogue, as he taught at Capernaum.*

While the first part of Jesus' discourse on the bread of life clearly refers to Jesus as the bearer of revelation, the second part focuses on him as the source of nourishment and life within the context of the sacrament of the Eucharist. That this section of the discourse refers to the Eucharist is first seen in the expressions used by Jesus: "eating the flesh of the Son of man" and "drinking his blood." These can in no way be interpreted as metaphors for a believing acceptance of his revelation. These expressions are indeed used metaphorically in the Old Testament, but always as expressions of hostility and destruction. To eat someone's flesh refers either to "uttering slander against someone" (Ps. 27:2) or destroying someone (Zech. 12:9). Drinking someone's blood is a metaphorical expression which refers to a brutal slaughter: "The sword shall devour and be sated, and drink its fill of their blood" (Jer. 46:10).

Secondly, the statement of Jesus, "and the bread which I shall give for the life of the world is my flesh," may very well be the Johannine form of the words of institution, which, as shall be noted further on, were probably displaced from John's account of Jesus' last supper discourse. The similarity between this Johannine formula of institution and the formulas preserved by Luke and Paul should be noted (Luke 22:19; 1 Cor. 11:24).

Scholars generally agree that the material in verses 51–58 was originally located within the Johannine narrative of the last supper, but, after being reshaped to conform to the first part of the bread of life discourse, was later moved to its present position in the gospel. Without this hypothesis, there would be no valid accounting for the absence of the institution narrative at the scene of the last supper, where the other evangelists placed it. Additionally, Jesus' statement on the Eucharist would have been more understandable within the context of the last supper when Jesus celebrated the Passover with his disciples on the evening of his redemptive death. Finally this hypothesis explains the striking similarity of verse 51 to an institutional formula.

Just as the first section of the discourse began with Jesus' statement that he is the bread of life, this section begins with his declaration that he is the living bread. In the Eucharistic discourse, however, Jesus promises life, not to those who believe in him, but to those who eat of this bread. The bread which he offers them to eat is his flesh, himself, *for the life of the world.* Jesus' statement, which is probably the Johannine formula of institution, is, as noted before, strikingly similar to the institution formulas in Luke 22:10 and Paul (1 Cor. 11:24); in all these formulas the connection between the Eucharist and the redemptive death of Christ is clear.

Jesus' declaration that "the bread I will give for the life of the world is my flesh" differs from the synoptic and the Pauline formulas, however, in that John uses the word *sarx* (flesh) while the others utilize *soma* (body). Since there is no specific Hebrew or Aramaic word for body, it is probable that the word actually used by Jesus at the last supper was either *basar*, the Hebrew, or *bisra*, the Aramaic word for flesh or the living body. At the beginning of the gospel, John stressed that the word became *sarx* (flesh, a human being). At this point, he stresses that it is this same human being who will be given to Christians as the food which brings them eternal life.

The Jews object at once, apparently interpreting Jesus' words in a cannibalistic sense. However, in order to convey to them beyond any shadow of a doubt that Jesus himself is really, and not figuratively, encountered and received within the Eucharist, he does not attempt to correct them. On the contrary, he repeats with even greater emphasis that if they are to have life, they must eat his flesh and drink his blood. In order to understand the full significance of Jesus' language at this point, it is vital to recall two facts: 1) the common Hebrew expression for human life, for the entire person, was flesh and blood; 2) since the Passover theme pervades this entire chapter, Jesus' decision to refer separately to flesh and to blood is undoubtedly colored and shaped by certain realities which were key elements of the original Passover event in Jewish history. The manna given to the Jews in the wilderness gave rise to the words of Jesus concerning bread-flesh-eating. The ritual of the blood of the covenant at Sinai (Exod. 24:8) provides the background for his statements about blood and drinking. Following the people's acceptance of the conditions of the covenant the Lord wishes to make with them, Moses ratified the covenant by taking the blood of the oxen which had been sacrificed, and throwing half of it on the altar (representing the Lord) and half upon the people. In this way, Moses expresses the establishment of a covenant between the Lord and the people: "Behold the blood of the covenant which the LORD has made with you in accordance with all these words." The relationship between the Eucharist and the covenant at Sinai is even more explicit in the institution formulas contained in Paul and the synoptics, which refer to the blood of the *new* covenant. Throughout the entire chapter and specifically the discourse on the bread of life, John repeatedly shows the superiority of the new Zion and the new Passover. Once more, before the completion of this discourse, Jesus stresses that the Eucharist is superior to the manna which their ancestors ate. While those who were fed with manna have died, those who eat this bread will have eternal life.

Up to this point, Jesus has promised that those who partake of the Eucharist will have eternal life. Jesus now describes what the Eucharist does for the Christian in another way: "He who eats my flesh and drinks my blood abides (*menei*, signifying a permanent relationship) in me, and I in him." The receiving of the Eucharist leads the Christian to an everlasting relationship with Jesus. Jesus adds that just as he lives through the life which comes to him through his Father, so the person who receives the Eucharist will live through the life which comes to him through Jesus. In other words, the eternal life which Jesus has promised the believer is a sharing in the very life of God himself.

[60]*Many of his disciples, when they heard it, said, "This is a hard saying; who can listen to it?"* [61]*But Jesus, knowing in himself that his disciples murmured at it, said to them, "Do you take offence at this?* [62]*Then what if you were to see the Son of man ascending where he was before?* [63]*It is the spirit that gives life, the flesh is of no avail; the words that I have spoken to you are spirit and life.* [64]*But there are some of you that do not believe." For Jesus knew from the first who those were that did not believe, and who it was that should betray him.* [65]*And he said, "This is why I told you that no one can come to me unless it is granted him by the Father."*

[66]*After this many of his disciples drew back and no longer went about with him.* [67]*Jesus said to the twelve, "Will you also go away?"* [68]*Simon Peter answered him, "Lord, to whom shall we go? You have the words of eternal life;* [69]*and we have believed, and have come to know, that you are the Holy One of God."* [70]*Jesus answered them, "Did I not choose you, the twelve, and one of you is a devil?"* [71]*He spoke of Judas the son of Simon Iscariot, for he, one of the twelve, was to betray him.*

Many of Jesus' disciples respond to his entire discourse with disbelief. They refuse to accept him as one who has come down from heaven, as one who has been sent. Responding to their refusal to commit themselves to him and to their willful rejection of his claim to be sent by the Father, Jesus asks about the kind of reaction they would have if they saw him "ascending to where he was before." If they cannot believe in him as one who has his origin in his Father, then how will they be able to accept the mysteries concerning his return to the Father, that is, his glorification (12:23; 17:5)?

Faced again with the same reaction of disbelief he had encountered among the Jewish leaders in Jerusalem (5:38, 40), Jesus once more insists upon the impossibility of belief in him without the power from above, the power of the Spirit, who gives the life promised by Jesus. This faith cannot be the product of the flesh, that is, the natural powers of the human person (1:14; 3:6). Jesus stresses that the words he has spoken to them in the entire discourse have the power, if accepted in faith, to communicate to believers the life of the Spirit, eternal life.

Once more the fourth gospel underlines the ever-present and painful awareness which Jesus had of the unbelief which surrounded him, an unbelief which he knew would lead some to betray him. In fact, that unbelief becomes immediately visible in his abandonment by many of his disciples. Jesus then turns to the twelve, who are mentioned for the first time in the fourth gospel, and asks whether they too are unbelievers, and whether they are ready to leave him. Answering for the others, Peter responds with what is the Johannine version of the confession of Peter narrated in the synoptics (Mark 8:27-30; Matt. 16:13-20; Luke 9:18-21). Peter confesses that for them, he, who has the words which can bring them eternal life, is their only hope. He acknowledges that they have come to accept him as the "Holy One of God," the Messiah, consecrated and set aside by the Father for the Father's own work in the world. While the fourth gospel seems to wish to end this episode on a note of the triumph of faith, it also appears to be unwilling to omit the ever-present theme of tragedy present in Jesus' ministry. Even as the words of Peter's confession ring in his ears, Jesus cannot but be painfully conscious of the fact that one of the twelve, whom he had chosen in a special way, would betray him.

Jesus at the Feast of Tabernacles (7:1–8:59)

When Jesus arrives in Jerusalem for the feast of Tabernacles, he makes no effort to soften his stance in order to avoid the growing hostility of official Jerusalem. Nor does he seek to offset the dangers he faces from the Jewish leaders by attempting to satisfy the popular thirst for a political Messiah. Jesus arrives determined to teach what he has been sent to teach, once more to affirm his origins, and once again to propose himself as the source of life. The feast, with its themes of life and the messianic era, is an appropriate setting for Jesus' invitation to the people to partake in the life which he is offering. Aware that his invitation not only falls on deaf ears but also further provokes the authorities, Jesus becomes more keenly conscious of the nearness of the end of his life and the moment of his return to the Father. The suffering and death which he will experience at the hands of his enemies will be the road to his glorification and return to the Father. In reality, it is that return which gives meaning to his life, for without it, he cannot offer life and salvation. Ironically, within the present scheme of things, it will be the Jewish leaders who will make possible the glorification and life-giving power of Jesus.

JESUS THE WATER OF LIFE (7:1–52)

¹After this Jesus went about in Galilee; he would not go about in Judea, because the Jews sought to kill him. ²Now the Jews' feast of Tabernacles was at hand. ³So his brothers said to him, "Leave here and go to Judea, that your disciples may see the works you are doing. ⁴For no man works in secret if he seeks to be known openly. If you do these things, show yourself to the world." ⁵For even his brothers did not believe in him. ⁶Jesus said to them, "My time has not yet come, but your time is always here. ⁷The world cannot hate you, but it hates me because I testify of it that its works are evil.

95

⁸Go to the feast yourselves; I am not going up to the feast, for my time has not yet fully come." ⁹So saying, he remained in Galilee.

¹⁰But after his brothers had gone up to the feast, then he also went up, not publicly but in private. ¹¹The Jews were looking for him at the feast, and saying, "Where is he?" ¹²And there was much muttering about him among the people. While some said, "He is a good man," others said, "No, he is leading the people astray." ¹³Yet for fear of the Jews no one spoke openly of him.

During the six-month period which intervened between the Passover, when the miraculous multiplication of the loaves and fishes occurred, and the feast of Tabernacles, Jesus remained in Galilee. He deliberately avoided the province of Judea, which was the center of power of the Jewish leaders who were convinced he was a blasphemer and who therefore planned to kill him. With the feast of Tabernacles approaching, a pilgrimage festival when the pious Jew would normally travel to Jerusalem, some of Jesus' brothers, that is, his near relations or perhaps even cousins, urge him to make the pilgrimage. Foremost in their minds is their conviction that Jesus has been losing an opportunity to advance his own religious and political career by limiting his ministry to Galilee. They want him to display his power to his disciples in Judea and Jerusalem (2:23; 4:1) by performing the types of miracles he had been performing in Galilee. It is clear from this conversation that these relatives continue to misinterpret the significance of Jesus' signs, and therefore are unwilling to accept him as the one who was sent by his Father and who came to bring them life. Once again Jesus is faced with the tragic fact that he is surrounded by people with a distorted perception of his person and his mission, a perception which is shaped by their own preconceived notions of the Messiah, deliberately resisting any challenge to those notions. Once again he is called upon to misuse his power. Just as he was tempted to take upon himself the role of political Messiah (6:15) and to prove his credibility by supplying miraculous bread (6:31), he is urged in this instance to provide a display of power for his disciples in Judea. In fact, the synoptics present Jesus as being so conscious of the popular messianic ideals of the magician and the warrior Messiah which prevailed at that time that he went out of his way to avoid publicizing his messianic role during his ministry (Mark 8:30; 9:9; 1:34; Luke 4:41). His rejection of those very temptations narrated in the fourth gospel in chapters 6 and 7, the temptation to display his power, to supply miraculous bread and to become a political Messiah, is presented in dramatic form by Matthew and Luke in the narrative of the temptation of Jesus in the desert (Matt. 4:1-11; Luke 4:1-13).

Jesus refuses to go, responding that his time has not yet come. Since the word John uses for time is not *chronos*, which would simply refer to chronological time, but *kairos*, it is clear that Jesus is referring to a decisive salvific moment. It is that moment, the moment of his glorification, of his return to his Father through his passion, death and resurrection, which has not yet come. As the hour approaches, John presents the picture of a Jesus who becomes more and more aware of his mission (7:30; 8:20; 12:23, 27; 13:1; 17:1). Jesus also states that his hour has not yet fully come. The Greek, *oupo peplerotai*, literally means that the hour is not yet fulfilled. This theme of the fulfillment of the divine plan as set forth in the Old Testament is ever-present in the New Testament, especially when Jesus speaks of his passion (Matt. 16:21; 17:22-23; 20:17-19; Luke 17:25). However, although the hour of Jesus' glorification is to be seen in its fullness some time in the future, his glorification is embryonically present during his ministry in the signs he performs and the words he speaks. The life which he offers to those who believe in him will be experienced in its fullness only when he has returned to the Father. It is that hour which Jesus awaits and which gives meaning to his entire life.

Jesus cannot speak of his hour without at the same time thinking of the world which hates him and will finally put him to death. The opposition to Jesus, which the fourth gospel explicitly described for the first time on the occasion of Jesus' healing of the man at the pool of Bethzatha, has grown into hatred and hostility, becoming more intense, explicit and deadly as time goes on. In describing Jesus' awareness of the hatred which he experiences, however, the fourth gospel seems to extend its horizons beyond the immediate historical situation of Jesus' personal ministry. At this point, Jesus is not only conscious of the hatred of the Jewish leaders, but also of the hatred of the world. In the second half of John's gospel, which describes the later stages of Jesus' ministry, the Greek word, *kosmos*, which can signify either the universe or the society of humans, refers more and more frequently to those who reject and actively oppose Jesus (9:39; 12:31; 14:17; 16:8-11). The powers in Jerusalem are only the first of a long line of the enemies who will unfailingly oppose and persecute Jesus and his followers throughout the centuries.

After very clearly indicating that he does not intend to go to Jerusalem, Jesus does in fact decide to travel to the city. What appears to be a deception on Jesus' part has puzzled and disturbed Christians over the centuries. In fact, it appears that the "yet" in verse 8 of some gospel manuscripts may have been added by a scribe in order to avoid any appearance of deception on Jesus' part. However, the difficulty disappears when we realize that what we have here is another example of the fourth gospel's use of a word which contains different levels of meaning at the same time. The Greek verb, *anabainein*, which means to go up in pilgrimage, also means to ascend to the Father (20:17). It is clear, especially if we take into consideration Jesus' statement about the hour to which he looks forward and which has yet to be fulfilled, that Jesus here refers to his return to his Father through his passion, death, resurrection and ascension. The hour of his suffering and death is but one phase of his glorification, and is followed, as naturally as the dawn follows the darkness of night, by the final phases of his glorification in his resurrection and ascension to the Father. In fact, the narrative of the passion and death of Jesus in the fourth gospel is more a history of a triumph than of a defeat, contrasting sharply with the narrative recorded by the synoptics. John omits the narrative of the agony in the garden and includes few of the humiliations and indignities suffered by Jesus at the hands of his judges. In the presence of Pilate, John has Jesus openly declare his kingship. When Jesus speaks of his hour and of going up to the Father, it is with the profound awareness that the glory foreshadowed in the signs he has performed awaits him at the end of the road of suffering.

After John indicates that Jesus finally did go to Jerusalem, he describes in vivid colors the charged atmosphere which Jesus enters. Jerusalem looks for Jesus, wonders where he is, and takes sides. However, John notes that whatever debates go on between those favoring Jesus and those who consider him a deceiver of the people, take place very quietly, since "for fear of the Jews [i.e. the Jewish leaders] no one spoke openly of him."

¹⁴About the middle of the feast Jesus went up into the temple and taught. ¹⁵The Jews marvelled at it, saying, "How is it that this man has learning, when he has never studied?" ¹⁶So Jesus answered them, "My teaching is not mine, but his who sent me; ¹⁷if any man's will is to do his will, he shall know whether the teaching is from God or whether I am speaking on my own authority. ¹⁸He who speaks on his own authority seeks his own glory; but he who seeks the glory of him who sent him is true, and in him there is no falsehood. ¹⁹Did not Moses give you the law? Yet none of you keeps the law. Why do you seek to kill me?" ²⁰The people answered, "You have a demon! Who is seeking to kill you?" ²¹Jesus answered them, "I did one deed, and you all marvel at it. ²²Moses gave you circumcision (not that it is from Moses, but from the fathers), and you circumcise a man upon the sabbath. ²³If on the sabbath a man receives circumcision, so that the law of Moses may not be broken, are you angry with me because on the sabbath I made a man's whole body well? ²⁴Do not judge by appearances, but judge with right judgment."

²⁵Some of the people of Jerusalem therefore said, "Is not this the man whom they seek to kill? ²⁶And here he is, speaking openly, and they say nothing to him! Can it be that the authorities really know that this is the Christ? ²⁷Yet we know where this man comes from; and when the Christ appears, no one will know where he comes from." ²⁸So Jesus proclaimed, as he taught in the temple, "You know me, and you know where I come from? But I have not come of my own accord; he who sent me is true, and him you do not know. ²⁹I know him, for I come from him, and he sent me." ³⁰So they sought to arrest him; but no one laid hands on him, because his hour had not yet come. ³¹Yet many of the people believed in him; they said, "When the Christ appears, will he do more signs than this man has done?"

³²The Pharisees heard the crowd thus muttering about him, and the chief priests and Pharisees sent officers to arrest him. ³³Jesus then said, "I shall be with you a little longer, and then I go to him who sent me; ³⁴you will seek me and you will not find me; where I am you cannot come." ³⁵The Jews said to one another, "Where does this man intend to go that we shall not find him? Does he intend to go to the Dispersion among the Greeks and teach the Greeks? ³⁶What does he mean by saying, 'You will seek me and you will not find me,' and 'Where I am you cannot come'?"

On the third or fourth day of the week-long feast, Jesus begins to teach in the temple. Since the ceremonies of the feast of Tabernacles, which will be elaborated upon later in this chapter, take place within the temple, Jesus finds a large audience for his teaching. His right to teach is immediately challenged by some in the crowd, since it was a well-known fact that Jesus had never gone through any formal training in the rabbinical schools. Jesus defends his right to teach, and responds to the crowd's skepticism by claiming that his doctrine originates in an authority which far exceeds the authority of any rabbinical school of the present or past. The teaching which Jesus proposes is not his, but "is his who sent me." Jesus claims that his truthfulness may easily be seen in the fact that he does not seek his own glory, is not speaking on his own behalf, but is a spokesperson for the Father, who is truthful (3:33; 8:26). Any person who has within himself a genuine desire to do the will of God will instinctively know where Jesus' teaching comes from.

Jesus' claim that he does not speak on his own authority and does not seek his own glory calls to mind his description of the relationship of absolute dependence existing between himself and the Father recorded by John in 5:19-20, 26, 30. Jesus merely declares what he has seen with the Father; it is the Father's words and teachings that Jesus proposes to people (3:34; 8:28; 12:49, 50; 14:24; 17:8, 14). Because there is such a unity between the Father and Jesus, and because Jesus is a faithful spokesperson, he is able to say to Philip, "He who has seen me has seen the Father. . . ." (14:9). The power and authority of Jesus' words are not lost on the crowds who listened to Jesus' words as recorded in the sermon on the mount (Matt. 5: 1–7:29): "And when Jesus had finished these sayings, the crowds were astonished at his teaching, for he taught them as one who had authority, and not as their scribes" (Matt. 7:28-29). The crowd's astonishment is not attributed to what Jesus said, but to his manner of teaching. Whereas the scribes stressed the continuity of their own teaching with the traditions, Jesus made no attempt to demonstrate his fidelity to tradition. In fact, in the sermon on the mount, he deliberately departed from tradition.

Having for the time being disposed of the question of his authority to teach, Jesus then takes the offensive by accusing the crowd of infidelity to the very law of Moses in which they take such pride, the law in which they received the formal education which Jesus lacks. While knowing that law and studying it, they seem to have no scruples about breaking it. It appears that the law to which Jesus is referring is the prohibition of murder, since he immediately follows up his statement by asking them to offer him the reason behind their plot to kill him. Jesus' accusation provokes anger, indignation and hatred as intense as similar feelings he provoked when he predicted that because they refused to believe in him, they would stand condemned by Moses, "on whom you set your hope" (5:45). To thus expose their infidelity to the very law in which they glory and which is the bed rock of their security, is to reveal to them and to others the hollowness and futility of their lives. That this kind of statement was fraught with danger is something of which Jesus was well aware: "The world cannot hate you, but it hates me because I testify of it that its works are evil."

Denying that they are plotting to kill Jesus, the crowd attributes Jesus' suspicions to his insanity (literally: You have a demon), considered to be the effect of demonic possession. Jesus attempts to prove to his enemies that his statement about their evil intention is grounded in reality when he reminds them that their desire to kill him can be traced back to the time when he healed the man at the pool of Bethzatha on the sabbath (5:18). Once more, Jesus sets out to justify his decision to heal on the sabbath. During this debate, Jesus does not again offer the theological justification which so enraged the Jewish leaders on the occasion of the healing (5:17). Jesus here justifies his healing on the sabbath by pointing to the superiority of his act of healing to the practice of circumcision, which the Jews allow on the sabbath, if the eighth day after a person's birth happens to fall on the sabbath. Circumcision, originally an initiation rite before marriage, became for the Israelites a sign of incorporation into the community of Israel and a sign of the covenant God made with Abraham and his descendants (Gen. 17:9-14; 34:14-16; Exod. 12:47-48). However, now that the one to whom the Scriptures bear witness (5:39) is here, now that the one of whom Moses wrote is here (5:46), ought not his work of healing the entire person take precedence even over circumcision? In other words, Jesus' deliberate decision to heal on the sabbath was one striking method he used to assert the superiority of his ministry to the law of Moses and the old order. The covenant between God and Israel is now supplanted by a new covenant with the coming of Jesus. The new order brings with it a salvation which is symbolized and effected in events such as the healing of the man at the pool of Bethzatha.

Some in the crowd, who witness the debate taking place between Jesus and his enemies, are puzzled over Jesus' ability to speak so openly. The failure of the Jewish leaders to stop Jesus raises the question of whether the authorities have already accepted him as the Messiah. Someone objects, however, that Jesus cannot be the Messiah, since they all know from where he comes (Nazareth). This group obviously belongs to the school of thought which held to the theory of the hidden Messiah, i.e., that the Messiah's origins would be unknown, that his arrival would be sudden, and that he would appear as if from nowhere. The irony of this statement is that they do not know the origins of Jesus, i.e., that he has his origin in the Father.

Jesus has heard those in the crowd who claim that they know where he has come from. As the Jesus of the fourth gospel does on many other occasions, he uses the misunderstanding of the crowd as a departure for developing a dialogue revealing a truth about himself. Once more Jesus speaks of his origin in the Father, of his dependency upon the one who sent him. Once more, he speaks of the special intimate relationship which he has with the Father (1:18; 6:46; 8:25; 17:25). Infuriated once more by Jesus' bold affirmation of his unique relationship to the divine, the authorities again make plans to arrest him. However, at this point, the fourth gospel brings to our attention the fact that Jesus is not a passive, helpless victim: whatever happens to him falls within the plan of God. Without the full consent of Jesus, the Jewish leaders would have no power over him: "So they sought to arrest him; but no one laid hands on him, because his hour had not yet come." When his hour does come according to the Father's plan, Jesus freely gives himself over to his enemies who come for him in the garden (18:6-8).

The nervousness of the chief priests and Pharisees about Jesus intensifies when they hear the crowd marveling about the many signs Jesus has performed. It appears that "many of the people believed in him." However, the emphasis placed by these believers upon the signs is an indication that this belief is incipient, a belief in which Jesus would not place much trust. He is seen as a wonder worker, a wizard. The tragedy of Jesus' ministry is that not only is he rejected, hated and actively opposed by one particular group, but that he is superficially understood by most of the people. When Jesus attempts to urge them to go beyond the limited understanding they evidence, he finds that they too reject him, since he does not fit into their notion of the Messiah.

Faced with the hatred of the Jewish leaders and always aware of their plots to kill him, Jesus perforce begins to think more of his final return to his Father, and addresses the crowd concerning that return. Constantly aware of his destiny and the purpose for which he was sent, and conscious of the fact that the hour, that is, the decisive moment, is approaching, Jesus tells the crowd that he will be with them only a little longer, an expression he will use on other occasions in the fourth gospel (12:35; 13:33; 14:19; 16:16). Implicit in this statement is Jesus' attempt to urge the Jews to seek after him while there is still time. Once he has returned to the Father and been glorified, they will have lost their opportunity. Their stubborn resistance to Jesus' message will have created in their hearts an alienation of such depth that they will have reached a point of no return: ". . . where I am, you cannot come."

At this point in the fourth gospel, it is essential to stop and reflect on the meaning of the expression, *ego eimi*, that is, "I am," used so often in John. We have already seen it used by Jesus during his conversation with the Samaritan woman (4:26) and during his attempt to calm his disciples who witnessed him walking on the water (6:20). It appears that the Johannine Jesus, in using this expression, is referring to his divinity. If we examine the *ego eimi* in the fourth gospel, we will recognize that it is used in three different grammatical constructions: 1) absolutely, without a predicate (8:24; 8:28; 8:58; 13:19); 2) where a predicate, while not expressed, may be understood (6:20; 18:5); 3) with a predicate nominative (e.g., 6:35, 51; 8:12; 10:7, 9; 11:25).

The Johannine usage of this expression which is taken to refer to Christ's divinity is best understood in the light of the Old Testament and of late Judaism. God tells who and what he is with the expression "I Yahweh" or "I God" without the Hebrew connecting verb (Gen. 28:13; Ezek. 20:5). The expression "I am Yahweh" is used when God wishes to assure his hearers of the validity of his statement, since it comes from him (Exod. 6:6; 20:1, 5). The expression is also used in many passages in Deutero-Isaiah (e.g., Isa. 43:10-13; 45:5-6, 18, 20-21; 46:9) to refer to the fact that there is no other to rival him. The Hebrew in Isa. 45:18 is translated simply in the Greek translation as *ego eimi*. This formula in the Septuagint came to signify not only the unicity of God, but also his very existence. In the Greek versions of Exodus 3:14, the all-important text for the meaning of the Hebrew word *Yahweh*, the Greek translates Yahweh as the existing one, thus stressing divine existence. In the Greek version of Isaiah 43:25, we read *ego eimi* twice, leading to the conclusion that the best translation seems to be "I am I AM who blots out transgressions."

In the light of this Old Testament background and of the fact that late Judaism considered "I am" a divine name, we can understand the Johannine usage of *ego eimi* in an absolute way, without any predicate. At the same time, the absolute use of *ego eimi* in John is the basis for the other uses, in particular when Jesus is quoted as describing himself in terms of his salvific activity on behalf of humankind: the bread of life, the light of the world, the shepherd, the resurrection and the life, the vine. Similarly, in the Old Testament, God described himself as "your salvation" (Ps. 35:3), "your healer" (Exod. 15:26), and so on in other passages.

When Jesus tells the crowd that they will be unable to follow him, they again misunderstand his statement, and debate whether Jesus is planning to travel to the Diaspora, that is, to the Jews who live outside the Holy Land, and to teach those who have been influenced by the Greek culture. We have in their mocking speculation another example of Johannine irony. Rejected by his own people, Jesus was finally accepted by the Gentiles who would receive the Word of God and would have the Holy Spirit poured out on them (Acts 10:44-48; 11:1).

[37]*On the last day of the feast, the great day, Jesus stood up and proclaimed, "If any one thirst, let him come to me and drink.* [38]*He who believes in me, as the scripture has said, 'Out of his heart shall flow rivers of living water.' "* [39]*Now this he said about the Spirit, which those who believed in him were to receive; for as yet the Spirit had not been given, because Jesus was not yet glorified.*

[40]*When they heard these words, some of the people said, "This is really the prophet."* [41]*Others said, "This is the Christ." But some said, "Is the Christ to come from Galilee?* [42]*Has not the scripture*

said that the Christ descended from David, and comes from Bethlehem, the village where David was?" ⁴³So there was a division among the people over him. ⁴⁴Some of them wanted to arrest him, but no one laid hands on him.

⁴⁵The officers then went back to the chief priests and Pharisees, who said to them, "Why did you not bring him?" ⁴⁶The officers answered, "No man ever spoke like this man!" ⁴⁷The Pharisees answered them, "Are you led astray, you also? ⁴⁸Have any of the authorities or of the Pharisees believed in him? ⁴⁹But this crowd who do not know the law, are accursed." ⁵⁰Nicodemus, who had gone to him before, and who was one of them, said to them, ⁵¹Does our law judge a man without first giving him a hearing and learning what he does?" ⁵²They replied, "Are you from Galilee too? Search and you will see that no prophet is to rise from Galilee."

On the last day of the feast of Tabernacles, Jesus stood up in the temple precincts and issued a solemn invitation: "If anyone thirst, let him come to me and drink." In order to better understand the significance of Jesus' invitation, it is essential at this point to explain the significance of the feast. Tabernacles was one of the three great pilgrimage festivals, together with the feast of Weeks and the feast of Unleavened Bread; in fact, it was the most important and best attended. The Hebrew name for the feast was *sukkot*, which can be translated either as Tabernacles, or Booths, or Tents, or Huts. An agricultural feast, it celebrated the harvest of the fields (Exod. 23:16), of the fullness of the threshing floors and of the wine and oil presses (Deut. 16:13). During this season, the farmers and their families would camp outdoors in huts of branches.

However, it was also an appropriate time to pray for rain for the following year, which the people hoped would be a year of plenty. On each of the mornings of the feast, as it was celebrated in Jerusalem, the people went in procession to the fountain of Gihon on the southeast side of the temple hill, the fountain from which the pool of Siloam received its waters. After the priest filled a golden pitcher with water, the procession moved to the temple, singing the Hallel (Ps. 113-118), carrying the *lulab* (a bunch of myrtle and willow twigs tied with palm) in the left hand. The *lulab* commemorated the branches used to construct the huts in which the Israelites were supposed to have lived following their liberation from Egypt (Lev. 23:43). In reality, the Israelites lived in tents during those days. When the procession reached the altar of holocausts in front of the temple, the priest went up to the altar to pour the water into a silver funnel through which it flowed onto the ground.

Finally, the feast was associated with the messianic era, the days in which the Lord would win his final victory in the world. The prophet Zechariah described the day when " . . . the LORD will become king over all the earth . . ." within the setting of the feast of Tabernacles (Zech. 14:9). Following the victory of Israel through the Lord's power over all nations, every surviving nation ". . . shall go up year after year to worship the King, the LORD of hosts, and to keep the feast of Booths" (Zech. 14:16).

Jesus' solemn invitation clearly refers to a solemn moment in the ceremony in which the water, symbol of life, was poured out over the earth. The translation proposed in the RSV has the "rivers of living water" flow out from the heart of the believer. However, for a number of reasons, other translations, possibly more accurate, would read in such a way that the rivers of living water would come out of Jesus. The translation would then read as follows: "If anyone thirst, let him come to me; and let him drink who believes in me. As the Scripture says, 'From within him shall flow rivers of living water.' " This translation better preserves the poetic parallelism between the first line, where the thirsty person comes to Jesus, and the second line, where the believer drinks from Jesus. Furthermore, and most importantly, this translation is clearly the more logical once the entire context is taken into consideration. The fourth gospel explains that the living water is the Spirit, and it is Jesus, not the believer, who gives the Spirit.

The Scripture passage to which the fourth gospel refers appears to be a combination of several passages. One set seems to be those which allude to the rock which gave forth water in the desert after Moses struck it (Exod. 17:6). In fact, the early Church saw this rock as a type of Christ (1 Cor. 10:4). According to Jewish legend, the rock from which Moses had struck water followed the Israelites during their wanderings in the desert. Paul compares the risen Christ to that rock, since he sees Christ as a source of nourishment for the faithful. The reference to this rock seems all the more logical in view of the fact that the fourth gospel makes many references to the events of the exodus (1:29; 3:14; 6:31; 6:12-21). Reference is also made to the life-giving rock in Isaiah 43:20; 44:3; 48:21. However, the Scripture passage which seems to be the closest in wording to the passage cited by Jesus is Psalm 78:15-16: "He cleft rocks in the wilderness, and gave them drink abundantly as from the deep. He made streams come out of the rock, and caused waters to flow down like rivers."

Two other texts which appear to provide the background for the text quoted by Jesus in verse 38 are Zechariah 14 and Ezekiel 47. As the early Church read the prophecies of these Old Testament apocalyptic authors who spoke of a new world which the Lord would create and of the final triumph of the world, it could not but help see that these prophecies were fulfilled in Jesus. The theme of Zechariah 14 is the suffering which the entire universe and Jerusalem, the center of the world empire, must pass through before the final day of the Lord's triumph. After the time of suffering, victory will emerge: "On that day living waters shall flow out from Jerusalem, half of them to the eastern sea and half of them to the western sea; it shall continue in summer as in winter. And the LORD will become king over all the earth; on that day the LORD will be one and his name one" (Zech. 14:8-9). Jerusalem is compared to life-giving water, and is celebrated as the source of abundant life for nations over the entire earth, i.e., east and west.

In Ezekiel 47 the prophet describes his own vision of the restored community of Israel. He shares this vision with the Jews in Palestine and, following the destruction of Jerusalem in 587 B.C., with the exiles in Babylon. Ezekiel promises that the new city and the new land will be a source of life: "Then he brought me back to the door of the temple; and behold, water was issuing from below the threshold of the temple toward the east . . . . And wherever the river goes every living creature which swarms shall live, and there will be very many fish; for this water goes there, that the waters of the sea may be fresh; so everything will live where the river goes" (47:1, 9). In this passage and many others in the Old Testament, water is a symbol of the life which God will bring to the world in the messianic age.

The background for John's description of Jesus as the source of living water appears then to be two sets of texts, one set dealing with the rock which is the source of life in the desert, the other the apocalyptic texts of the two prophets. Jesus, the source of life, effects the new exodus and brings about God's final triumph in the world.

John explains that the water flowing from Jesus and bringing life is the Spirit, whom believers will receive. To the Hebrew mind, the relationship between water and the Spirit seemed very natural. Isaiah 44:3 describes the giving of the Spirit as the pouring of the Spirit, just as he speaks of the pouring of water on the thirsty land. What more apt metaphor could a Hebrew, who lived in a land where water was so precious and so vividly connected with life, use to describe the life-giving and creative power which was God's Spirit? John adds, however, that Jesus will be the source of living water only at the hour of his glorification, that is, when he has returned to his Father.

On the other hand, Jesus is the source of life and living water inasmuch as he is the source of revelation. Jesus' invitation here is reminiscent of the invitation of divine wisdom (Prov. 1:20; 8:2-3). In the Old Testament, water is used as a symbol of the word of God, which is compared to the rain which waters the earth and makes it fertile (Isa. 55:10-11). The absence of God's word from the earth is compared by Amos to a drought (Amos 8:11); wisdom's teaching is lifegiving water (Isa. 55:1; Sir. 15:3; 24:25-31).

When the crowds hear Jesus refer to himself as the source of living water, they immediately think of the prophet like Moses, an association easily made once we understand that the background to Jesus' statement is the rock from which Israel drank in the desert. Others in the crowd wonder whether Jesus may be the Messiah. This would also be a natural conclusion for those who thought of the association between the feast of Tabernacles and the messianic hope. Others immediately object that Jesus cannot be the Messiah since he was born in Nazareth and not in Bethlehem, which was to be the birthplace of the Messiah. The passage implicitly referred to by the crowd (Micah 5:2) in reality was a reference only to the Davidic origin of the Messiah; however, later thought imposed a more literal interpretation on the text. Again we have another example of Johannine irony in the crowd's ignorance of Jesus' real birthplace.

When questioned by the chief priests and Pharisees as to why they failed to arrest Jesus, the officers responded that they had never heard anyone speak like Jesus. A similar awe was experienced by the crowds who where astonished at the teachings Jesus had given on the mountain: "And when Jesus finished these sayings, the crowds were astonished at his teachings, for he taught them as one who had authority, and not as their scribes" (Matt. 7:28-29). The Jewish leaders express their exasperation with the timidity and naiveté of the police, and point out that the only ones who believe in Jesus are those who know nothing of the law. They show their contempt for the ordinary people, who were not educated in the law and who did not treat the law with the exaggerated meticulousness which the leaders considered of such importance. On the other hand, they refuse even to listen to Nicodemus' call for an open mind on their part, and retort that Jesus cannot be a prophet, since it is clear that no prophet can come from Galilee. This statement appears to be made in desperation and without thought, since no basis for it can be found.

With the reading of the fourth gospel's account of Jesus' appearance in Jerusalem during the feast of Tabernacles, the reader is made more vividly aware of Jesus' uncompromising determination to focus on his unique role in human salvation and on his special relationship to the divine, as well as his refusal to bend in order to win over either the leaders or the crowds. There is also an unmistakable escalation of the tempo of Jesus' movement towards the decisive moment of his life, made evident not only in the explicit attempts on the part of the leaders to arrest him, but also in the more frequent references to that moment which Jesus himself makes.

JESUS AND THE ADULTERESS (7:53–8:10)

The story of Jesus and the adulteress reveals Jesus as a judge who is capable of combining an uncompromising demand for obedience to God's law with a gentle and understanding readiness to forgive those who are willing to change their lives. In the discourse which follows this story, Jesus proclaims himself as the light of the world, warning the unbelieving crowds to seize the opportunity for life which he offers them before it is too late and they die in their sin. Not only do they reject Jesus, but they have already transferred their allegiance from God to the devil. They will become, in fact, the devil's agents as they prepare to destroy Jesus, the light and the truth they cannot tolerate.

[53]*They went each to his own house,* [1]*but Jesus went to the Mount of Olives.* [2]*Early in the morning he came again to the temple; all the people came to him, and he sat down and taught them.* [3]*The scribes and the Pharisees brought a woman who had been caught in adultery, and placing her in the midst* [4]*they said to him, "Teacher, this woman has been caught in the act of adultery.* [5]*Now in the law Moses commanded us to stone such. What do you say about her?"* [6]*This they said to test him, that they might have some charge to bring against him. Jesus bent down and wrote with his finger on the ground.* [7]*And as they continued to ask him, he stood up and said to them, "Let him who is without sin among you be the first to throw a stone at her."* [8]*And once more he bent down and wrote with his finger on the ground.* [9]*But when they heard it, they went away, one by one, beginning with the eldest, and Jesus was left alone with the woman standing before him.* [10]*Jesus looked up and said to her, "Woman, where are they? Has no one condemned you?"* [11]*She said, "No one, Lord." And Jesus said, "Neither do I condemn you; go, and do not sin again."*

While the story of the adulteress was not an original part of the fourth gospel, having been included at a later date, it does appear to be an ancient story about Jesus. The most likely reason for its initial omission was that the earlier Church, in which a strict penitential discipline was the rule, found difficulty in reconciling itself to what may have seemed to them an inappropriate liberality in Jesus' readiness to forgive the adulteress. During the second century, while Christians believed that all sins were forgiven through baptism, serious sins committed after it, such as idolatry, blasphemy, murder, adultery, fornication, false-witness and fraud could not be forgiven again. While Tertullian seemed to allow for a second repentance for certain sins, apostasy, adultery, and murder were so deadly that these would remain unforgiven. Little by little, as time went on, a greater variety of serious sins was being forgiven within the Church; however, there was no unanimity of opinion, particularly on the question of adultery. In view of this, it is easy to see why this passage might have been omitted due to what appeared to be an almost cavalier attitude on Jesus' part.

Many scholars do not consider the story to be Johannine, but think that it had its origin in the gospel of Luke. Its position at this particular section of the fourth gospel may very well be connected with two of Jesus' statements in chapter 8. First, Jesus asserts that whereas the Pharisees judge according to the flesh, that is, according to human standards, Jesus himself judges no one (v. 15). The second passage is Jesus' challenge to the Jews to convict him of any sin (v. 46). Both of these statements will be discussed later in this chapter.

While Jesus is again teaching in the temple precincts, the scribes and Pharisees bring before him a married woman who was being charged with adultery, and who had in fact been observed having sexual relations with her lover. According to Deuteronomy 19:15, there had to be a least two witnesses, exclusive of the woman's husband, for any formal charges to be brought against her. The scribes and Pharisees present the woman to Jesus, and ask him to advise them concerning the most appropriate way to deal with this sinner. The fourth gospel characterizes their question as a trap and considers the entire situation as merely another way of getting at Jesus. Jesus knew, of course, without having to be instructed by them, that the law of Moses, as set forth in Leviticus 20:10, commanded that both the married woman and her lover must be killed. While no method of death was formally prescribed, it is clear from Ezekiel 16:38-40 that stoning was the normal penalty for adultery, and was still the practice in Jesus' time. Where then was Jesus' dilemma? It is important to recall that the Sanhedrin itself was no longer empowered to try and to execute the woman, since the Romans had deprived them of the right of imposing capital punishment. If Jesus had spoken in favor of stoning her to death, he could have been accused of setting himself up in opposition to Roman authority. If, on the other hand, he hesitated to make that judgment, then he could be accused of being unfaithful to the law of Moses. Once again, as can be seen so frequently in the synoptics, the Jewish leaders deliberately avoid entering into an honest dialogue with Jesus, but seek another way of discrediting Jesus and of removing him from their midst. They are totally insensitive to the plight of this woman, and use her as an object, as a weapon against him. The fourth gospel presents a picture of Jesus, surrounded by his enemies, continuing to press him for an answer, while Jesus calmly writes with his finger on the ground. While there have been many attempts to cast some light on the meaning of Jesus' action, there is no one of them which can be considered conclusive. Perhaps the simplest and most plausible is that this was merely his way either of showing his contempt for their hypocrisy, dishonesty and insensitivity, or of showing them that their seemingly ingenious traps left him unpreturbed.

Instead of responding directly to their question, Jesus throws out a direct challenge to them: "Let him who is without sin among you be the first to throw a stone at her." Jesus' statement, of course, is not intended to be made into an absolute principle. Otherwise, no person on this earth could pass judgment on anyone else, nor could anyone rightfully impose an appropriate penalty for a crime. Jesus' challenge must be understood within the context of this particular situation, for Jesus can see into the hearts of the scribes and Pharisees who have no interest in the law or in this woman. Since Jesus knows that their indignation and their professed love of the law are merely a charade, and that their prime interest is to destroy him, he can challenge their right to be either judge or executioner in this particular case. They have compromised themselves in such a way that any attempt on their part to carry out the demands of the law of Moses would be a mockery of that law.

Jesus' challenge intimidates the accusers, and "they went away, one by one, beginning with the eldest. . . ." Since all the witnesses and the accusers have gone, the woman is free to go. However, while Jesus does not condemn her, he clearly does not condone her action: ". . . do not sin again." As has been quite evident in Jesus' discourses, he is a demanding teacher, one who calls for a faith in him which is an active commitment, i.e. one which leads to action. Due to the unsympathetic portrait of the scribes and Pharisees presented in the fourth gospel and the picture of an apparently weak and helpless woman about to be stoned to death, the reader might be inclined to interpret Jesus' action here as justification for a sentimental and irresponsible attitude toward the standards of sexual morality. His action must be seen, rather, as indicative of his love for sinners, a love which moves him to reach out and heal them and to destroy the power which Satan has over their lives (5:14). While justice and devotion to truth compel Jesus to confront human persons with their sinfulness, his mercy and his desire to save impel him to forgive all persons of their sins.

JESUS THE LIGHT OF THE WORLD (8:12–59)

12Again Jesus spoke to them, saying, "I am the light of the world; he who follows me will not walk in darkness, but will have the light of life." 13The Pharisees then said to him, "You are bearing witness to yourself; your testimony is not true." 14Jesus answered, "Even if I do bear witness to myself, my testimony is true, for I know whence I have come and whither I am going, but you do not know whence I come or whither I am going. 15You judge according to the flesh, I judge no one. 16Yet even if I do judge, my judgment is true, for it is not I alone that judge, but I and he who sent me. 17In your law it is written that the testimony of two men is true; 18I bear witness to myself, and the Father who sent me bears witness to me." 19They said to him therefore, "Where is your Father?" Jesus answered, "You know neither me nor my Father; if you knew me, you would know my Father also." 20These words he spoke in the treasury, as he taught in the temple; but no one arrested him, because his hour had not yet come.

Jesus continues to teach within the temple precincts. The discourse on the light of the world takes place near the temple treasury in the Court of the Women. Just as he had proclaimed himself the bread of life (chap. 6) and the source of living water (chap. 7), so he now proclaims himself to be the light of the world. He promises that "he who follows me will not walk in darkness, but will have the light of life."

In the Old Testament, there is an inextricable relationship between light and life. Darkness is the lot of infants who die before birth (Job 3:16; Ps. 58:9). Those who die are said to go to the "land of gloom and deep darkness" (Job 10:22). A person who dies "will never more see the light" (Ps. 49:19). A person who is rescued by God from death is said to "walk before God in the light of life" (Ps.

56:13). Even within the framework of this life, light is connected with the protection and blessing of God (Job 29:3; Ps. 27:1) and joy (Ps. 97:11; Isa. 60:20).

The Johannine opposition of light and darkness, as the symbol of the opposition of the two worlds of good and evil seems, however, to be rooted more directly in the teachings of the Essenes rather than in the Old Testament. The teachings of the Essenes (a Jewish religious, quasi-monastic group in Palestine at the time of Christ) are preserved for us primarily in the Qumran texts. The *Rule of the Community*, which is the essential rule book of the Qumran community, has as its theme the belief that this community was the fulfillment of the new covenant foretold by Jeremiah 36:37-41. The Qumran writings describe the struggle between the prince of lights and the angel of darkness to dominate humankind. In the fourth gospel, the light (Jesus) shown in the darkness (the forces of evil, Satan), and could not be overcome by the darkness (1:5).

In this particular discourse in the fourth gospel, however, which has as its setting the feast of Tabernacles, Jesus' description of himself as the light of the world appears to be occasioned by the ritual of the lighting of the four golden candlesticks in the Court of the Women. The meaning of Jesus' proclamation may be discerned through the study of the same biblical passages which threw light on Jesus' description of himself as the source of living water. For example, immediately prior to the prophet's description of the living waters which shall flow out from Jerusalem on the day of the Lord, Zechariah 14:7 predicts that there shall be one continuous day, "not day and not night, for at evening there shall be light." The Book of Exodus, which provides the story of the rock of living water, also describes God's special presence leading Israel through the desert as a pillar of cloud by day and a pillar of fire by night (Exod. 13:21-22). This pillar of fire is compared in the Wisdom of Solomon 18:3-4 to "the imperishable light of the law," which, as has been noted, was considered by the Jews as the source of nourishment and life. Jesus, who had already used images of the law, such as the bread of life and the source of living water, to describe himself, here uses another image of the law in referring to himself as the light of the world. In utilizing this title, Jesus once more portrays his role as the revealer of the Father through his words and deeds.

Once again, Jesus is confronted by the Pharisees and must address himself to the question of the validity of the testimony which he offers on his own behalf as he had done during the discourse at the pool of Bethzatha (cf. commentary on 5:22-29). Jesus characterizes the judgment which the Pharisees pass upon him as a judgment according to the flesh, that is, one that is limited by narrow human standards. This remark leads Jesus to address the question of judgment. Jesus himself does not judge, in the sense that he does not evaluate human actions. This type of judgment is superficial and powerless. Jesus is the judge, however, in the sense that his words and actions create the milieu which forces people to make a decision for life or for death, that is, to live in a way which will either lead to damnation or to salvation (cf. commentary on 5:22-30).

[21]Again he said to them, "I go away, and you will seek me and die in your sin; where I am going, you cannot come." Then said the Jews, "Will he kill himself, since he says, 'Where I am going, you cannot come?' " [23]He said to them, "You are from below, I am from above; you are of this world, I am not of this world. [24]I told you that you would die in your sins, for you will die in your sins unless you believe that I am he." [25]They said to him, "Who are you?" Jesus said to them, "Even what I have told you from the beginning. [26]I have much to say about you and much to judge; but he who sent me is true, and I declare to the world what I have heard from him." [27]They did not understand that he spoke to them of the Father. [28]So Jesus said, "When you have lifted up the Son of man, then you will know that I am he, and that I do nothing on my own authority but speak thus as the Father taught me. [29]And he who sent me is with me; he has not left me alone, for I always do what is pleasing to him." [30]As he spoke thus, many believed in him.

As he had done in the discourse on the source of living water, Jesus again warns the crowd that he is returning to his Father, and that the opportunity to gain eternal life through him will soon be lost to them. Since they refuse to believe in him and his Father (v. 19) they will be unable to follow him into the community he enjoys with his Father. One can almost detect a note of pleading in Jesus' voice, a last-ditch effort to break through their unbelief. Unless they seek him now, they will not be able to find him in the future. The tragedy of the situation is that it is already too late. Jesus' enemies have already alienated themselves to such a degree that Jesus can predict that they will die in their *sin*. *Hamartia*, the singular form of the Greek noun for *sin*, indicates that in Johannine thought there is one radical sin. The root of all other sins is people's refusal to believe in Jesus; all other sins are but a reflection of their unbelief. Without a faith in Jesus, the human person becomes more deeply and more irretrievably set in resistance to goodness, light and truth. The synoptics dealt with this sin when they spoke of the sin against the Spirit (Matt. 12:31-32; Mark 3:28-30; Luke 12:10). It is an unforgiveable sin, not because of any limitation on God's mercy and forgiveness, but because once people have freely rejected the advances of a loving God, they have deprived themselves of all hope. Light cannot be seen by people who are blind; and by their fundamental rejection of Jesus, the enemies of Jesus have blinded themselves. During Jesus' earthly ministry, before the coming of the Spirit, who will come only after Jesus' glorification, no rejection is truly final. However, after Jesus has returned to the Father and has freed the Spirit to testify within the human heart, no other opportunities *can* be given. Persons who reject the Spirit will go to their graves, eternally trapped within themselves, forever lost in the darkness they have freely chosen to embrace.

When it becomes clear that the Jews have again failed to understand Jesus' words, he makes another effort to convince them that they live in a world which does not have life and which in fact is opposed to life. He comes from the world above, from his Father, and he comes with life for them. However, he can give it only if they believe in him as one who bears the divine name ("I am he") and as one who has been sent by the Father. Otherwise, they will die in their sin. Their inability to overcome their sin and to come to life is reminiscent of the position of the sick man at the pool of Bethzatha before Jesus came to him.

In response to Jesus' affirmation that "I am he," the crowd, persisting in its ignorance and obduracy, again demands to know who he is. Jesus responds by referring them to statements which he made concerning his identity from the very beginning. He has already told them that he has come from the Father (3:13, 31-35; 6:33, 35, 38, 51, 58; 7:28), and that he speaks for the Father (5:19-24, 26-27, 30, 43; 6:37-41; 7:16-18). Jesus once more affirms that the message which he delivers to them is not his own; he proclaims only what he has heard from the one who sent him.

The dialogue between Jesus and the crowd moves along as a give-and-take between an uncomprehending audience and a teacher who uses all his strength to break through their ignorance. When he realizes that the crowd has not understood that the one who Jesus said has sent him is the Father, he then makes the prediction that his true nature will be made manifest when they "have lifted up the Son of man." At that moment, they will understand that Jesus rightfully bears the divine name ("I am he") and that he represents the Father in everything that he says and does. The Greek verb, *hyposete* (you have lifted up) refers, of course, not merely to Jesus' crucifixion and death. This occurrence in itself would obviously not suffice to manifest Jesus' true identity. It is intended to embrace his resurrection and ascension, that is, his glorification by and his return to his Father. The fourth gospel refers to the "lifting up of the Son of man" on two other occasions in Jesus' ministry, one during his discourse with Nicodemus (3:14-15) and once during his discourse to the crowd following his triumphant entry into Jerusalem (12:32). These statements seem to be the Johannine equivalent of the three predictions of the passion and death of Jesus in the synoptics (Matt. 16:21; 17:9-13; 20:17-27, and parallels). While Jesus looks forward eagerly to his hour, the time of his glorification, he stresses, however, that even now, at this moment, there exists a basic unity between himself and his Father: " . . . he has not left me alone."

The fourth gospel points out that Jesus' words move some in the crowd to believe in him. The reader can become so conscious of the conflict in Jesus' ministry and the hatred of the Jewish leaders for him that it is easy to forget that his word touched the hearts of many and drew them to believe in him. We need only think of the apostles, Nicodemus, the Samaritans and others whom Jesus was able to reach through his words and his actions.

[31]*Jesus then said to the Jews who had believed in him, "If you continue in my word, you are truly my disciples,* [32]*and you will know the truth, and the truth will make you free."* [33]*They answered him, "We are descendants of Abraham, and have never been in*

bondage to any one. How is it that you say, 'You will be made free'?"

[34]Jesus answered them, "Truly, truly, I say to you, every one who commits sin is a slave to sin. [35]The slave does not continue in the house for ever; the son continues for ever. [36]So if the Son makes you free, you will be free indeed. [37]I know that you are descendants of Abraham; yet you seek to kill me, because my word finds no place in you. [38]I speak of what I have seen with my Father, and you do what you have heard from your father."

[39]They answered him, "Abraham is our father." Jesus said to them, "If you were Abraham's children, you would do what Abraham did, [40]but now you seek to kill me, a man who has told you the truth which I heard from God; this is not what Abraham did. [41]You do what your father did." They said to him, "We were not born of fornication; we have one Father, even God." [42]Jesus said to them, "If God were your Father, you would love me, for I proceeded and came forth from God; I came not of my own accord, but he sent me. [43]Why do you not understand what I say? It is because you cannot bear to hear my word. [44]You are of your father the devil, and your will is to do your father's desires. He was a murderer from the beginning, and has nothing to do with the truth, because there is not truth in him. When he lies, he speaks according to his own nature, for he is a liar and the father of lies. [45]But, because I tell the truth, you do not believe me. [46]Which of you convicts me of sin? If I tell the truth, why do you not believe me? [47]He who is of God hears the words of God; the reason why you do not hear them is that you are not of God."

[48]The Jews answered him, "Are we not right in saying that you are a Samaritan and have a demon?" [49]Jesus answered, "I have not a demon; but I honor my Father, and you dishonor me. [50]Yet I do not seek my own glory; there is One who seeks it and he will be the judge. [51]Truly, truly, I say to you, if any one keeps my word, he will never see death." [52]The Jews said to him, "Now we know that you have a demon. Abraham died, as did the prophets; and you say, 'If any one keeps my word, he will never taste death.' [53]Are you greater than our father Abraham, who died? And the prophets died! Who do you claim to be?" [54]Jesus answered, "If I glorify myself, my glory is nothing; it is my Father who glorifies me, of whom you say that he is your God. [55]But you have not known him; I know him. If I said, I do not know him, I should be a liar like you; but I do

know him and I keep his word. ⁵⁶*Your father Abraham rejoiced that he was to see my day; he saw it and was glad."* ⁵⁷*The Jews then said to him, "You are not yet fifty years old, and have you seen Abraham?"* ⁵⁸*Jesus said to them, "Truly, truly, I say to you, before Abraham was, I am."* ⁵⁹*So they took up stones to throw at him; but Jesus hid himself, and went out of the temple.*

While Jesus addresses his next words to the believers in the crowd, it is clear from the nature of the dialogue that follows that the response comes from those who not only do not believe in him, but who are also intent upon bringing about his death. Jesus affirms that his true disciples are those who continue (remain, abide) in his word. This expression is reminiscent of Jesus' assertion that unbelievers do not have God's word abiding in them (5:37-38). The logical consequence of that statement, of course, is that believers have God's word abiding in them, and that they respond to that word in faith. The genuine disciple of Jesus, therefore, is one who abides in Jesus' word in a spirit of obedience to that word. Once again, it cannot be overly stressed that believing *in* Jesus involves a commitment to him and his word, and therefore leads the believer to carry out that word in his life.

To these true disciples, to those who believe, then, Jesus promises that they will know the truth, and that the truth will bring them freedom. The truth, of course, is the revelation of the Father by Jesus, a revelation which has already been compared to the bread of life, the living water, and the light of the world. The crowd objects that they have no need of being liberated, since, as descendants of Abraham, they have never been in bondage to anyone. Although this assertion at first may seem strange coming from a nation which has fallen under the rule of Egypt, Babylonia, and now the Romans, it is important to recall that the Jews genuinely believed that as descendants of Abraham, their political bondage could never be real or lasting; it was merely a temporary condition inflicted upon them by God as a punishment. The promises that God had made to Abraham were their assurance that they would always be a free nation. Aware that their thinking is, as it always has been, on a lower level of reality, Jesus corrects their perception by clarifying his statement and by affirming that his truth and revelation free the believer from the bondage of sin, not from the oppression of a foreign government. The real slavery is the slavery to sin. The real freedom, promised by Jesus, is the freedom from sin: "So if the Son makes you free, you will be free indeed."

The theme of slavery to sin and of liberation from slavery is developed in Pauline theology. Paul's theology of sin focuses on *hamartia* (sin), the great power which entered the world through one man, Adam, and which has exercised a tyranny in the world since that time. In his Letter to the Romans, Paul describes sin as a power which dominates and enslaves all people, both Jews and Greeks (3:9). The results of sin's tyranny in the world are described by Paul in the first three chapters of his letter. Because people did not honor God," . . . God gave them up in the lusts of their hearts to impurity, to the dishonoring of their bodies among themselves . . . . " (Rom. 1:24). "And since they did not see fit to acknowledge God, God gave them up to a base mind and to improper conduct. They were filled with all manner of wickedness, evil, covetousness, malice. Full of envy, murder, strife, deceit, malignity, they are gossips, slanderers, haters of God, insolent, haughty, boastful, inventors of evil, disobedient to parents, foolish, faithless, heartless, ruthless. Though they knew God's decree that those who do such things deserve to die, they not only do them but approve those who practice them" (Rom. 1:28-31). The world before Jesus was a world in which the tyranny of sin was only too evident and in which humans were incapable of escaping from its domination. With each new sin, human beings found themselves more and more under the power of sin: " . . . you once yielded your members to impurity and to greater and greater iniquity . . ." (Rom. 6:19). We are reminded of Jesus' warning that unbelievers would die in their sin when we hear Paul describe the consequences of a life in which sin has been the dominant force: "For the wages of sin is death . . . " (Rom. 6:23). The tragedy of sin's power over humanity and of the consequences of that power for human beings is compounded by what Paul seems to describe as an almost complete helplessness: "I do not understand my own actions. For I do not do what I want, but I do the very thing I hate . . . . So then it is no longer I that do it, but one which dwells within me. For I know that nothing good dwells within me, that is, in my flesh. I can will what is right, but I cannot do it. For I do not do the good I want, but the evil I do not want is what I do. Now if I do what I do not want, it is no longer

I that do it, but sin which dwells within me" (Rom. 7:15-20). Is it any wonder that Jesus refers to sin as slavery? The fulfillment of Jesus' promise to free believers from the bondage of sin is described by Paul when he states that the old self which suffered under the domination of sin has been crucified and destroyed (Rom. 6:6) and that we shall be united to the risen Jesus and walk in newness of life (Rom. 6:4). The power that dominates the life of the Christian is the power of God. In fact, we may call ourselves "slaves of God" (Rom. 6:22). This slavery, however, is a blessing, which leads to eternal life.

At this point, Jesus confronts the crowd on their insistance that they are the descendants of Abraham and tries to shake their self-satisfaction and complacency. He warns them, in a brief parable, that they are in danger of losing their place in the house: "The slave does not continue in the house for ever; the son continues for ever." This parable recalls the story of Ishmael, the son of Abraham and Hagar, the slave-girl, who was cast out of Abraham's house and disinherited (Gen. 21:1-12). Jesus' indirect warning here is more explicit in Matthew (3:7-10; 8:11-12).

Jesus presses the crowd further in his efforts to disturb their unjustified sense of security which they base upon their relationship to Abraham. As he had promised the crowds that even Moses would reject them (5:45-57), so now he attacks the validity of their claim that they are Abraham's children. The true descendants of Abraham would not plot to kill Jesus. Jesus urges them to do what they have heard from their Father, God, and to turn back from the course they have set for themselves. When the crowd insists again that they have Abraham for their father, Jesus challenges them again, pointing out that this claim has no validity as long as they do not follow Abraham's example. It appears that Jesus is stressing what Abraham has done rather than Abraham's belief. However, Jesus may also be making an implicit reference to Abraham's faith contrasting it indirectly to the unbelief of the Jews, since he speaks of the "truth which I heard from God."

The drift of Jesus' discourse becomes more apparent when Jesus claims that in planning to kill him, they have effectively given evidence that they do not have Abraham as their father. They do what their father did. It soon becomes clear that the father Jesus refers to is the devil. The Jews immediately respond that they are the children of God, and that they are not "born of fornication." Some have interpreted this response of the crowd to be a protest against Jesus' charge that they are the children of the devil. Infidelity to God was described as prostitution or fornication in prophetic literature, which often depicted the relationship between Yahweh and his people in terms of a marital relationship. Other commentators believe that the Jews may have been casting some doubt on the legitimacy of Jesus' own birth, a slur which later became a part of Jewish-Christian polemics.

Jesus responds that the sign of a true child of the Father is a person's acceptance of Jesus. Jesus had already explained that the Father bore witness to Jesus in the human heart, and that a true son of the Father would instinctively recognize the validity of Jesus' words (5:37-38). Jesus concludes that those who reject him have in effect turned away from the Father and have silenced his voice in their hearts, thus showing that they can no longer be considered his children. Jesus now understands the root of their inability to understand him: "It is because you cannot bear to hear my word." The construction of the Greek verb in this sentence (*akouein*, to hear, with the objective case) indicates that the Jews cannot even *physically* hear what Jesus is saying. Such is the intensity of their hatred for Jesus and their resistance to his words. This radical alienation from Jesus and his Father can only mean that they have given themselves over to another, the devil himself, who is the personified opposition to truth, "a liar and the father of lies."

As there is a fundamental opposition between truth and falsehood, between light and darkness, so there is an impassible chasm between Jesus, who is the truth (14:6), and the devil, the father of lies. The crowd will not believe Jesus, precisely because he speaks the truth. The person whose entire life is dominated by evil hates the truth and the light, since he cannot bear to have his life seen for what it is: "And this is the judgment, that the light has come into the world, and men loved darkness rather than light, because their deeds were evil. For every one who does evil hates the light, and does not come to the light, lest his deeds should be exposed. For he who does what is true comes to the light, that it may be clearly seen that his deeds have been wrought in God" (3:19-21). There exists within the human being an instinctive inclination to do what is right. If the good and the right become difficult to do, however, then the human mind finds a way of convincing itself that the evil it has chosen to do is the good. The Jewish leaders and the others who opposed Jesus had come to an understanding with their consciences, and they were comfortable with all the compromises they had made. They loved the darkness, and they had to destroy the light which revealed their true natures to them: "The world cannot hate you, but it hates me because I testify that its works are evil" (7:7).

As Jesus looks into the faces of the crowd, the faces of the people who were even then plotting his death, he charges that since they belong to their father, the devil, they are one in their desires with the evil one. It is, in fact, perfectly natural for them to want to kill Jesus, since Satan ". . . was a murderer from the beginning. . . ." The fourth gospel is probably referring to the belief that it was Satan who moved Cain to kill Abel: ". . . we should love one another, and not be like Cain who was of the evil one and murdered his brother. And why did he murder him? Because his own deeds were evil and his brother's righteous. Do not wonder, brethren, that the world hates you" (1 John 3:11-13). Cain and the world are the instruments of Satan, who is the ultimate agent of their murderous work.

The enemies of Jesus are like their father, the devil, not only in their willingness to destroy what is good, but also in their aversion to the truth. In fact, because they cannot bear to live with the truth, they have no choice but to destroy those who speak the truth: Satan ". . . has nothing to do with the truth, because there is no truth in him. When he lies, he speaks according to his nature, for he is a liar and the father of lies." In fact, the devil's first appearance in human history is as a deceiver. The serpent lies to Eve by claiming that eating of the fruit of the tree in the middle of the garden will not bring death (Gen. 3:4). While the fourth gospel emphasizes the opposition between light and darkness, the First Letter of John gives a prominent position to the struggle between truth and false-hood. Anyone who claims to have fellowship with God but who lives an immoral life is not living "according to the truth" (1:6). The person who denies that he is a sinner is a liar (1:8). The person who claims to know God but disobeys God's commandments "is a liar, and the truth is not in him" (2:4). The one who claims to love God but hates the neighbor is a liar (4:20). A genuine belief in and commitment to truth is made visible in action. Since the enemies of Jesus will not follow the example of their father, Abraham, or hear the word of the Father, they truly merit Jesus' description of them as the children of the devil and the disciples of falsehood.

The Jews who oppose Jesus continue to resist him and to reject his word, although they are unable to find any sin in him. In fact, they cannot believe in him precisely because he tells them the truth. It is the truth with which they cannot bear to live, since they belong to the devil, the father of lies, and not to the Father. They cannot tolerate the truth, since they cannot bear to see themselves as they truly are.

When the crowd retorts with an *ad hominem* argument that it is Jesus himself who is under the power of the devil, Jesus merely points to the fact that he honors the Father. The ultimate judge of the truth, however, the one who will vindicate Jesus' life and teaching is not Jesus himself: Jesus will be vindicated by the Father who will glorify him. Once again, as Jesus faces the hostility and lies of an unbelieving crowd, he eagerly anticipates the decisive hour of his glorification, the moment when the world will see him in his glory. That glory was already present in a hidden way in his signs (2:11) which revealed the divinity of Jesus and his unique relationship with the Father. His true nature will be fully manifest in the future. In the Old Testament, the glory of God refers to the visible manifestation of God, in fire and smoke, in cloud, in natural disturbances, in the heavens, or in some special form of a divine theophany. In the fourth gospel, the glorification of Jesus, the manifestation of his true nature, will take place through his passion, death, resurrection, and ascension. This moment of glory wil be effected by his Father, and it is a moment for which Jesus begins to pray and long more and more intensely (12:23; 17:1-5).

When Jesus again promises eternal life to those who keep his word, the crowd once more objects, reminding Jesus that Abraham and the prophets have died. Who is this man, who places himself above Abraham and the prophets? Rather than responding directly to their limited interpretation of the meaning of life and death on the physical level, Jesus once more proclaims his true nature to them. He first points to himself as the fulfillment of the ages, and affirms that Abraham rejoiced in the foreknowledge that he was to see the day of Jesus, and that, in fact, Abraham did see his day and was glad. This appears to be a reference to the day of Isaac's birth, an event in the life of Abraham which contained a meaning far beyond itself. The birth of Isaac was the beginning of the fulfillment of God's promise to Abraham (Gen. 12:1-3; 18:19-21), a promise which would find its culmination in the coming of Jesus into the world.

In answering their objection concerning the impossibility of a meeting between Abraham and Jesus, who was not yet fifty years old, Jesus once again claims divinity as his prerogative: "Jesus said to them, 'Truly, truly, I say to you, before Abraham was, I am.'" This seems to be the clearest evidence of Jesus' claim to divinity found in the gospels. It is so clear to the crowd that they immediately take up stones to inflict the appropriate penalty upon this blasphemer, in conformity with Leviticus 24:16. Later, when they finally succeed in killing Jesus, the primary charge against him in the presence of the Roman procurator was his claim to divinity: "The Jews answered him, 'We have a law, and by that law he ought to die, because he has made himself the Son of God'" (19:7).

The Healing of the Blind Man (9:1-41)

The restoration of sight to the man born blind is another of the signs performed by Jesus presented in the fourth gospel. It is again essential to look beyond the physical result of the healing to the higher reality which is symbolized by the sign. The bestowal of physical sight by Jesus was a sign of the spiritual enlightenment which enabled this man to move gradually from a superficial perception of Jesus' identity to a clear vision of him as the one sent by God, as the "Lord" whom he finally brought himself to worship. The note of tragedy, however, always present in the fourth gospel, enters again with the continued and by now predictable rejection of Jesus by the Jewish leaders. Their unyielding and perverse opposition to Jesus, the light, leads them further into the darkness and assures their eternal blindness. While one man moves from darkness to light, others willfully choose the darkness and condemn themselves to live in it for all eternity.

¹As he passed by, he saw a man blind from his birth. ²And his disciples asked him, "Rabbi, who sinned, this man or his parents, that he was born blind?" ³Jesus answered, "It was not that this man sinned, or his parents, but that the works of God might be made manifest in him. ⁴We must work the works of him who sent me, while it is day; night comes, when no one can work. ⁵As long as I am in the world, I am the light of the world." ⁶As he said this, he spat on the ground and made clay of the spittle and anointed the man's eyes with the clay, ⁷saying to him, "Go, wash in the pool of Siloam (which means Sent). So he went and washed and came back seeing. ⁸The neighbors and those who had seen him before as a beggar, said, "Is not this the man who used to sit and beg?" ⁹Some said, "It is he"; others said, "No, but he is like him." He said, "I am the man." ¹⁰They said to him, "Then how were your eyes opened?" ¹¹He answered, "The man called Jesus made clay and anointed my eyes and said to me, 'Go to Siloam and wash'; so I went and washed and received my sight." ¹²They said to him, "Where is he?" He said, "I do not know."

¹³They brought to the Pharisees the man who had formerly been blind. ¹⁴Now it was a sabbath day when Jesus made the clay and opened his eyes. ¹⁵The Pharisees again asked him how he had received his sight. And he said to them, "He put clay on my eyes, and I washed, and I see." ¹⁶Some of the Pharisees said, "This man is not from God, for he does not keep the sabbath." But others said, "How can a man who is a sinner do such signs?" There was a division among them. ¹⁷So they again said to the blind man, "What do you say about him, since he has opened your eyes?" He said, "He is a prophet."

¹⁸The Jews did not believe that he had been blind and had received his sight, until they called the parents of the man who had received his sight,¹⁹and asked them, "Is this your son, who you say was born blind? How then does he now see?" ²⁰His parents answered, "We know that this is our son, and that he was born blind; ²¹but how he now sees we do not know, nor do we know who opened his eyes. Ask him; he is of age, he will speak for himself." ²²His parents said this because they feared the Jews, for the Jews had already agreed that if any one should confess him to be Christ, he was to be put out of the synagogue. ²³Therefore, his parents said, "He is of age, ask him."

²⁴So for the second time, they called the man who had been blind, and said to him, "Give God the praise; we know that this man is a sinner." ²⁵He answered, "Whether he is a sinner, I do not know; one thing I know, that though I was blind, now I see." ²⁶They said to him, "What did he do to you? How did he open your eyes?" ²⁷He answered them, "I have told you already and you would not listen. Why do you want to hear it again? Do you too want to become his disciples?" ²⁸And they reviled him, saying, "You are his disciple, but we are disciples of Moses. ²⁹We know that God has spoken to Moses, but as for this man, we do not know where this man comes from." ³⁰The man answered, "Why, this is a marvel! You do not know where he comes from, and yet he opened my eyes. ³¹We know that God does not listen to sinners, but if any one is a worshiper of God and does his will, God listens to him. ³²Never since the world began has it been heard that any one opened the eyes of a man born blind. ³³If this man were not from God, he could do nothing." ³⁴They answered him, "You were born in utter sin, and would you teach us?" And they cast him out.

³⁵*Jesus heard that they had cast him out, and having found him he said, "Do you believe in the Son of man?" *³⁶*He answered, "And who is he, sir, that I may believe in him?" *³⁷*Jesus said to him, "You have seen him, and it is he who speaks to you." *³⁸*He said, "Lord, I believe"; and he worshiped him. *³⁹*Jesus said, "For judgment I came into this world, that those who do not see may see, and that those who see may become blind." *⁴⁰*Some of the Pharisees near him heard this, and they said to him, "Are we also blind?" *⁴¹*Jesus said to them, "If you were blind, you would have no guilt; but now that you say, 'We see,' your guilt remains."*

As Jesus and his disciples walk through Jerusalem one day, Jesus observes a man who had been blind from birth. The question of the disciples reflected a Jewish belief, still in vogue at the time of Jesus, of a causal relationship between sin and sickness. In fact, the specific affliction of blindness was seen as a punishment for sin (Gen. 19:11). In Deuteronomy 28:15-68, the people of Israel are warned that if they refuse to obey God and are careless about "his commandments and statutes," they will be cursed and punished by God in a variety of ways. Among those punishments are enumerated "madness and blindness and confusion of mind . . . " (Deut. 28:28). In the view of the disciples, then, this man was blind either because of some sin he would commit some day, or because of a sin which his parents had committed (Exod. 20:5; Deut. 5:9). Jesus himself appeared to support this view when, after having healed the man at the pool of Bethzatha, he warned that if the man sinned again, something worse might befall him (5:14). However, while Jesus did consider sickness to be one sign of Satan's power in the world, he never claimed that one person's specific illness was necessarily a result of personal guilt (cf. commentary on 5:14). In response to the remark of the disciples on this occasion, in fact, Jesus explicitly denies that the man was born blind either because of his sins or because of transgressions committed by his parents. This blindness, Jesus affirms, is an occasion for God to manifest his *works* through Jesus. Once again, Jesus affirms the unity between himself and the Father and the continuity between his own ministry and the ongoing activity of the Father in the world. In the fourth gospel, Jesus always refers to his miracles as "works" (*erga*), a word used in the Greek version of the Old Testament to describe God's creative and redemptive actions

128

(Gen. 2:2; Exod. 34:10; Ps. 66:5; 77:12). Jesus' consciousness that his ministry is continuous with the activity of his Father was also made explicit when he healed the man at the pool of Bethzatha (cf. commentary on 5:36).

As Jesus looks at the blind man, he expresses a note of urgency, which the fourth gospel perceived not only in Jesus' attitude towards his own personal ministry, but also in the attitude which his disciples and the Church had towards their mission in the world: "We must work the works of him who sent me, while it is day; night comes, when no one can work." Jesus, increasingly aware of the powers of darkness which are gathering about him, knows that once they have their way with him, he will be unable to carry out his work. The "we" used at the beginning of Jesus' statement suggests that the fourth gospel, conscious of the opposition from the world that the Church would always experience and the ever-present danger of persecution and death, is urging Christians to continue Jesus' work before the world can put an end to their ministry.

As he prepares to restore vision to the blind man, Jesus again refers to himself as the light of the world, thereby making explicit the connection between the role which he claimed for himself during the feast of Tabernacles (8:12). The blind man will not only receive the vision which will enable him to see the physical world around him, but will also be rescued from the spiritual darkness in which he has been living. The connection between *work* and *word* which we have seen in the other signs of Jesus is made very clear during John's narration of this incident. However, while the other signs of Jesus *preceded* the word which illuminated the significance of the sign, the *work* of the healing of the blind man *follows* the *word* which raises human understanding to the reality beyond the physical cure. Where as the multiplication of the loaves was an *action* which symbolized a reality infinitely surpassing the natural reality of nourishing bread, the *word* in which Jesus describes himself as the light of the world carried within itself the power to restore vision on someone living in darkness from the moment of birth.

Jesus then turns to the man and performs a ritual, which was taken by the early Church to be a sign of baptism. Jesus first of all made clay out of his own spittle and dirt and anointed the man's eyes with it. Spittle, which was used by Jesus in other miracles (Mark 7:33; 8:23), was believed to have medicinal properties.

Anointing itself was part of the baptismal rite from early times, and the use of spittle became a part of the ceremonies at a later date. That the Church was justified in finding a baptismal interpretation in this chapter is evident from a study of the text itself. First, the man in this chapter, as opposed to the man at the pool of Bethzatha (5:1-14), was actually healed by his washing in the water. Second, the fourth gospel makes a special effort to connect these waters with Jesus, and thereby to imply that they have their healing power through Jesus, by stating that the name of the pool, *Siloam*, means "sent." In the fourth gospel, Jesus is time and again described as the one who is sent. Furthermore, the pool where the man washed and through which he received his sight was the pool south of Jerusalem from which water was brought for the ceremonies of the feast of Tabernacles. It was in reference to the solemn moment during this feast when the water, the symbol of life, was poured out on the earth, that Jesus issued his solemn invitation to all who thirst to drink from him, the source of living water. Through the waters of baptism, Jesus gives life to all.

Another theme of this chapter, which appears to justify the baptismal interpretation, is the connection between blindness and sin. While Jesus denies that this man's blindness was caused by any specific sin on his part or on the part of his parents, Jesus heals him in his role as the light of the world and removes him from the darkness, which is the symbol of the power of sin and evil. Finally, the restoration of sight to the blind man was the sign of an enlightenment of that man vis-à-vis the nature of Jesus. He begins by seeing Jesus as "the man" and ends up by worshiping him as "Lord." Baptism itself was spoken of as "enlightenment" in the early Church (Heb. 6:4; 10:32) and in the writings of the fathers of the Church. Justin Martyr, who wrote in the second century, referred to baptism as "illumination," since those who learn the Christian teachings are enlightened from within (Apol. I. 61:12). Justin also explains how, after the baptism of the new Christian, the assembly offers prayers for themselves and for "the one who has been illuminated" (Apol. I. 65:1).

After the blind man washes at the pool and suddenly receives his vision, he is observed by his neighbors and questioned concerning the restoration of his sight. After he describes the ritual by which Jesus healed him and identifies the one who healed him as "the man called Jesus," he is brought before the Pharisees, to whom he again explains how he came to be healed. At this point, the fourth gospel offers yet another example of the unwillingness of the Jewish authorities to consider the works of Jesus with an open mind and to make an effort to perceive the reality beyond the physical healing. Rather than focusing on the wonder of this event and the meaning of the miracle, of which there is no example in the Old Testament (Tobit, who experienced a miraculous restoration of sight [Tob. 11:12-13], was not born blind), the Pharisees find fault with Jesus' violation of the sabbath and offer this as evidence that he cannot be from God (cf. commentary on 5:16). The more open-minded among the authorities argue that if Jesus were a sinner, he would be incapable of working such wonders. Although the individuals who argue on Jesus' behalf show some evidence of faith in him, theirs was an incipient faith, based on Jesus' ability to perform miracles. Jesus was never content with that kind of faith (2:23-25; 3:2-3; 4:45-48; 7:3-7). In fact, while it was generally true that a sinner could not perform a miracle, there were exceptions to that rule. Pharaoh's magicians, for example, were able to duplicate the miracles of Moses and Aaron (Exod. 7:12, 22; 8:7). Deuteronomy 13:1-5 warns that even false prophets may be able to perform signs and wonders, and that the ultimate criterion of whether God is the source of those wonders is the teaching of those wonder-workers. If they teach rebellion against the Lord who brought Israel out of Egypt and urge Israel to leave the way the Lord commanded them to walk, then they are false teachers. Jesus himself warned his disciples that false Messiahs and false prophets would be able to perform miracles so convincing that "even the elect might be led astray (Matt. 24:24; Mark 13:22). In the final analysis, therefore, although a healing may very well be a sign that its author is an authentic messenger from God, it is absolutely essential to go beyond the material phenomenon itself and examine the meaning of the miracle. It was this inability of even those who believed in Jesus to see beyond the natural and physical level of the miracle that was a constant source of frustration to Jesus.

The more profound effect of Jesus' healing of the blind man becomes more and more evident as we follow the dramatic confrontation that takes place between him and the Jewish leaders. After having argued among themselves without reaching any satisfactory conclusion, the Pharisees once again turn to the man and ask him his opinion about Jesus. Jesus is no longer seen as "the man called Jesus" but is now described by the man as "a prophet," that is, as an extraordinary person who has received power from God to perform a wonder the likes of which has never been seen. The response of Jesus' adversaries is to question the veracity of the man and to challenge the authenticity of Jesus' miracle. They appear to suspect that the blind man himself may be a trickster in collusion with Jesus, and that he may never have been blind from birth. In order to find a way to discredit him, the Pharisees call the man's parents before them and question them about their son. His parents will admit only that he is indeed their son, and that he was born blind. They refuse to make any statements beyond those since, as the fourth gospel explains, ". . . they feared the Jews, for the Jews had already agreed that if any one should confess him to be the Christ, he was to be put out of the synagogue." It appears that the fourth gospel is here anticipating the ultimate outcome of Jewish hostility towards Jesus, that is, the expulsion from the synagogues of Christians who believed in him, which occured at the end of the first century. During the period of Jesus' ministry, and of his followers' activities as narrated in the Acts of the Apostles, there was some form of ostracism, although the hostility did not reach its extreme and final form until A.D. 90, when the Jews attempted to drive from the synagogues all Jews who accepted Jesus as the Messiah.

When the Pharisees decide to question the man for the second time, they use an oath formula, "Give God the praise," an expression used before taking testimony, commanding him to speak the truth as *they* see it, that is, that Jesus is a sinner. Far from being intimidated by them, however, the man's courage grows progressively stronger, and he refuses to enter into a debate with them concerning Jesus' sinfulness. He limits his response, simply pointing to the fact that he was blind, and now he can see. When the authorities appear to make an effort to trip him up by having him repeat his description of Jesus' method of healing him, he becomes exasperated and asks sarcastically whether they also wish to become his disciples. Reacting angrily to what they consider his insolence, the Pharisees respond that while the man may be Jesus' disciple, they are the "disciples of Moses," a title sometimes used in referring to the Pharisees. They have no doubt concerning Moses' credentials, since

God had certainly spoken to him (Exod. 33:11; Num. 12:2-9). As for Jesus, they know nothing about his origin. This statement of theirs may be merely another denial of Jesus' claim to be from above, or may also be a slur upon the legitimacy of his birth. The man then expresses his astonishment that they could doubt that Jesus has his origin in the Father, since ". . . God does not listen to sinners, but if any one is a worshiper of God and does his will, God listens to him." The principle affirmed here is also enunciated in various passages of the Old Testament: Isaiah warns the people of Israel that because of their sinfulness, their prayers will have no impact on God as long as they remain unrepentant and their sinfulness remains a barrier between themselves and their God (Isa. 1:15; 59:2); the prophet Micah warns the secular leaders of the community that the Lord will never hear those who have been guilty of sins of social injustice (Mic. 3:4). The man again tries to call their attention to the stupendous nature of Jesus' deed, and reminds them that the restoration of sight to a person born blind is an event without precedent in history. It is self-evident, as far as he is concerned, that one with this kind of power must be from God.

After the Pharisees finally eject the man from their presence, Jesus hears of his plight and calls him to make an act of faith in the Son of man. While the title, "Son of man," which Jesus appropriates to himself at this point, sets the stage for the theme of judgment which is to follow, the title used by the man in his confession of faith, is "Lord," applied to Jesus in the early preaching of the resurrected Christ (Acts 2:36; 7:59). The Greek noun, *kyrios* (Lord), was used to translate the Hebrew *YHWH*, which referred to the God of Israel. The fourth gospel also points to the accompanying gesture made by the man when he professes his faith in Jesus, the gesture of worship. The Greek verb, *proskynein*, (bowing down in worship), is used elsewhere in John to describe the worship due to God (4:20-24; 12:20). In the man's words of faith and in his gesture of worship, we witness the triumphant conclusion of a person's journey from darkness through the first faint glimmer of dawn to the bright noon-day brilliance of a trusting and obedient acceptance of Jesus as Lord.

In this miracle of the restoration of sight to the man born blind, we witness the fulfillment of the prophecy of Isaiah, who foretold the coming of a new world in which the eyes of the blind would be opened (42:7), and light and release would be granted to those who are held captive in the darkness of prison (61:1). Those who had resisted the word of God and had become blind and deaf to God's presence would now be able once more to see and hear. However, the blind had to confess their blindness and their need for healing before the gift of sight could be restored. The blind man's acceptance of Jesus brought him the gift of natural sight and the gift of spiritual vision which enabled him to see Jesus' true identity.

As Jesus rejoices in the man's liberation from darkness, he cannot help but become aware of his rejection by the authorities who deliberately remain fixed in their blindness. Once more, Jesus affirms his role as judge: "For judgment I came into the world, that those who do not see may see, and that those who see may become blind." A superficial reading of this text might lead the reader to the conclusion that Jesus came into the world as the judge who set out to enlighten certain people and to cast others into the darkness of blindness. We ought first to recall, however, that Jesus is not a judge in the sense that he separates the good from the evil. He is a judge only in the sense that his presence and his revelation are a challenge to his hearers to make a decision, and that neutrality is not possible once he has spoken. It is Jesus' challenge which provides the forum in which human beings judge themselves, and make the free decision to accept or reject Jesus. Human beings are the judges who choose freely whether they will stand among the saved or among the damned. Jesus did not come to condemn but to bring all people to the light, since he is the light of the world. For those who admit their blindness and reach out for vision, Jesus' coming is an occasion for the restoration of sight. For those who cannot tolerate the light of truth and who prefer the darkness where their deeds will remain hidden, the coming of Jesus is the occasion for their plunge into a deeper darkness.

Another set of texts, which deals with the decisive effect of Jesus' presence on human beings and which seems to suggest that Jesus came in order to condemn certain people to spiritual blindness and therefore to damnation, are the synoptic accounts discussing the purpose of the parables (Matt. 13:10-17; Mark 4:10-12; Luke 8:9-10). These passages appear to be saying that Jesus preached in parables in order to confuse those who resisted his preaching: "That is why I speak to them in parables, because seeing they do not see, and hearing, they do not hear, nor do they understand" (Matt 13:13). The Marcan version appears even more harsh: ". . . so that they may indeed see but not perceive, and may indeed hear but not understand; lest they should turn again, and be forgiven" (4:12) However, the true purpose of the parables is disclosed in Mark 4:33 "With many such parables he spoke the word to them, as they were able to hear it." Jesus used the parable, which was an already existing stylistic form, to make his message more persuasive and to move his hearers to make a decision. By preaching in parables, Jesus was creating a situation in which his listeners were forced to choose either him and light or Satan and darkness.

How then do we explain the expression, "that those who see may become blind" in verse 39 of this chapter and similar expressions found in the synoptic texts just referred to? Was this blinding of the eyes and the hardening of the hearts the actual purpose of the parables of Jesus and of his ministry? These expressions are taken from Isaiah 6:10, the classical Old Testament passage used in the New Testament to explain the failure of Jesus' mission to the Jews. In commanding Isaiah to preach to the Israelites of his day, the Lord commands, "Go, and say to this people: 'Hear and hear, but do not understand; see and see, but do not perceive.' Make the heart of this people fat, and their ears heavy, and shut their eyes; lest they see with their eyes and hear with their ears, and understand with their hearts, and turn and be healed." Just as the texts quoted from John and the synoptics seem to affirm that Jesus' purpose in his parables and his ministry was to harden the hearts of his Jewish adversaries, so it appears in this text that the prophet set out intentionally to harden the hearts of the people of Israel in his day. Although such a purpose may seem contrary to our notions of Jesus' intention, we must endeavor to comprehend the mentality of the biblical writers.

It is important to recall that biblical writers were unable to conceive of a divine purpose which failed to achieve its result, just as they could not conceive of the existence of a reality unless it were willed and intended by the Lord. Therefore, within the context of this mentality, the failure of the Jews to understand and to believe in Jesus was willed by God, and was the purpose of Jesus' ministry. From our point of view, this is an oversimplification, and does not take into account the interplay of God's call and free will and the relationship between God, the primary cause, and created agents, human and otherwise, the secondary causes. It is true that, in the *ultimate* plan and design of God, the primary cause of all things, the stubborn resistance of the Jewish authorities to Jesus' person and message and their eventual inability to hear and to see was intended by God. However, on the level of secondary causality, the purpose of Jesus' ministry was to enlighten *all* his listeners, the Pharisees as well as the man born blind. In the Old Testament, the purpose of Isaiah's preaching was to move the people of Israel to leave the paths of infidelity and to return once again to their Lord. The biblical writers, however, emphasized the primary causality of the Lord and his purpose, and neglected to emphasize secondary causality.

Furthermore, the failure of the people of Israel to respond to Isaiah and the failure of the Jewish leaders to believe in Jesus were the result of their own free and deliberate choice to seek the glory which comes from humans rather than that which comes from God. While always affirming that all reality is the result of God's will and purpose, biblical writers at the same time affirmed that human beings were free in making the choices they did. The reconciliation of these two truths was apparently not a matter of concern to biblical writers, who were content to affirm the validity of both beliefs. The attempt to understand the mysterious relation between God's power and human freedom became the perennial task of Christian theologians who have struggled with the problem throughout the centuries.

Because the Pharisees could not live with the truth which Jesus preached, they freely and knowingly rejected the truth (8:45). Because they loved the darkness, they preferred to remain blind. Confronted by the light of the world, they sought to escape from that light by every imaginable intellectual ruse, thereby condemning themselves to an increasingly deeper and incurable blindness. When they ask Jesus whether he considers them to be blind, he refuses to allow them such a facile escape from responsibility for the stance they had taken. If their inability to see had been inflicted on them from without, as in the case of the man born blind, they would have no guilt. However, since their failure to see and understand is attributable to them, their guilt remains.

Jesus as Sheep Gate and Shepherd;
Messiah and the Son of God (10:1–42)

The love and the concern which Jesus has for his people and his awareness of the uncaring and callous manner with which the Jewish authorities exercise their offices lead him to attack them as thieves and robbers and as strangers lacking in love for the people they are to nourish. While they leave the sheep to the mercies of the wolf and abandon them to death, Jesus loves with an intensity and depth which drive him to lay down his life not only for his own sheep, but even for those who are not of his fold. When the authorities, whose hatred for Jesus grows with every effort of his to make them face the truth, again challenge him to state whether he is the Messiah, he repeats his affirmation of his unique relationship with his Father. When they try to kill him for what they consider his blasphemy, he calls upon them to open their minds to the significance of the works which he does in his Father's name. When he sees that their only reaction to his words is one more attempt to arrest him, he realizes that the point of no return has been reached, and leaves them, bringing to a tragic close the period of his public ministry.

JESUS THE GOOD SHEPHERD (10:1–21)

[1]*"Truly, truly, I say to you, he who does not enter the sheepfold by the door but climbs in by another way, that man is a thief and a robber;* [2]*but he who enters by the door is the shepherd of the sheep.* [3]*To him the gatekeeper opens; the sheep hear his voice, and he calls his own sheep by name and leads them out.* [4]*When he has brought out all his own, he goes before them, and the sheep follow him, for they know his voice.* [5]*A stranger they will not follow, but they will flee from him, for they do not know the voice of strangers."* [6]*This figure Jesus used with them, but they did not understand what he was saying to them.*

⁷So Jesus again said to them, "Truly, truly, I say to you, I am the door of the sheep. ⁸All who came before me are thieves and robbers; but the sheep did not heed them. ⁹I am the door; if any one enters by me, he will be saved, and will go in and out and find pasture. ¹⁰The thief comes only to steal and kill and destroy; I came that they may have life, and have it abundantly. ¹¹I am the good shepherd. The good shepherd lays down his life for the sheep. ¹²He who is a hireling and not a shepherd, whose own the sheep are not, sees the wolf coming and leaves the sheep and flees; and the wolf snatches them and scatters them. ¹³He flees because he is a hireling and cares nothing for the sheep. ¹⁴I am the good shepherd; I know my own and my own know me, ¹⁵as the Father knows me and I know the Father; and I lay down my life for the sheep. ¹⁶And I have other sheep, that are not of this fold; I must bring them also, and they will heed my voice. So there shall be one flock, one shepherd. ¹⁷For this reason the Father loves me, because I lay down my life, that I may take it again. ¹⁸No one takes it from me, but I lay it down of my own accord. I have power to lay it down, and I have power to take it again; this charge I have received from my Father."

¹⁹There was again a division among the Jews because of these words. ²⁰Many of them said, "He has a demon, and he is mad; why listen to him?" ²¹Others said, "These are not the sayings of one who has a demon. Can a demon open the eyes of the blind?"

The discourse in which Jesus compares himself with the sheep gate and the shepherd serves, in conjunction with chapter 9, as a point of transition between the discourses at the feast of Tabernacles and the discourse at the feast of Dedication. This chapter, in fact, begins with Jesus' continuation of his attack upon the Jewish leaders which he commenced in the aftermath of the incident of the man born blind. At the same time, his criticism of their leadership includes the contrasting description of his own attitude toward the sheep who have suffered for so long from the false shepherds of Israel.

Jesus' attack upon the destructive manner in which the Jewish leaders have exercised their offices takes the form of two parables (vv. 1-3a and vv. 3b-5). The first parable contrasts two methods of entering the sheepford, that of the thief and robber and that of the shepherd. The type of sheepfold described here seems to be a pen surrounded by a low stone wall near the home of the owner of the sheep, constructed to protect them from wild animals and thieves. The gate through which the shepherd enters was merely an opening in the enclosure. Jesus is saying that what distinguishes the genuine shepherd from the thief and robber is the manner in which they approach the sheep. The uncaring and sneering attitude shown by the Jewish leaders in their treatment of the man born blind (chap. 9) is but one example of the kind of leadership that Jesus is condemning in this passage. In Jesus' eyes a true shepherd would not approach his sheep with the contempt which the Jewish leaders showed for the ordinary people, "who do not know the law," and who were considered damned since they did not treat the law with the meticulousness considered so important by the leaders (7:49).

In the second parable, Jesus contrasts the reaction of the sheep toward the shepherd, whom they know and who knows them, with their fearful reaction toward the stranger. The use of the figure of the shepherd to describe the leaders of Israel, commented upon in greater depth later in this commentary, has a long history in Jewish thought. For example, when Moses learns from the Lord that he will see the land which has been given to Israel, but that he will not be allowed to enter it, Moses petitions God to provide for a leader to replace him: "Let the LORD, the God of the spirits of all flesh, appoint a man over the congregation, who shall go out before them and come in before them, who shall lead them out and bring them in; that the congregation of the LORD may not be as sheep which have no shepherd" (Num. 27:16-17). The true shepherd knows each sheep, since each can be called by its own name, and the sheep know the shepherd's voice. Jesus describes an intimacy and a personal relationship here, which is implied in the verb "know," the implications of which will be explored more deeply later.

The Jewish leaders, whom Jesus had described as blind (9:39-41) and as incapable of hearing (8:43, 47), are unmoved by Jesus' attack upon them. They were unable to understand the figure of speech (*paroimia*) which Jesus used with them. The Greek word, *paroimia*, translates the Hebrew word, *masal*, a broad term which includes almost all types of figurative speech. Once again confronted with the now almost insurmountable wall which separates Jesus from the Jewish leaders, he nonetheless makes an effort to reach them.

Jesus explains the first parable (vv. 1-3a), contrasting the way in

139

which the shepherd approaches the sheep with the manner in which the thief and robber approaches them, by describing himself as the door of the sheep. In verses 7 and 8, he explains that *he* is the proper way to reach the sheep, and that those who have gone before him, that is the Jewish leaders, are thieves and robbers. It is important to note at this point that Jesus' condemnation of the Jewish leaders in the fourth gospel focuses primarily on their refusal to accept him as the one sent by the Father and their refusal to listen to his word with open hearts and minds. He has never dealt as explicitly with their manner of leadership as he does during this discourse. In his explanation of the first parable, Jesus seems to be saying that since *he* is the *proper way* to teach the sheep, the leaders, who have not and will not accept him as truly sent by the Father to bring life, are thieves and robbers, in that they attempt to reach the sheep by some other way.

In Jesus' second reference to himself as the door (vv. 9-10), he seems to be making a different point. Whereas the first comparison concerns the relationship between Jesus, the door, and the Jewish leaders, this second comparison deals with the relationship between the door and the sheep: "I am the door; if any one enters by me, he will be saved, and will go in and out and find pasture." Jesus is the entrance to salvation. He will later describe himself as ". . . the way, and the truth, and the life; no one comes to the Father, but by me" (14:6). The theme of Jesus as the source of life (3:16, 36; 5:40; 6:33, 35, 48, 51; 14:6; 21:31) returns once again in the fourth gospel. He has described himself as the living water (4:10), as the bread of life (6:35), as the source of living water (7:38), and as the light of life (8:12). Now he offers pasture. While Jesus assures the sheep that they will find life through him, he warns them against the thief, the one who comes "to steal and kill and destroy." Jesus' description of this evil intruder is reminiscent of his description of the devil during his discourse at the feast of Tabernacles: "You are of your father, the devil, and your will is to do your father's desires. He was a murderer from the beginning . . ." (8:44). Although the Jewish leaders may certainly be included within the ranks of those who steal and kill and destroy, the fourth gospel here may in fact be broadening the scope of Jesus' attack to include Satan and all his representatives who are described as the world. It is the world which hates Jesus and his followers (7:7; 15:19; 16:33; 1 John 3:13).

Jesus then goes on to explain the second parable, concerning the relationship between the sheep and the shepherd, by describing himself as the good shepherd. In order to more fully understand the meaning of the parable as well as Jesus' explanation, we must examine the Old Testament background of the shepherd figure which symbolized the rulers of the people of Israel. From the period of the patriarchs until well after their settlement in Palestine, the culture of Israel was strongly pastoral, and therefore lent itself to the imagery of shepherding. Within that civilization, the figure of the shepherd seemed a very apt symbol for the ruler. The shepherd, while being the leader of the sheep, was also a protector and a caring companion. He had to protect the sheep against wild beasts (Gen. 31:39; 1 Sam. 17:34-37), and was responsible for leading them to the nourishment of the pastures (Ps. 23:1-4) and the refreshment of water (Exod. 2:16). The shepherd is sensitive to the needs and the condition of his flock, and treats them with care and solicitude (Gen. 33:13). The patriarchs, Moses and David, were themselves literally shepherds. In time the rulers of Israel came to be called shepherds (Jer. 2:8; 3:15; 10:21; Ezek. 34:3-23).

Although Jesus did not explicitly refer to the Jewish leaders as evil shepherds, his condemnation of the manner in which they carried out their office can better be understood in the light of the Old Testament's condemnation of the evil shepherds of Israel. In Jeremiah 10:21, we hear of the "stupid shepherds" who "have not prospered" and the "scattered flock." The kings of Judah were not interested in carrying on the work of Moses and the charismatic judges as God had willed them to do, but were more concerned about their political futures. In fact, the rulers rebelled against God (Jer. 2:8). The evil kings had in fact destroyed and scattered the sheep of the pasture, and the Lord will replace them (Jer. 23:1-4).

The Old Testament text which can shed most light on this discourse is the thirty-fourth chapter of Ezekiel, who prophesied at the time of the Babylonian captivity. In this chapter the rulers of Israel, the shepherds of Israel, are condemned by the Lord because they had ruled with harshness, had fed themselves instead of caring for the sheep, and had been responsible for allowing their sheep to be scattered over the face of the earth into exile. Because of the carelessness of the shepherds, the sheep have become food for wild beasts (that is, foreign conquerors). The Lord will take away the office of those who have failed and will himself become the shepherd. He will seek out his sheep, rescue them from the places where they have been scattered, and will feed them with good pasture. He will judge between the oppressors and the victims of injustice. The Lord finally promises to place his servant, David, as shepherd over them, a shepherd who will feed them. The chapter concludes, "And you are my sheep, the sheep of my pasture, and I am your God, says the Lord GOD."

Jesus' severe criticism of the Jewish leaders' exercise of their role and of the plight of the sheep who have not been properly cared for calls to mind the synoptic references to Jesus' compassion for the crowds: "When he saw the crowds, he had compassion on them, because they were harassed and helpless, like sheep without a shepherd" (Matt. 9:36). In Jesus' mind, the scribes and Pharisees had become so enamored with the perfection they had reached in their knowledge and observance of the law, and had become so focused on themselves, that they had set themselves apart from the very people they were to nourish. In fact, they spoke of the people with contempt and treated them in like manner rather than giving them the nourishment they craved. The gospel of Mark also makes note of the compassion which Jesus felt for the spiritually starved crowds, immediately preceding the miraculous multiplication of loaves and fishes, when he would bring them the bread of revelation. Ezekiel's prophecy against the shepherds of Israel and the Lord's promise to rescue the scattered sheep find an unmistakable echo in Jesus' discourse.

Who are the Jewish leaders so strongly condemned by Jesus, both here and in the synoptics? While the synoptics describe them as Pharisees, scribes, Sadducees, Herodians and the chief priests, the fourth gospel simply refers to the Pharisees and the chief priests or speaks merely of the Jews, which in most instances meant the Jewish leaders. The scribes, scholars who were expert in the law, belonged to the sect of the Pharisees. While the synoptics make frequent reference to them, the fourth gospel only mentions them once (8:33). It must be remembered that for the author of the fourth gospel, who wrote after the destruction of Jerusalem and the temple, most of the distinctions noted by the synoptics had lost their importance. In the fourth gospel, the only two categories which retained any significance were those of the chief priests, who presided over Jesus' trial and death, and the Pharisees, the one sect which survived the destruction of the temple in A.D. 70.

The Pharisees, who appeared as an organized movement in Jewish history around 140 B.C., were primarily a lay group which espoused a rigorous observance of the law. For them, the criterion of righteous behavior and piety was not only the written Torah, but also the oral Torah, a collection of detailed interpretations of the law set forth by the religious lawyers (the scribes) since the fifth century before Christ. Those interpretations were eventually codified in the Mishnah and the Talmud of rabbinical literature. The Pharisees took great pride in their knowledge and meticulous observation of the law and of its 613 prescriptions and prohibitions. However, they also considered themselves an elite, and felt contempt for the rabble that did not know the law and therefore could not observe it. It was this pride and this sense of being above the crowds which Jesus condemned in them. In our evaluation of the Pharisees, it is important to recall that the picture of this sect which we have from the gospels is limited in perspective and is very colored by an apologetic and polemic perspective. On many points their development of the teachings was faithful to the original spirit of the Old Testament revelation. Their dedication to the law, although eventually misguided and distorted, was a dedication which they believed had been revealed to Moses by the Lord. It was the lifeblood of the people of Israel, and its observance was a sign of their fidelity to the Lord. A reading of Psalm 119 will give the reader some indication of the reverence with which Israel thought of the law and the love directed towards this great gift of God: "Oh, how I love thy law! It is my meditation all the day . . . . How sweet are thy words to my taste, sweeter than honey to my mouth" (vv. 97, 103). Even the codified interpretations of the law were meant to protect it and to assist the Jew in its observance. It is also important to recall that it was the Pharisees who preserved Judaism from utter destruction after the Romans destroyed Jerusalem and the temple. Pharisaism, then, was in itself a constructive spiritual force in Jewish history, which, like so many other basically wholesome religious institutions, developed the serious and destructive tendencies which Jesus so strongly condemned.

Perhaps Jesus' strongest attack is contained in Matthew 23. This chapter, reflecting the experiences of the community of Palestine and the destruction of Jerusalem in A.D. 70, is a diatribe against the scribes and Pharisees which concludes the controversy stories and introduces the eschatalogical discourse of chapter 24. It is important to note that Jesus never attacks the teaching authority of the Jewish leaders, but censures their practices. The scribes and Pharisees lay heavy burdens on others through their unnecessarily severe interpretations of the law. They are filled with a sense of their own self-importance, and "love the place of honor at feasts and the best seats in the synagogues" (Matt. 23:6). They practice a casuistry and twist the law to serve their own ends. They dwell on trivia, and ignore the vital matters of justice, mercy, and faith. While being preoccupied with ritual cleanliness, they ignore the moral rot within themselves. Jesus finally condemns them for having murdered the prophets in the past, and predicts that they will crucify him and persecute his followers.

While in the synoptics, as in Matthew above, Jesus' condemnation of the Jewish leaders is based upon their moral and social behavior, in the fourth gospel his attack is based primarily on their refusal to accept him. By the time this gospel is written, the primary issue is the acceptance of Jesus as the one sent by the Father. However, in this discourse at the beginning of chapter 10, he does condemn their failure of spiritual leadership.

The final category of Jewish leader specifically named in the fourth gospel are the chief priests. They were a distinct social set, the families who descended from the high priests who had been appointed at the pleasure of foreign rulers since 37 B.C. Prior to the period of the exile, during the period in which Israel was ruled by kings, the head of the clergy was simply called the priest and had a strictly religious role in Israel. He was a man set apart and dedicated completely to the Lord's service; his place was in the sanctuary. However, after the people of Israel returned from exile, the priest assumed civil leadership, becoming a political and secular ruler. It may well be that the fourth gospel here intended to have Jesus include the chief priests within the scope of his attack upon the Jewish leaders. The feast of Dedication (10:22) would have brought to mind the memory of the evil priests who had introduced

Hellenic practices prior to the revolt of the Maccabees (1 Macc. 1:11-15; 4:21-50).

Having examined the Old Testament background of the shepherd imagery utilized here by Jesus, we can now proceed to Jesus' explanation of the second parable (vv. 3b-5), which concerns the relationship between the shepherd and the sheep. Jesus is the good shepherd (other translations have *model shepherd*, or *noble shepherd*) because he is willing to die for his sheep: "The good shepherd lays down his life for his sheep." Once more, Jesus stresses the freedom and the purpose with which he dies. No one takes his life from him. He offers it, as he freely chooses, to give his flesh for the life of the world (6:51). Jesus later reminds his disciples that he is laying down his life for them, his friends (15:13). This is the measure of his love for his sheep. In sharp contrast to Jesus' readiness to lay down his life for his sheep, is the cowardliness and lack of care and love on the part of the hireling, who leaves the sheep at the first sign of danger and allows them to be scattered by the wolf. We are again reminded of the evil shepherds in Ezekiel who allowed the sheep to be scattered and to become food for all the wild beasts. The failure of the Jewish leaders to care with love for the people of Israel had indeed left them as a flock without a shepherd. In Jesus, the good shepherd, we find fulfillment of the Lord's promise: "And I will bring them out from the peoples, and gather them from the countries and will bring them into their own land; and I will feed them on the mountains of Israel, by the fountains, and in all the inhabited places of the country. I will feed them with good pasture, and upon the mountain heights of Israel shall be their pasture; there they shall lie down in good grazing land, and on fat pasture they shall feed on the mountains of Israel. I myself will be the shepherd of my sheep, and I will make them lie down, says the Lord GOD" (Ezek. 34:13-15).

In further explaining the second parable, Jesus describes the relationship between himself and his sheep as one of deep love and intimacy: " . . . I know my own and my own know me, as the Father knows me and I know the Father. . . ." The sheep are his own since they have been given to him by the Father (6:37, 44, 65; 17:6-7). Those who believe in Jesus can do so only because the Father has given them to Jesus, that is, has given them the power to believe in Jesus. The bond between Jesus and the believer is almost a bond of ownership, properly understood. It is so powerful a bond that Jesus will not cast out the believer (6:37), so powerful that Jesus can lose nothing of what the Father has given him (6:39). We are here reminded of Paul's statement that the Christians who have died to the law through the body of Christ now "belong to another, to him who has been raised from the dead in order that we may bear fruit for God" (Rom. 7:4).

The mutual knowledge existing between Jesus and his own is not to be understood merely as the conclusion of an intellectual process. In biblical language, "to know" another person is to personally and intimately encounter that person and to eventually arrive at a relationship of love. The prophet Amos (3:2) gives notice to the people of Israel: "You only have I known of all the families of the earth; therefore I will punish you for all your iniquities." The Hebrew verb, *yada*, here refers to the gratuitous entering of the Lord into an intimate relationship with the people of Israel. They are to be punished, since this knowledge is intended to be mutual and demands a fidelity on the part of the people whom God has known. God knew Jeremiah even before the prophet was formed in the womb (Jer. 1:5). Paul teaches that if one loves God, he or she must remember that the first knowing was by God (Gal. 3:9). The Christian cannot have a knowledge of God or love God unless having been first chosen and loved by God, God enters into a personal relationship with that person. On our part, knowledge of God implies that we freely accept the gift of the relationship which God offers and are faithful to the relationship or covenant by obeying God's word. The mutual knowledge which exists between Jesus and his sheep is modeled after the intimate union of love which Jesus enjoys with the Father (3:35; 5:20; 7:29; 13:3; 17:25).

The union which exists between Jesus and his sheep moves him to think of the other sheep, which are not yet within the fold. He wishes to bring them in, so that they too may heed his voice. In this way the fourth gospel introduces the idea of the mission to the Gentiles, a mission which took on importance only during the later stages of Jesus' ministry. Initially he had decided to limit his preaching and ministry to the Jews and commanded his disciples to follow his example (Matt. 10:5, 6; 15:24; Mark 7:27). However, faced with rejection by his own people, Jesus began to give various indications that his message was now destined to extend even to the Gentiles (Matt. 8:11; 22:7-10; 11:17; Luke 13:28-30). After his glorification, it becomes very clear that the twelve are to make disciples of all nations (Matt. 28:19), to preach the Gospel to all creation (Mark 16:15) and to be his witnesses to the ends of the earth (Acts 1:9). In spite of his command, however, it took the early Christians some time to understand the full implications of his word. Even then, they approached the other sheep only with some reluctance and hesitation (Acts 10:11).

The gathering of the Gentiles into the one flock under one shepherd will take place, however, only through the glorification of Jesus in his death and resurrection: "For this reason the Father loves me, because I lay down my life, that I may take it again. No one takes it from me, but I lay it down of my own accord. I have power to lay it down, I have power to take it again; this charge I have received from my Father." His death will bear fruit only if he lives again. As we have indicated before (cf. commentary on 7:8), the suffering and death of Jesus is but one phase of his glorification, and must be perfected and completed by his resurrection and ascension to the Father.

In laying down his life, Jesus is obeying the charge he has received from his Father. The will of the Father, to which Jesus has conformed during his entire life, appears here under the form of a command. Since his death was willed by the Father, Jesus gives it up freely and without hesitation. The will of his Father has been the governing principle of his life, and it will be the governing principle of the manner in which he will leave this world (12:49-50; 14:31). Jesus' food is to do the will of him who sent him, to accomplish his work (4:34). During his entire ministry, he has sought not his own will but the will of him who sent him (8:29). If it is necessary for him to die to bring life and unity to his sheep, then he will do it, since it is the will of his Father that all who come to Christ should have resurrection and eternal life (6:38ff.). Because he has done the will of his Father, and is willing to lay down his life, he is loved by his Father.

This discourse of Jesus is again an occasion of division among his listeners. The belief among some that he is insane is repeated.

Others, however, who do not yet accept him, are not ready to reject him because of the works which he has performed: "These are not the sayings of one who has a demon. Can a demon open the eyes of the blind?"

THE FEAST OF DEDICATION (10:22–42)

22It was the feast of the Dedication at Jerusalem; 23it was winter, and Jesus was walking in the temple, in the portico of Solomon. 24So the Jews gathered round him and said to him, "How long will you keep us in suspense? If you are the Christ, tell us plainly." 25Jesus answered them, "I told you, and you do not believe. The works that I do in my Father's name, they bear witness to me; 26but you do not believe, because you do not belong to my sheep. 27My sheep hear my voice, and I know them, and they follow me; 28and I give them eternal life, and they shall never perish, and no one shall snatch them out of my hand. 29My Father, who has given them to me, is greater than all, and no one is able to snatch them out of the Father's hand. 30I and the Father are one."

31The Jews took up stones again to stone him. 32Jesus answered them, "I have shown you many good works from the Father; for which of these do you stone me?" 33The Jews answered him, "We stone you for no good work but for blasphemy; because you, being a man, make yourself God." 34Jesus answered them, "Is it not written in your law, 'I said, you are gods'? 35if he called them gods to whom the word of God came (and scripture cannot be broken), 36do you say of him whom the Father consecrated and sent into the world, 'You are blaspheming,' because I said, 'I am the Son of God'? 37If I am not doing the works of my Father, then do not believe me; 38but if I do them, even though you do not believe me, believe the works, that you may know and understand that the Father is in me and I am in the Father." 39Again they tried to arrest him, but he escaped from their hands.

40He went away again across the Jordan to the place where John at first baptized, and there he remained. 41And many came to him; and they said, "John did no sign, but everything that John said about this man was true." 42And many believed in him there.

The next confrontation between Jesus and his adversaries takes place during the feast of Dedication, also known as the feast of Hannukah or the feast of Lights. It had its origins in the aftermath of the persecution of the Jews by the Greek king Antiochus IV. Moved by a desire to achieve unity throughout his realm, he forced Greek culture on all his subjects, including the Jews. Antiochus forbade Jewish sacrifices and circumcision and, in 167 B.C. desecrated the temple and its altar and replaced it with a pagan altar. This became known as the Abomination of Desolation (1 Macc. 1:54-59; Dan 9:27; 11:31). On that altar the first sacrifice to Zeus Olympios was offered in December of 167 B.C. Three years later, the victorious Judas Maccabeus purified the sanctuary, erected a new altar and rededicated the temple. The feast of Dedication was the annual celebration of that event.

Jesus' encounter with the Jewish leaders takes place on Solomon's Portico, located in the outermost court of the temple. The Jewish leaders press Jesus to state plainly whether he is the Messiah. They had challenged him to identify himself during his discourse at the feast of Tabernacles (8:53), and many had questioned whether he was the Messiah (7:26, 31, 41-42; 9:22). The Sanhedrin will address this question to Jesus in the synoptic version of the passion (Matt. 26:63-68; Mark 14:61-65; Luke 23:67-71). The Jews' question on this particular occasion was very natural in view of the fact that Jesus had described himself as the good shepherd. The shepherd was a frequent symbol of the Davidic king, who, under the Lord, will unite the nation in a new covenant of peace: "My servant David shall be king over them; and they shall all have one shepherd. . . . My dwelling place shall be with them; and I will be their God, and they shall be my people. Then the nations will know that I the LORD sanctify Israel, when my sanctuary is in the midst of them for ever more" (Ezek. 37:24, 27-28). Jesus' response is very similar to the response he gave the Jews when they had asked him to identify himself during his discourse at the feast of Tabernacles (8:25). He refers them back to what he had already told them, that he is from the Father, and that he speaks for the Father. His answer always frustrates them, since he very carefully avoids giving an unqualified answer concerning his messianic role. Jesus in fact consistently went out of his way to prevent any rumors that might prove an obstacle to his mission. Jesus realized that the Jews of his time had one basic image of the Messiah, the image of a political and secular savior who would overthrow the foreign oppressor. The figure of the Messiah, from the Aramaic word for "anointed," was a concept which underwent an evolution in Jewish history. During the first days of the Davidic monarchy, every anointed king was considered a savior sent by God to his people. Later, when the Jews were governed by unworthy kings, they pined for the coming of a king who would be like David. After the exile, however, when the Davidic line was no longer in power, they looked forward to one supreme king whom the Lord would send to save his people. Through this Messiah, God would intervene in history in the same way as he had intervened in the events of the exodus. The secular, political, and nationalistic coloring of the concept was always there, and was a natural development of Jewish thinking. It could not be considered a corruption only by the Jews of Jesus' time. Jesus was not attempting to restore a concept which had been lost, but struggled to raise the expectations to a new and higher level, and to introduce the Jews into a world which had not existed before his coming.

Jesus, refusing to give up his efforts to overcome the blindness and deliberate ignorance of his listeners, expands upon and clarifies his response by recalling for them the works which he has done in his Father's name, that is, the signs or miracles he has performed. These works stand as eternal witnesses to Jesus as the giver of life, the bread of life, the source of living water, the light of life, the one sent by the Father. Jesus explains to them that they are unable to see beyond the external works just as they are unable to hear and understand the words he speaks to them because they do not believe in him. They have never taken the first step towards entering into the knowledge of him which his sheep possess. He had previously explained their inability to hear the words of God by stating that they were not of God (8:47).

While the Jewish leaders, who do not belong to Jesus' sheep, cannot hear his voice and will therefore die in their sin, Jesus' flock, which hears his voice and follows him, receives eternal life. They are Jesus' own, and cannot be snatched out of his hand. The ultimate guarantor of their safety is, of course, the Father. Again we are reminded that Jesus will not lose any of those whom the Father has given him. We might summarize Jesus' response, then, by stating that Jesus presents himself as the one sent by his Father to continue the work begun by his Father, the work of giving life. Eternal life belongs to those who accept the gift of faith in Jesus, and it belongs to them eternally, never to be lost.

Jesus concludes his response to the Jews by once again stressing his unity with the Father: "I and the Father are one." The oneness of purpose and activity which Jesus shares with the Father is also a recurrent theme in the fourth gospel: Jesus was sent into the world by the Father to save it (3:17); he is loved by the Father (3:35) and has been given all things by the Father, including judgment (5:22, 27), life (5:26), power over all flesh (17:2), followers (6:37), what to say (12:49; 17:8), the divine name (17:11, 12) and glory (17:22); Jesus has come into the world to do the Father's will and to carry out his work (4:34; 6:38-40); He does only what he sees the Father doing (5:19), and his teaching is the teaching of the one who sent him (7:16). Jesus therefore speaks of a unity of will, of power, and of operation.

The Jewish response to Jesus' affirmation of his unity with the Father is to take up stones to try to kill him. On two other occasions in the fourth gospel, Jesus has placed himself in mortal danger by stressing the uniqueness of his relationship to the Father (5:17-18; 8:59). Returning to the theme of the good works of the Father he has performed, Jesus ironically asks which of the good works have moved them to this violent act. His would-be executioners respond that they wish to kill him because he has blasphemed by claiming that he, a human, is God. While it is not absolutely clear as to what constituted blasphemy during the period of Jesus' ministry, it is certain that he was not condemned for any claim to be the Messiah, but for making himself God (10:33), making himself equal to God (5:18), making himself the Son of God (18:7). It will ultimately be this charge which serves as the basis of their justification for killing him.

Jesus defends his affirmation by citing a verse from Psalm 82, which reads, "I say, 'You are gods, sons of the Most High, all of you; nevertheless, you shall die like men, and fall like any prince' " (vv. 6-7). The psalmist is writing about a condemnation by God of corrupt judges who have favored the wicked and undermined the bases of earthly society. Although they are gods in that they share in the specifically divine function of judging, they shall die like men. Jesus argues that if the Old Testament could refer to human judges as gods, they should not object to his calling himself the Son of God. This defense of Jesus may appear very weak to our Western logic. It seems clear *to us* that Jesus' claim to be *God* with a capital "G" is not the same as the Psalm's description of the judges as gods. However, it seems that Jesus' argument, which followed the rules of scriptural interpretation commonly accepted in his day, does not cause any problem for his audience. Jesus continues to press his argument further. According to Jesus' interpretation, the judges were called gods because the word of God came through them. If they can be called gods for that reason, why then should the Jews object to the title Son of God being applied to someone who has been consecrated and sent into the world as the vehicle of God's word. He had been sent by the Father to bring into the world the Father's teaching (7:16), to declare to the world what he had heard from the Father (8:26) and what he had seen with the Father (1:18; 3:11; 8:38). Jesus is the special vehicle of the Father's words and teachings (3:34; 8:28; 12:49-50; 14:24; 17:8, 14). Jesus' claim that he is consecrated, set within the feast of Dedication, calls to mind the prologue's statement that Jesus "pitched his tent among us," and was seen as the new tabernacle. Jesus also claimed that he would be the new temple (2:19-22). The body of the risen Christ is to be the locus of the worship of the Father in spirit and truth. Jesus will be the new temple from which the living waters flow (7:37-39).

Jesus once again points to his works, and tries to convince his listeners at least to give them credence, which ought to be evidence that the Father is in him and he is in the Father. Jesus is assuming here that the Jewish leaders will accept his works as the works of the Father, and that therefore they would be forced to conclude that Jesus and the Father are one. Of course, without basic faith in Jesus, his listeners cannot see Jesus' miracles as works of the Father. Remaining unconvinced, they once again try to arrest Jesus, but are unable to lay hands upon him.

Jesus leaves Jerusalem and returns to Bethany in the Trans-Jordan, where John had baptized, and where Jesus' public life had begun. Jesus remains there, where many believed in him. His public ministry ends, and all that remains before him is his deliberate final journey to Jerusalem at the time of the Passover, when he would freely place himself in the hands of his adversaries and lay down his life for his sheep.

Jesus Raises Lazarus from the Dead
And Is Condemned to Death by the Sanhedrin
(11:1–57)

Jesus, who has life in himself and bestows that life on those who believe in him, transforms tragedy and sadness into an event of glory, a moment in which the power of his Father becomes visible in Jesus' action. His listeners, who have already heard Jesus proclaim himself as the bread of life, the source of living water, and the light of the world, now witness his triumph over death in the existence of another human being, Lazarus, a triumph to be surpassed only by Jesus' own resurrection. As in all his other signs, however, Jesus is anxious that those who see the miracle perceive the reality beyond the sign. The life Jesus has come to give exceeds in infinite measure the physical life he restores to Lazarus. The life which Jesus gives, symbolized by the restoration of physical life, is the eternal life by which God himself lives. While for some this miracle was an event which led to faith, for the Jewish authorities it was the act which sealed Jesus' fate. As they gather to bemoan his growing impact on the crowds, they conclude that his continued presence and ever-increasing influence may bring down the fury of the Roman Empire upon their small and helpless nation. It is then that the statement is made that Jesus must die in order to save the nation. It is a prophetic statement, the ultimate significance of which infinitely surpasses the intent of the group of conspirators who have condemned Jesus.

THE RAISING OF LAZARUS (11:1–44)

¹Now a certain man was ill, Lazarus of Bethany, the village of Mary and her sister Martha. ²It was Mary who anointed the Lord with ointment and wiped his feet with her hair, whose brother Lazarus was ill. ³So the sisters sent to him, saying, "Lord, he whom you love is ill." ⁴But when Jesus heard it he said, "This illness is not unto death; it is for the glory of God, so that the Son of God may be glorified by means of it."

⁵Now Jesus loved Martha and her sister and Lazarus. ⁶So when he heard that he was ill, he stayed two days longer in the place where he was. ⁷Then after this he said to the disciples, "Let us go into Judea again." ⁸The disciples said to him, "Rabbi, the Jews are but now seeking to stone you, and you are going there again?" ⁹Jesus answered, "Are there not twelve hours in the day? If any one walks in the day, he does not stumble, because he sees the light of this world. ¹⁰But if any one walks in the night, he stumbles, because the light is not in him." ¹¹Thus he spoke, and then he said to them, "Our friend Lazarus has fallen asleep, but I go to awake him out of sleep." ¹²The disciples said to him, "Lord, if he has fallen asleep, he will recover." ¹³Now Jesus had spoken of his death, but they thought that he meant taking rest in sleep. ¹⁴Then Jesus told them plainly, "Lazarus is dead; ¹⁵and for your sake I am glad that I was not there, so that you may believe. But let us go to him." ¹⁶Thomas, called the Twin, said to his fellow disciples, "Let us also go, that we may die with him."

¹⁷Now when Jesus came, he found that Lazarus had already been in the tomb four days. ¹⁸Bethany was near Jerusalem, about two miles off, ¹⁹and many of the Jews had come to Martha and Mary to console them concerning their brother. ²⁰When Martha heard that Jesus was coming, she went and met him, while Mary sat in the house. ²¹Martha said to Jesus, "Lord, if you had been here, my brother would not have died. ²²And even now, I know that whatever you ask from God, God will give you." ²³Jesus said to her, "Your brother will rise again." ²⁴Martha said to him, "I know that he will rise again in the resurrection at the last day." ²⁵Jesus said to her, "I am the resurrection and the life; he who believes in me, though he die, yet shall he live, ²⁶and whoever lives and believes in me shall never die. Do you believe this?" ²⁷She said to him, "Yes, Lord, I believe that you are the Christ, the Son of God, he who is coming into the world."

²⁸When she said this, she went and called her sister Mary, saying quietly, "The Teacher is here and is calling for you." ²⁹And when she heard it, she rose quickly and went to him. ³⁰Now Jesus had not

yet come to the village, but was still in the place where Martha had met him. [31]When the Jews who were with her in the house, consoling her, saw Mary rise quickly and go out, they followed her, supposing that she was going to the tomb to weep there. [32]Then Mary, when she came where Jesus was and saw him, fell at his feet, saying to him, "Lord, if you had been here, my brother would not have died." [33]When Jesus saw her weeping, and the Jews who came with her also weeping, he was deeply moved in spirit and troubled; [34]and he said, "Where have you laid him?" They said to him, "Lord, come and see." [35]Jesus wept. [36]So the Jews said, "See how he loved him." [37]But some of them said, "Could not he who opened the eyes of the blind man have kept this man from dying?"

[38]Then Jesus, deeply moved again, came to the tomb; it was a cave, and a stone lay upon it. [39]Jesus said, "Take away the stone." Martha, the sister of the dead man, said to him, "Lord, by this time there will be an odor, for he has been dead four days." [40]Jesus said to her, "Did I not tell you that if you would believe you would see the glory of God?" [41]So they took away the stone. And Jesus lifted up his eyes and said, "Father, I thank thee that thou hast heard me. [42]I knew that thou hearest me always, but I have said this on account of the people standing by, that they may believe that thou didst send me." [43]When he had said this, he cried with a loud voice, "Lazarus, come out." [44]The dead man came out, his hands and feet bound with bandages, and his face wrapped with a cloth. Jesus said to them, "Unbind him, and let him go."

As has already been noted in the conclusion of the commentary on chapter 10, it appears, as some critics would have it, that Jesus' public ministry came to close with his discourse at the feast of Dedication and his departure for Bethany in the Trans-Jordan area of Palestine. His next journey to Jerusalem would be his last, for he would then be ready to face the hour of his departure out of this world to the Father (13:1). These critics suggest that chapters 11 and 12 were added to the gospel and inserted at this point by an editor at a later time, and that the material contained therein concerns events which in reality occurred during an earlier period of Jesus' ministry. Among the reasons offered by these scholars are two which will be mentioned here. First, the chronology they suggest is in agreement with the itinerary described in the synoptics, who have Jesus travelling from the Trans-Jordan area through Jericho to Jerusalem, with Bethany (in Judea) as his domicile. The sequence of journeys made by Jesus in chapters 11 and 12 is complicated, and difficult to reconcile with the synoptic itinerary. A second reason is that the expression, "the Jews," in chapters 11 and 12 is used to refer to the ordinary people of Jerusalem and Judea who give evidence of sympathy for Jesus, while the same expression in chapters 1 to 10 refers primarily to the hostile Jewish authorities.

Another issue that must be touched upon briefly is the historicity of the miracle. Some critics have held that the narrative of raising Lazarus from the dead is a story which is not literally true. Their skepticism is not based on any doubt that Jesus could have performed such a miracle, but on the difficulty of explaining the synoptics' omission of such a stupendous miracle, a miracle which led the authorities to the final decision to kill Jesus. In response, it is important to underline the fact that the fourth gospel, while sharing material with the synoptics, also draws from an independent historical tradition. As to the statement that the synoptics would not have omitted a miracle which was the proximate cause of Jesus' death, another explanation may be in order. While the synoptics indicate that Jesus' condemnation by the Sanhedrin was the result of the words and deeds of his entire ministry, the fourth gospel, for pedagogical and theological reasons, chose to make this miracle the specific deed which brought the Sanhedrin to its decision. No other miracle showed so dramatically the very *raison d'être* for Jesus' coming into the world, that is, " . . . that they may have life, and have it abundantly" (10:10).

The narrative begins by noting that a man named Lazarus of Bethany, the town of Mary and Martha, was ill. It specifically notes that it was the town of Mary and Martha in order to distinguish it from Bethany in the Trans-Jordan, where Jesus had taken refuge before his final trip to the holy city. Bethany was the town where Jesus normally stayed when he went to Jerusalem (Mark 11:11; 14:3), and, judging from the deep friendship which the fourth gospel suggests Jesus enjoyed with Lazarus and his sisters, their home was where he remained. Martha and Mary are mentioned in Luke 10:38-42 as two women who offered him hospitality on another occasion.

Luke's description of the sisters is in perfect conformity with the portrait here painted by John. John further adds that Mary was the woman who anointed the Lord with ointment and wiped his face with her hair, referring to an occurrence which would be narrated in chapter 12.

When Jesus receives the message that the friend whom he loved is ill, his response is an unmistakable indication that the miracle which will follow is intended by Jesus to be another of his signs, pointing to a reality beyond itself which will be visible only to the eyes of the believer. Jesus affirms that this illness will not end in death, and that it will serve as the manifestation both of God's glory and of Jesus' own glorification. Jesus' reference to the *glory of God* can be fully understood only through a brief examination of the Old Testament background of that expression. The Greek, *doxa tou theou* (the glory of God), is a translation of the Hebrew, *kebod yahweh*, which referred to the presence of God *made visible through deeds of power*. In the Old Testament, the glory of God was visible in fire and smoke, in the lightning and thunder of nature's storms (Ps. 29), in the winds of Sinai (Exod. 19:16), in earthquakes (Ps. 18) and in the spectacular beauty of the heavens (Ps. 19). In the fourth gospel, Jesus is the visible manifestation of God, a manifestation made visible through his deeds of power (2:11). In fact, the glory of God is made visible in all of Jesus' works, which are the works of the Father. Jesus considers Lazarus' illness as an occasion for the manifestation of his Father through a deed of power, that is, the calling forth of Lazarus from the tomb. Furthermore, as the fourth gospel will note (11:45-53), this miracle will provoke the Jewish leaders to finalize their plans to bring about Jesus' death, the death which will be the first phase of his glorification and return to the Father. Thus Lazarus' illness and this miracle will result in the glorification of the Son of God, which in turn will bring about the manifestation of his Father's glory.

The fourth gospel then couples its statement that Jesus, after hearing about Lazarus' illness, delayed his departure for two days, with the affirmation of Jesus' love for Lazarus and his sisters. This seeming paradox disappears when it becomes clear that the gospel is attempting to explain that it was not a lack of love which led to Jesus' delay, but that his action was guided by his perception that this illness was intended to serve as an occasion for the manifestation of God's glory. If Jesus delayed long enough so that Lazarus would have been dead for four days by the time of his arrival in Bethany, then there would be no doubt about the finality of Lazarus' death, for the Jews of that period believed that the soul of the dead person hovered nearby for three days, and only departed after that. There could be, therefore, no doubt concerning the genuineness of Jesus' miracle. His delay is easily explained once it is understood that his primary interest here was the glory of the Father, and not the assistance of friends, whom he truly loved.

Jesus' discussion with his disciples concerning his trip to Judea deals with two distinct and separate issues, that of the death of Jesus and that of helping Lazarus. The discussion of the connection between going to Jerusalem and the danger he thereby faced was probably added by the editor in order to establish a proper sequence between this chapter and the one preceding, which described Jesus' escape following the attempt of the Jewish authorities to stone him. Jesus responds to the objections of the disciples by emphasizing the importance of taking advantage of the light, as he had done in his discussion with them preceding his healing of the man born blind (9:4). There is a parallel to the disciples' fears and to the anticipation of Jesus' death in Jerusalem in Mark 10:32-35.

The discussion of the trip to Judea as it related to helping Lazarus begins with Jesus' statement that Lazarus had fallen asleep, a euphemism referring to his death (Mark 5:39). When the disciples show by their response that they have not understood Jesus, he makes it clear that Lazarus has died. His expression of joy is obviously not over the death of his friend, but over his knowledge that Lazarus' death and subsequent return from the grave will strengthen his disciples' faith in him, a faith that they had already acquired after witnessing the first of his signs in Cana of Galilee (2:11). All of the signs performed by Jesus, as presented by John, are intended to confirm and deepen the faith of those who already believe (20:31).

When Jesus arrives with his disciples at Bethany, he is told that Lazarus has been in the tomb four days, and that many of the Jews from Jerusalem had come to Bethany to console Mary and Martha. The fourth gospel gives two accounts of his meeting with the two sisters, one of his meeting with Martha, and one of his meeting with

Mary. Some critics believe that the "Martha" account, the more developed of the two accounts, was original, and that a later one was added for Mary, who was the better known of the two sisters.

Jesus' joy over the opportunity to accomplish another of his Father's works which will strengthen the faith of his disciples is based on the obvious assumption that their faith is still inadequate. The validity of that assumption is exhibited very clearly in the case of Martha, who greets Jesus by affirming her faith that Jesus could have prevented her brother from dying, but whose faith does not include a confidence in his power to restore life. On the other hand, she seems to be open to that possibility, since she states that she knows that "whatever you ask from God, God will give you." Jesus' greeting concerning her brother's future resurrection is misunderstood by Martha as a conventional Jewish confession of belief in the final resurrection, the quickening of the dead, held not only by the Pharisees but by many Jews of Jesus' day. Jesus corrects Martha, proclaiming that he is the resurrection and the life for people, *now*. Whereas Martha thinks of the future intervention of God who will bring about the resurrection of the dead (final eschatalogy), Jesus insists that resurrection and life are offered by him in the present (realized eschatology). Whoever believes in Jesus, the resurrection, though he die physically, shall live with eternal life, that is, with the inner life of God himself. Whoever is alive spiritually and believes in Jesus, the life, shall never die spiritually.

Martha responds to Jesus by professing her faith in him as "the Christ, the Son of God, he who is coming into the world," reflecting her acceptance of him as the Messiah and the prophet who is to come into the world. While these titles carried within themselves a more profound meaning to be discovered gradually by the believing community in which the fourth gospel was written, they had only the limited and traditional meaning for this woman who was about to witness an event which would ultimately raise her faith in Jesus to a level never before dreamt in this world.

While the "Mary" account adds nothing in terms of the perceptions of Lazarus' family in this situation, it does contain a reference to the strong emotions evoked in Jesus when he witnesses the mourning of Mary and the Jews who had accompanied her: "When Jesus saw her weeping, and the Jews who came with her also weeping, he was deeply moved in spirit and troubled . . . . " The Greek verb, *enebrimesato*, expresses a very deeply felt anger, whose depth and intensity are not clearly communicated by the RSV. The same verb was used to express anger and indignation in Mark 14:5, describing the reaction of the guests to the action of the woman who poured the precious ointment over Jesus' head. Jesus' anger would not have been directed toward the mourners for any lack of faith on their part, since he himself also wept over his friend's death. It may very well have been directed, however, at the power of darkness, Satan, whose hand Jesus saw in human death and sickness (cf. commentary on 5:14). This is the power, "the ruler of this world," whom Jesus would cast out through his glorification and return to the Father (21:31). Jesus' attack upon the empire of Satan through his expulsion of devils and his casting out of sickness is much more clearly expressed in the synoptics (cf. commentary on 5:14).

At Jesus' request, he is led to the tomb of Lazarus, where he again gives evidence of his love for his friend by openly weeping. Martha's remark at Jesus' order that the stone be rolled away from the tomb reflects, as has already been noted, a faith that has not yet matured to the point of seeing Jesus as having the absolute power over life. Jesus calls upon Martha to exercise the faith which she professes to have, and promises that she will now see the glory of God, that is, his presence in the world made visible through an act of power, the power which Jesus has to give life (5:21).

When the rock is rolled away from the tomb, Jesus lifts his eyes, an action normally connected with prayer, and thanks his Father for having heard him. It thus appears that Jesus had already requested the Father to empower him to raise Lazarus from the dead, although no such prayer has been mentioned here. However, in view of the fourth gospel's emphasis upon the unity between Jesus' will and the "will of him who sent me" (4:34), it seems clear that Jesus is thanking his Father for hearing, not a formal request for the power to perform this specific miracle, but for hearing Jesus' constant prayer and desire, that the Father's will be done. While the fourth gospel does not explicitly contain this as a prayer on Jesus' part, the synoptics provide several such instances (Matt 6:10; 26:39; Mark 14:36; Luke 11:2-4). Whatever Jesus seeks to bring about, including the resurrection of Lazarus, is sought by him because it is his Father's will (5:30). Jesus' food is to do the will of him who sent him, and to accomplish his work (4:34). Jesus does in fact see his miracles, which he calls his works, as a continuation of the works of the Father (5:17), the work of giving life and of judging. In view of this, it is clear that as he stands before the tomb of Lazarus, Jesus is expressing his joy and gratitude not only for the raising of Lazarus, but for all the life-giving works which the Father enables him to do.

Jesus' explicit prayer of thanksgiving is offered "on account of the people standing by, that they may believe that thou didst send me." All throughout this narrative, Jesus' sole concern is for the glory of God and for others' belief in himself as God's emissary. By thanking God formally and publicly in this way, he tries to assure that the miracle which the people are now about to witness will be seen by them as a work of his Father, as a visible manifestation of the Father's glory. Through that prayer, he also hopes that the witnesses will come to believe that the Father has sent him, not for Jesus' own glory (8:50), but so that they will come to know the Father through Jesus. For it is through Jesus, the door of the sheep (10:9), that they will have life in the Father.

Jesus then calls to Lazarus, who had been dead four days, to come out of the tomb. His friend, hands and feet bound with bandages and his face wrapped with a cloth, walks from the tomb in full view of the mourners. To the eye of the unbeliever, this is merely another one of the inexplicable miracles of a troublesome wonder-worker and magician. To the believer, however, who can see beyond the victory over physical death, this deed was a sign of Jesus' ability to give eternal life to a human person, a sign of his power to raise up the spiritually dead. In fact, some critics see this miracle as the dramatized expression of the truth which Jesus proclaimed following his healing of the sick man at the pool of Bethzatha: "For as the Father raises the dead and gives them life, so also the Son gives life to whom he will . . . . Truly, truly, I say to you, the hour is coming, and now is, when the dead will hear the voice of the Son of God, and those who hear will live . . . . Do not marvel at this; for the hour is coming when all who are in the tombs will hear his voice and come forth . . . . " (5:21, 25, 28-29).

This miracle is a visible and powerful manifestation of Jesus' affirmation to Martha that he is the resurrection who can grant eternal life to those who believe in him, even though they are physically

<u>dead.</u> Through this sign, Jesus shows that he is life itself (11:25; 16:6) and that the life he gives to humankind (10:10), the life by which God himself lives (5:26; 6:57), cannot be destroyed by death.

SESSION OF THE SANHEDRIN (11:45–57)

⁴⁵*Many of the Jews therefore, who had come with Mary and had seen what he did, believed in him;* ⁴⁶*but some of them went to the Pharisees and told them what Jesus had done.* ⁴⁷*So the chief priests and the Pharisees gathered the council, and said, "What are we to do? For this man performs many signs.* ⁴⁸*If we let him go on thus, every one will believe in him, and the Romans will come and destroy our holy place, and our nation."* ⁴⁹*But one of them, Caiaphas, who was high priest that year, said to them, "You know nothing at all;* ⁵⁰*you do not understand that it is expedient for you that one man should die for the people, and that the whole nation should not perish."* ⁵¹*He did not say this of his own accord, but being high priest that year he prophesied that Jesus should die for the nation,* ⁵²*and not for the nation only, but to gather into one the children of God who are scattered abroad.* ⁵³*So from that day on they took counsel how to put him to death.*

⁵⁴*Jesus therefore no longer went about openly among the Jews, but went from there to the country near the wilderness, to a town called Ephraim; and there he stayed with the disciples.*

⁵⁵*Now the Passover of the Jews was at hand, and many went up from the country to Jerusalem before the Passover, to purify themselves.* ⁵⁶*They were looking for Jesus and saying to one another as they stood in the temple, "What do you think? That he will not come to the feast?"* ⁵⁷*Now the chief priests and the Pharisees had given orders that if any one knew where he was, he should let them know, so that they might arrest him.*

While the stupendous event at Bethany had resulted in an increase in the number of believers and in the deepening of the faith of those who already accepted Jesus, it caused fear and panic in others who went immediately to the Pharisees to report on what had happened. Their report moves the chief priests and the Pharisees, specifically the scribes who belong to the Pharisaic sect, to call together the

Sanhedrin, the supreme governing council of the Jewish people, in existence since the time of Judas Maccabeus (1 Macc. 7:33). During the period of Jesus' ministry, it included the elders, who represented the lay aristocracy, the chief priests, former high priests and members of the families from which the high priest was normally selected, and the scribes, religious lawyers most of whom belonged to the sect of the Pharisees. Under the Romans, this assembly was the supreme governing body of the Jews, regulating religious affairs with complete freedom and having limited power over civil affairs. As the fourth gospel makes clear (18:31), they could pronounce the sentence of death, but had to depend upon the Roman procurator for its ratification and execution. Although this particular session of the Jewish authorities is not recorded in the synoptics, they do indicate that two days before the Passover, the chief priests and scribes were seeking to find a way to arrest him quietly and dispose of him quickly without upsetting the crowds (Mark 14:1-2; Luke 22:1-2). Matthew in fact alludes to a gathering of the chief priests and elders of the people in the palace of the high priest, Caiaphas, a preliminary meeting where plans for killing Jesus were discussed (Matt. 26:3). The fourth gospel, as has already been noted in the commentary on this chapter, selects the miracle at Bethany as the point of no return for the Jewish leaders. While Jesus continues to perform his miracles and more and more people believe in him, the authorities become more aware than ever that they have had no impact on this dangerous phenomenon. They are now driven by a growing anger and a sense of helplessness, recalling the many occasions in which they have tried to arrest or even to kill Jesus, but have failed (7:30, 44; 8:59; 10:31, 39). Their anger intensifies when they also consider the people's awareness of what appears to be their inaction and inability to control Jesus (7:25-26). Their primary reason for wanting Jesus dead was his arrogant affirmation that he is equal to God (5:18; 8:59; 10:33). However, they are also genuinely concerned with his growing power to convince the crowds that he is the Messiah and with the dangerous divisions he has created among the people (7:32, 43-44). Some of the members of the Sanhedrin think that unless they take action, more believers will gather to his cause, thus forcing the Romans to move decisively against the Jews in what was becoming an explosive revolutionary situation.

It is at this point that Caiaphas, while offering what he considers is the wisest political solution to the problem, also utters what the fourth gospel considers an unconscious prophecy concerning the effects of Jesus' death. It is important to recall that the Judaism of the first century had a belief in unconscious prophecy, and that this power was especially associated with the high priesthood. Caiaphas proclaims that their course of action should be very clear. If one person should be sacrificed in order to assure the survival of the nation, then so be it. The fourth gospel comments that by this remark, Caiaphas unconsciously predicts that the death of Jesus would accomplish far more than assure the survival of the nation, a survival that ironically would only be the stay of a death-sentence upon the Jewish nation. Jesus' death would in fact effect the salvation of the nation and also enable him "to gather into one the children of God who are scattered abroad." The shepherd would lay down his life for his sheep to save them from "the thief who comes only to steal and kill and destroy," and to bring them life in abundance (10:10-11). By his death, Jesus in effect was taking the first step in the process of glorification, which would enable him to finally bestow upon humankind the life-giving Spirit (7:39). Moreover, Jesus' death will bring life not only to the sheep of his fold, i.e., to those who already believe in him, but also to the "other sheep, that are not of this fold" (10:16). Caiaphas's statement recalls the vision of the Old Testament prophets, who dreamt of a day when the Lord would gather the dispersed people of Israel and set them together like sheep in a fold and a flock in its pasture. Theirs was a vision and a dream which would now find fulfillment in the death of the shepherd (Isa. 11:12; Mich. 2:12; Jer. 23:3; Ezek. 34:16). As Jesus' death approaches, the fourth gospel underlines the salvific meaning of that death, and the universal scope of God's love manifested in the entire ministry of Jesus. He, who was sent by the Father to save the world (3:17; 10:36; 12:47), to take away the sin of the world (1:29), and to give life to the world (6:33, 51), approaches the moment of his glorification, the very *raison d'être* of his existence (12:27-28).

The life which Jesus offers will be given to humanity, not as to isolated individuals, but within the context of community. The nations and the children of God scattered abroad are to be gathered into one. There will be one flock and one shepherd (10:16). The unity of the children of God, which would reflect the unity of the Father with Jesus, would be the object of Jesus' prayer: ". . . that

164

they may all be one; even as thou, Father, art in me, and I in thee, that they also may be in us . . . The glory which thou hast given me I have given to them, that they may be one as we are one, I in them and thou in me, that they may become perfectly one . . . . " (16:21-23).

Jesus, always aware of the hatred directed against him and of the authorities' plans to destroy him, flees from public view into a wilderness, where he will await the appropriate moment to return of his own volition and then freely lay down his life. While Jesus waits in a town called Ephraim, and the pilgrims gathered in Jerusalem for the Passover discuss Jesus, the chief priests and Pharisees put the finishing touches on their plans for Jesus' arrest and destruction.

Anointing at Bethany; Entry into Jerusalem; Concluding Discourses (12:1–50)

While the Sanhedrin's response to the stupendous miracle of Bethany is a decision to take away the life of the one who is the source of life, a grateful sister of Lazarus responds with an act of love, a prophetic act which prepares Jesus for his burial. In addition, there are many others, whose response is an enthusiastic and spontaneous attempt to turn Jesus into a political Messiah and to turn his entry into Jerusalem into the triumphant procession of a conquering hero. Jesus reacts by correcting their nationalism and their distorted view of his mission by symbolically underlining the universal nature and scope of his mission, a theme reinforced by the arrival of Gentiles seeking an audience from him. Their arrival, together with Mary's prophetic action and the activity of his enemies, brings Jesus to an ever-deepening awareness of his approaching death and to a reflection on the meaning of life and death. Jesus' final words to his enemies before the events of his glorification are words of warning to his listeners, encouraging them to believe in him, the light, before darkness falls over his world and theirs.

THE ANOINTING (12:1–8)

[1]Six days before the Passover, Jesus came to Bethany, where Lazarus was, whom Jesus had raised from the dead. [2]There they made him a supper; Martha served, but Lazarus was one of those at table with him. [3]Mary took a pound of costly ointment of pure nard and anointed the feet of Jesus and wiped his feet with her hair; and the house was filled with the fragrance of the ointment. [4]But Judas Iscariot, one of his disciples (he who was to betray him), said, [5]"Why was this ointment not sold for three hundred denarii and given to

the poor?" ⁶This he said, not that he cared for the poor but because he was a thief, and as he had the money box he used to take what was put into it. ⁷Jesus said, "Let her alone, let her keep it for the day of my burial. ⁸The poor you always have with you, but you do not always have me."

The theme of Jesus' impending death, developed in chapters 11 and 12, first appears in this chapter in John's account of the anointing of Jesus at Bethany at a supper given for him. The scene of a woman anointing Jesus at table is one which John has in common with all three synoptics. Critics believe that the incident described by John is the same as that recorded by Mark and Matthew, while the incident described by Luke is a different incident. Since the account offered by Matthew 26:6-13 is completely dependent upon Mark 14:3-11, we may omit Matthew's report in any discussion of the various accounts. John and Mark are describing an incident which took place in Bethany in the house of Simon the leper, whereas Luke 7:36-38 narrates an incident in Galilee in which a sinful woman weeps on Jesus' feet, and after drying them, anoints them with ointment. Critics point out, however, that while Mark presents the pure form of the incident at Bethany, the fourth gospel incorporates into its report of that incident some of the details from Luke's account of the anointing by Jesus by the sinful woman. For example, John's version has the woman, whom he identifies as Mary of Bethany, anointing Jesus' feet, a detail which appears in the Lucan version. In Mark's description of the incident, the woman anoints Jesus' head, which was common practice. Furthermore, the fourth gospel has the woman wipe away the ointment she has poured on Jesus' feet with her hair, an action which is, to say the very least, somewhat unusual since it nullifies the effect of the anointing. In Luke's account, the woman uses her hair to wipe away her tears from Jesus' feet, an action which makes sense. Moreover, the loosening of a Jewish woman's hair in public, considered a scandalous action, would fit the character of the sinful woman in Galilee but certainly not that of a respectable woman like Mary of Bethany. How this transferral of details between the accounts of two separate and, as we shall see, very different incidents, took place is easily understood once we recall the nature of the method by which the material for the gospels was transmitted within the Christian community. During the period intervening between the end of Jesus' life and the first written accounts of that life, his words and deeds were circulated in a living manner by his followers through oral tradition. It is easy to see how it was possible for details of the incident recorded by Luke to become incorporated into John's account of the anointing at Bethany, and how details from Mark's account of the anointing at Bethany could have been transferred to Luke's incident of the sinful woman at Galilee. Similarly, the Church in later centuries confused Mary Magdalene with Mary of Bethany and with the repentant woman mentioned in the Lucan version of the anointing of Jesus. For many centuries, in fact, the Latin Church continued to identify the three women by honoring them together under the title of St. Mary Magdalene on July 22. Most of Christian art depicted Mary Magdalene as a repentant woman weeping at Jesus' feet.

Six days before the Passover, Jesus was a guest at a supper given for him in Bethany. The fourth gospel's explicit description of Bethany as the village of Lazarus, the man whom Jesus had raised from the dead, seems somewhat unusual and unnecessary to the reader, who is well acquainted with Bethany from the Lazarus incident described in chapter 11. However, it is important to recall that since the Lazarus story and the account of the anointing were at first separate from each other, this identification would originally have had to be clearly made. While Mark indicates that Jesus' host on this occasion was Simon the leper, the fourth gospel names only the characters who are important to the meaning of this story (Mary and Judas). John also names Martha and Lazarus, who have no part to play in this scene, primarily to connect chapters 11 and 12. While Jesus is at table, Mary takes a pound of very expensive ointment or perfume made from the root of the nard plant, which grows in the mountains of northern India, and anoints Jesus' feet. She then wipes off the ointment with her hair. As we have already pointed out, this action would not have made much sense and probably did not take place during this incident, but was a detail which was transferred from Luke's description of the incident at the house of the Pharisee in Galilee.

The Jews, who lived in a hot and arid climate, anointed themselves with olive oil, especially after bathing, in order to keep the skin from drying. The wealthy used a perfumed oil which had to be prepared by a professional perfumer. In Mark's account, the woman anoints Jesus' head, which was the normal Jewish usage. The anointing of the feet would make sense only in the case of a dead person, whose entire body was anointed after having been washed. The aromatic oils were intended to counteract the unpleasant odors which came from the corpse. Jesus' response to Judas' complaint, in fact, indicates that Jesus did interpret Mary's act of gratitude for her brother's life within the context of Jesus' own burial. Jesus admonishes Judas, pointing out that the purpose of this ointment was to prepare Jesus for burial. That Jesus did consider Mary's act as prophetic and as symbolizing the preparation of his body for burial is even clearer from Mark: "She has done what she could; she has anointed my body beforehand for burying" (14:8).

The other major character in the Johannine account of this incident is Judas, who, as the instrument through which the Jewish leaders would finally achieve their aim of the destruction of Jesus, is another reminder of the approaching passion and death of Jesus. When Judas witnesses Mary's act, he criticizes her for what he considers an irresponsible extravagance, pointing out that the ointment she used could have been sold for three hundred denarii and the proceeds donated to the poor. When we recall that in Jesus' day, the normal wage for one day's work was one denarius, then we can understand the shocked reaction of someone who could not see beyond the material worth of the ointment or comprehend the profound love and gratitude expressed by this gesture. John's evaluation of Judas' statement, however, reflects what must have been the common tendency in the Christian community of his time to depict Judas as a disciple whose greed and cupidity led him first to thievery and then to treachery against his teacher and friend. While Matthew and Mark do not accuse Judas of having stolen from the common fund, they do attribute his willingness to betray Jesus into the hands of his enemies to his inordinate love of money (Mark 14:11; Matt. 26:15). The more primitive and fundamental explanation of Judas' deed of infamy was that Satan had taken possession of him (Luke 22:3; John 13:2, 27). In the conversation with the disciples following the discourse on the bread of life, in fact, Jesus calls Judas a devil (6:70-71).

Jesus' counter to Judas concerning the inevitable continuance of the poor in the world appears to be a paraphrase of Deuteronomy 15:11: "For the poor will never cease out of the land; therefore I command you, you shall open wide your hand to your brother, to the needy and to the poor, in the land." Jesus' statement is of course not reflective of a lack of concern for the poor, but is expressing a rabbinic opinion of that time which considered burial, a work of mercy, as more perfect than giving to the poor, a work of justice.

Triumphal Entry (12:9–19)

9When the great crowd of the Jews learned that he was there, they came, not only on account of Jesus but also to see Lazarus, whom he had raised from the dead. 10So the chief priests planned to put Lazarus also to death, 11because on account of him many of the Jews were going away and believing in Jesus.

12The next day a great crowd who had come to the feast heard that Jesus was coming to Jerusalem. 13So they took branches of palm trees and went out to meet him, crying, "Hosanna! Blessed is he who comes in the name of the Lord, even the King of Israel!" 14And Jesus found a young ass and sat upon it; as it is written,
15"Fear not, daughter of Zion;
behold, your king is coming,
sitting on an ass's colt!"
16His disciples did not understand this at first; but when Jesus was glorified, then they remembered that this had been written of him and had been done to him. 17The crowd that had been with him when he called Lazarus out of the tomb and raised him from the dead bore witness. 18The reason why the crowd went to meet him was that they heard he had done this sign. 19The Pharisees then said to one another, "You see that you can do nothing; look, the world has gone after him."

Before narrating the crowd's acclamation of Jesus as he makes his way to Jerusalem, the fourth gospel once more keeps the Lazarus theme alive by reporting that a large crowd came to Bethany in order to see both Jesus and the man he had raised from the dead. At the same time, John again brings to the fore the hatred and desperation of the Jewish authorities, who now plan even the death of Lazarus, since his very existence leads many Jews away from the influence of their leaders to Jesus' side. The day after he is anointed by Mary at Bethany, Jesus sets out for Jerusalem, and is met by a crowd of pilgrims. While the synoptics record how the disciples, at Jesus' directions, bring him a colt and then by their example inspire the crowd to accompany Jesus in spontaneous demonstration (Matt. 21:1-9; Mark, 11:1-10; Luke 19:28-38), John indicates that the crowd, enthused by the miracle of Lazarus, goes out expressly to meet Jesus and to welcome him. In the synoptic account of this scene, Jesus appears to be making an effort to present himself as the Messiah who has come to take possession of his city and to cleanse it of the evils which have filled it. In John, the crowd, inspired by the Lazarus miracle, comes out with palms as if to form a triumphal procession, reminiscent of the fronds of palm held by the Jews following the purification of the temple by Judas Maccabeus (2 Macc. 10:7) and of the palm branches the people carried when they entered the citadel of Jerusalem captured by Juda's brother Simon. Although this carrying of palm branches could be associated with the feasts of Tabernacles or of Dedication, it appears here to be a gesture of the crowd welcoming Jesus as a national liberator. The very words which the crowd uses in welcoming Jesus betray the spirit of nationalism that was rampant in the crowd on that day. The expression, "Hosanna!," a plea for help in distress, was used in addressing a king (2 Sam. 14:4; 2 Kings 6:26). The verse which is shouted by the crowd (Ps. 118:26) comes from a psalm which is connected with the pilgrim's entrance into the temple. The words added by the crowd, however, "even the King of Israel," shows Jesus the real intent of the crowd. When Jesus had met this situation following the multiplication of the loaves and fishes, he escaped from the crowd (6:15). Here, however, he attempts to dispel their vision of him as a political and national leader by obtaining a young ass and sitting upon it. Whereas in the synoptic version, he enters upon the animal in a triumphant procession, in the fourth gospel he uses this animal to communicate a message to the crowd. That Jesus' use of the ass was a prophetic action is clear in the citation of Zephaniah 3:16: "On that day it shall be said to Jerusalem: 'Do not fear, O Zion; let not your hands grow weak.' " This text occurs within the prophecy that after the Lord has punished all the nations of the world and after they have experienced "all the heat of my anger," they will undergo a conversion. "Yea, at that time I will change the speech of the peoples to a pure speech, that all of them may call upon the name of the LORD and serve him with one accord" (Zeph. 3:9). The introduction of this universalistic text shows that Jesus wishes to be acclaimed a king, yes, but only as a king of all nations, and not a nationalistic king. The other text cited in the fourth gospel at this point is taken from the prophet Zechariah (9:9): "Behold, your king is coming, sitting on an ass's colt." Since John is not concerned with stressing the humility of Jesus, he omits the verse, "humble and riding on an ass," which Matthew includes. The citation of Zechariah also stresses the universality of Jesus' mission, since the very next verse of Zechariah states that the king "shall command peace to the nations; his dominion shall be from sea to sea, and from the River to the ends of the earth." God will have a universal empire, uniting the entire civilized world from the Mediterranean to the Persian Gulf.

The universalist theme stressed in this scene of Jesus' entry into Jerusalem runs as a common thread throughout chapters 11 and 12. Caiaphas's statement that Jesus should die for the people is interpreted by John as a prophecy that Jesus would die "to gather into one the children of God who are scattered abroad" (11:49-52). The Pharisees look helplessly at the crowd which goes out to meet Jesus and despair because "the world has gone after him." After Jesus is told that some Gentiles have come to see him, he predicts that "when I am lifted up from the earth, I will draw all men to myself," significance of Jesus' gesture; they comprehend its full implications only after his glorification.
only after his glorification.

THE GREEKS AT THE FEAST (12:30–36)

²⁰*Now among those who went up to worship at the feast were some Greeks. ²¹So these came to Philip, who was from Bethsaida in Galilee, and said to him, "Sir, we wish to see Jesus." ²²Philip went and told Andrew; Andrew went with Philip and they told Jesus. ²³And Jesus answered them, "The hour has come for the Son of man to be glorified. ²⁴Truly, truly, I say to you, unless a grain of wheat falls into the earth and dies, it remains alone; but if it dies, it bears much fruit. ²⁵He who loves his life loses it, and he who hates his life in this world will keep it for eternal life. ²⁶If any one serves me, he*

must follow me; and where I am, there shall my servant be also; if any one serves me, the Father will honor him.

27"Now is my soul troubled. And what shall I say, 'Father, save me from this hour'? No, for this purpose I have come to this hour. 28Father, glorify thy name." Then a voice came from heaven, "I have glorified it, and I will glorify it again." 29The crowd standing by heard it and said that it had thundered. Others said, "An angel has spoken to him." 30Jesus answered, "This voice has come for your sake, not for mine. 31Now is the judgment of this world, now shall the ruler of this world be cast out; 32and I, when I am lifted up from the earth, will draw all men to myself." 33He said this to show by what death he was to die. 34The crowd answered him, "We have heard from the law that the Christ remains for ever. How can you say that the Son of man must be lifted up? Who is this Son of man?" 35Jesus said to them, "The light is with you for a little longer. Walk while you have the light, lest the darkness overtake you; he who walks in the darkness does not know where he goes. 36While you have the light, believe in the light, that you may become sons of light." When Jesus had said this, he departed and hid himself from them.

The universalist theme continues into this next section of chapter 12 with the reported effort of "some Greeks" to see Jesus. The people referred to here are not necessarily inhabitants of Greece, but Gentiles of the Roman Empire influenced by Greek culture. Their presence in Jerusalem "to worship at the feast" shows that they were proselytes, full-fledged converts to Judaism who had been circumcised and who observed the other tenets of the Mosaic law. They were distinguished from another group of Gentiles called the "God-fearers," who, while inclining towards Judaism, did not submit to circumcision or follow the Mosaic law. They approach Philip, the only disciple of Jesus who spoke Greek, and make their request. Once we are told that Philip and Andrew approach Jesus and inform him of the visitors' request, the Gentiles drop out of sight. Some commentators believe that the lack of any further mention of them is an indication that Jesus refused to see them. After all, the hour of his mission to the Gentiles had not yet arrived. However, it may very well be that John was not interested in either affirming or denying that Jesus actually spoke with the Gentiles, since his sole interest was to announce the fact that the Gentiles came to Jesus, an ironic fulfillment of the remark recently made by the Pharisees that "the world has gone after him" (v. 19).

The presence of the Gentiles, "the other sheep, that are not of this fold" (10:16), reminds Jesus that the hour of his glorification, of his laying down of his life and taking it up again (10:17) has arrived. The salvific and decisive moment for which he came into the world and to which he has alluded with an eagerness and sense of mission is at hand (2:4, 7:30; 8:20; 12:27; 13:1; 17:1). As will be evident in verses 27 to 30, this eagerness and sense of mission are tempered and profoundly touched by the human emotion of fear which borders on terror, arising from his anticipatory inner experience of the death he must experience before the final and triumphant phase of his glorification. Before the fourth gospel expands upon Jesus' fear of that hour, however, it introduces a series of sayings dealing with the themes of life and death. As Jesus begins to contemplate the death which will be the channel through which life will come to the world, he turns to nature and becomes aware that the same paradox of life through death is also present there. The death of the grain of wheat is the condition for its passage to a higher life. The Johannine parable of the grain of wheat brings to mind Mark's parable of the grain of mustard seed (4:30-32). While Mark's parable about the growth of the kingdom of God does not focus on the necessity of death for the growth of the kingdom, it does touch upon the element of the fruit which John here sees as the result of the death of the grain of wheat. Mark's parable focuses on the wonder of the enormous results of the preaching and ministry of Jesus, which had such a modest and almost imperceptible beginning. Mark's description of the kingdom of God as "the greatest of all shrubs . . . [which] puts forth large branches, so that the birds of the air can make nests in its shade" seems to be an allusion to Daniel 4:20-22, where the kingdom of God is compared to the kingdom of Nebuchadnezzar, whose empire encompassed all peoples. The kingdom of God in the parable of the mustard seed will encompass the Gentiles as well as the Jews. The abundance of fruit which comes about through the death of Jesus is the life which Jesus will be able to grant to all peoples, as Caiaphas unconsciously prophesied (11:50-52). If there is any doubt about the meaning of the Johannine parable of the grain of wheat, then the saying which follows in verse 25 brings us to absolute clarity: "He who loves his life will lose it, and he who hates his life in this world will keep it for eternal life." We are confronted here not with the normal meaning of love and hate, but with the Semitic usage of vivid contrasts to express preferences (Deut. 21:15; Matt. 6:24; Mark 14:26). If a person values physical life over commitment to Christ and refuses to die when called upon to do so, then all will be lost. Only the person who "hates his life in this world" will be capable of being where Jesus is and of gaining eternal life. A similar statement is found also in the synoptics (Mark 8:35; Matt. 10:39; 16:25; Luke 9:24; 17:33).

Jesus then makes even more explicit his requirement that his disciples must be willing to die in order to gain eternal life. Anyone who wishes to serve Jesus must be ready to follow him. Within this context, following Jesus is defined by the larger context of his glorification (his death on the cross), of the death of the grain of wheat, and by the prayer of his willingness to accept the Father's will even if it entails a death which Jesus fears. The Church is called upon to take the risks Jesus has taken, and to follow him in his suffering. It goes without saying that this willingness to give one's life out of fidelity to Jesus, the ultimate gift (15:13), encompasses the readiness to accept every other conceivable hardship and sacrifice which falls short of the ultimate gift. To those who are willing to serve Jesus with their lives, he promises that they will be where he is, that is, in the place in the Father's house he has prepared for them (14:3), a place where they can behold his glory (17:24). They will be honored by the Father, or, as it is expressed in verse 25, they will possess eternal life.

Although the fourth gospel has continuously painted for us the picture of a Jesus whose entire ministry was guided and inspired by his vision of the future decisive hour which gave meaning to his entire ministry and who was always aware that his ability to give life would come only through his death, we are here faced with another portrait of Jesus, a portrait which underlines the reality of his humanity as vividly as the scene of his open weeping for his dead friend, Lazarus: "Now my soul is troubled. And what shall I say, 'Father, save me from this hour'?" The Jesus we see here is a person who experiences fear, even terror, as he contemplates the suffering and death which his enemies plan to inflict upon him. This portrait of the inner struggle in Jesus is presented by the synoptics in an even more dramatic form (Matt. 26:36-46; Mark 14:32-42; Luke 22:39-46). However, in this gospel, the majesty emanating from Jesus' strength is preserved even in this moment of human agonizing. As has already been noted in the commentary on 7:6-8, the fourth gospel presents the passion and death of Jesus as the history of a triumph, and therefore tends to omit certain details found in the synoptics which emphasize the humiliation and defeat of Jesus. The prayer for pity he utters in the synoptic accounts is absent here. He does not fall to the ground, as in the other gospel accounts. There is a control and a calm in John's portrait of the suffering Christ, which emphasizes John's insistence that when Jesus dies, it will be because he freely surrenders himself into the hands of his enemies.

While the synoptics report Jesus' inner struggle in a dramatic manner in their account of his agony in Gethsemane, John makes reference to Jesus' deeply felt fear of his future suffering and death and his courageous acceptance of that hour elsewhere in the gospel. In 14:30-31, Jesus speaks of the coming of "the ruler of this world," an expression which brings to mind his description of the moment of his arrest as the hour of "the power of darkness" (Luke 22:53). Jesus' statement that he does as the Father commands so that the world may know that he loves the Father reminds us of the expression of his acceptance of the Father's will in the synoptic accounts. In 18:11, Jesus speaks of the cup which the Father has given him, an expression referring to the suffering which awaits him also used by the synoptics. The fourth gospel's presentation of the dramatic struggle that took place within Jesus' soul as a struggle he experienced at many points during his ministry is probably much more realistic than the synoptics' presentation. How could he not have experienced that fear, for example, when he found himself face to face on so many occasions with the Jewish authorities, whose hostility only grew in its ferocity each time they confronted Jesus and of whose murderous intent Jesus was always only too vividly aware.

Jesus' fear, very real and very profound, growing probably into terror, was overcome by the strength of his union of will with his Father: "Father, glorify thy name." In this prayer, Jesus expresses his willingness to embrace the destiny which awaits him. The Father's name will be glorified only when Jesus has gone through every single phase of his glorification, beginning with the hour of his passion and death. The Johannine expression uttered here by Jesus is the equivalent of his affirmation of absolute conformity to the Father's will which is expressed in the synoptic accounts of his agony in Gethsemane (Matt. 26:39, 42; Mark 14:36; Luke 22:42). Both expressions are in fact reminiscent of the Our Father, which Jesus taught to his disciples as the model after which all their prayers should be patterned. The first three petitions of this prayer (Matt. 6:9-13) are synonymous with each other and with the Johannine prayer that the Father's name be glorified. While in Matthew, where the theme of the kingdom of God is predominant, the prayer is for the realization of God's rule in the world, in John the prayer is that God's presence be made visible through the deeds and words of Jesus.

The Father's response to Jesus' expression of absolute obedience is a theophany in which the Father pledges that his name will be glorified in the future as faithfully as it has been in the past. In the fourth gospel, the Father has been glorified, that is, made visible through Jesus' deeds of power (2:11), and in all the works of Jesus, which are the works of the Father. The Father promises that his power will be made visible in the future through the passion, death, and resurrection of Jesus. The Father's response through a theophany is the first occurrence of this type of phenomenon in the fourth gospel. Other theophanies are recorded in the synoptic accounts of Jesus' baptism (Mark 1:11; Matt. 3:13-17; Luke 3:21-22) and of his transfiguration (Mark 9:1-8; Matt. 17:1-8; Luke 9:28-36). This extraordinary sign of the Father's approbation recorded by John is not intended to reassure Jesus, but to move the crowds to an understanding of Jesus' relationship with the Father. However, because they have been constant in their rejection of Jesus, the crowds are not attuned to the Father's voice, and therefore hear only thunder or some sound that vaguely resembles a voice.

Whatever the power and depth of Jesus' fear of the destiny which awaits him, its hold over him is nil because of the strength of his love for the Father. That fear is also vanquished by Jesus' awareness that the hour of his glorification will bring about the destruction of Satan's power in this world (14:30; 15:11). While the ruler of this world remains and the evil influence of his power is never completely absent from the world, his dominant position can no longer remain unchallenged. The author of the fourth gospel, while rejoicing in the victory of Jesus' glorification over evil, is not naive enough to believe that the tension and the struggle between light and darkness have come to an end. In fact, in 1 John 5:12, we hear that "the whole world is in the power of the evil one." The reality of evil and its power is a reality of which the Church is only too aware. On the other hand, while keeping in mind that the ruler of this world never lets up in the desire to dominate humanity, "we know that any one born of God does not sin, but He who was born of God keeps him, and the evil one does not touch him" (1 John 5:18). While Jesus' glorification has not driven evil from the world, the life which believers receive through the Spirit provides them with the power to cope with Satan and to gain mastery in the struggle. In fact, it is because of the salvific effect of Jesus' glorification that Satan's power can no longer run rampant in the universe. When Jesus is lifted up from the earth, he will draw all to himself, that is, he will enable them to believe in him and to receive the eternal life which he came to give to humankind. While the "lifting up" clearly refers to the manner of his death, it also alludes to the other phases of his glorification, that is, his resurrection and his ascension to heaven (3:13, 14; 8:28; 6:62). Once Jesus has been glorified, be becomes capable of giving life through the Spirit (7:39). At the same time, the lifting up of Jesus will be the source of condemnation of those who reject him, as is suggested in Jesus' response to the Jews who called upon him to reveal his true identity (8:28).

As has already been pointed out in the commentary on Jesus' conversation with Nicodemus (3:14), the use of this expression, "being lifted up," in the fourth gospel identifies Jesus with the suffering servant of Isaiah (chaps. 52 and 53). This mysterious figure, the subject of four songs in the book of Isaiah, represents the perfect Israelite whose obedience to the Lord, even in suffering, takes away the sins of many (Isa. 53:12). The suffering servant, in addition to representing collectively all the greatest leaders of Israel throughout her history, was also seen as an individual who would appear in the future, and who would be greater than any Israelite of the past. In prophesying that the servant would prosper, would be exalted and lifted up and be very high, Isaiah was announcing the triumph of the servant. For the fourth gospel, Jesus was the suffering and obedient servant in whose triumph Israel could rejoice.

Although Jesus makes no explicit reference to himself as the Son of man or the Messiah at this point, his listeners again question his claim to be the Messiah. They remind him that the Son of man must remain forever, probably referring to the Old Testament teaching that the rule of the Messiah will be everlasting. If Jesus is to be lifted up, then how can he rightfully claim to be the Messiah? Once again, we have another example of Johannine irony. As on other occasions, (7:27, 35), Jesus' adversaries, while believing that they have successfully challenged his claims, have in fact ironically corroborated essential truths concerning his nature and mission. Little did they realize that the one whom they addressed, this Son of man and Messiah, would have an everlasting rule, and that this rule was made possible by means of and not in spite of "his being lifted up."

Rather than responding directly to their objection, Jesus contents himself with directing another warning at them about the shortness of time. His death will mean the withdrawal of light from them: "The light is with you for a little longer." Unless they accept him now and choose freely to walk in his light, he will be taken from them, and they will walk in the darkness, unable to see where they are going. He warns them that now is the time for them to decide whether they wish to walk in darkness (live an evil life) or believe in him, the light, and become children of light. In his discourse to the crowd at the feast of Tabernacles, he had already warned them that he was going away, and that unless they accepted the opportunity he was offering them, they would be lost forever (8:21). Jesus' warning about the withdrawal of the light, however, has no effect upon the crowd. Tragically, as the fourth gospel notes, it is their last chance, for when Jesus finishes his discourse, "he departed and hid himself from them."

THE CONCLUSION OF THE PUBLIC MINISTRY (12:37–50)

[37]*Though he had done so many signs before them, yet they did not believe in him;* [38]*it was that the word spoken by the prophet Isaiah might be fulfilled:*

"Lord, who has believed our report,
and to whom has the arm of the Lord been revealed?"
[39]*Therefore they could not believe. For Isaiah again said,*

⁴⁰*He has blinded their eyes and hardened their heart,*
lest they should see with their eyes and perceive with
     their heart,
and turn for me to heal them."

⁴¹*Isaiah said this because he saw his glory and spoke of him.*
⁴²*Nevertheless many even of the authorities believed in him, but for*
fear of the Pharisees they did not confess it, lest they should be put
out of the synagogue: ⁴³*for they loved the praise of men more than*
the praise of God.

⁴⁴*And Jesus cried out and said, "He who believes in me, believes*
not in me but in him who sent me. ⁴⁵*And he who sees me sees him*
who sent me. ⁴⁶*I have come as light into the world, that whoever*
believes in me may not remain in darkness. ⁴⁷*If any one hears my*
sayings and does not keep them, I do not judge him; for I did not
come to judge the world but to save the world. ⁴⁸*He who rejects me*
and does not receive my sayings has a judge; the word that I have
spoken will be his judge on the last day. ⁴⁹*For I have not spoken on*
my own authority; the Father who sent me has himself given me
commandment what to say and what to speak. ⁵⁰*And I know that*
his commandment is eternal life. What I say, therefore, I say as the
Father has bidden me."

At this point, John looks back in order to evaluate the ministry of
Jesus and its effects. The tragic fact is that the signs performed by
Jesus, those visible manifestations of God's power and presence,
have failed to move his hearers to believe him. Notwithstanding the
works which the Father has granted him to accomplish, the inner
testimony of the Father, and the validation of Jesus' claims by the
Scriptures themselves, his own people have received him not (5:32-
40; 1:10). Because they have freely chosen to be blind and deaf in
his presence, nothing that Jesus says or does can penetrate through
the unyielding unbelief that characterizes their reaction to him (8:47;
9:40-41). The fourth gospel, faced with the mystery of this unbelief,
seeks an answer in the prophet Isaiah. John avers simply that the
Jews did not believe in Jesus because that unbelief had been foretold
by Isaiah the prophet, and the prophecy had to be fulfilled. Although
it may appear incomprehensible to us, the text of the fourth gospel
at this point, "it was that the word spoken by the prophet Isaiah
might be fulfilled," clearly means that the prophecy was the cause

of the unbelief. The text cited by John is taken from the fourth song of the suffering servant, and expresses the astonishment of the Gentiles that Israel had rejected the servant, who was one of their own (Isa. 53:1). In light of that text, then, Jesus, who was seen in the fourth gospel as the triumphant suffering servant prophesied by Isaiah, had also to be rejected by his own people. Israel's refusal to believe in Jesus is part of the divine plan. The fact that the root of the Jews' unbelief lies in the divine causality is clear also in the verses which immediately follow the citation of Isaiah 53:1. The fourth gospel clearly states that ". . . they *could not* believe." The gospel cites another reason for the unbelief with which Jesus had met during his entire ministry: "He has blinded their eyes and hardened their hearts, lest they should see with their eyes and perceive with their hearts, and turn for me to heal them" (Isa. 6:10). This passage is used in Acts 28:26-27 and in the synoptic gospels to explain the failure for the Jews of Jesus' time to believe in him. In the text from Isaiah, the Lord commands the prophet to dull the heart and senses of the people so that they will not be able to see or hear or understand. In the fourth evangelist's reading of this text, God is the one who blinds the eyes and hardens the heart. John then traces the resistance of the Jewish people to Jesus to the ultimate cause of all reality, that is, to the Lord, and ignores secondary causality. He is primarily interested in explaining this unbelief in the context of the divine plan.

While the gospel's explanation of the unbelief of the Jews seems to carry with it a note of determinism, it is important also to recall that John points out that many believed in Jesus. Both statements must be accepted as John's perception of the realities of belief and unbelief. While God is both the source and cause of belief and unbelief, the human being is ultimately free in whatever decision is reached.

After having cited Isaiah, the fourth gospel, recalling the prophet's initial vision of the Lord, states that Isaiah saw "his glory and spoke of him," referring to Jesus. Some critics explain this statement by pointing out that the early Church had believed that Jesus was active in the Old Testament, and that Isaiah's vision of the glory of God was a veiled vision of Jesus who is himself the glory of God (1:14).

John makes note of the fact that there were many who believed in Jesus, and that some of these believers could be found in positions of leadership. However, even this belief was not a genuine one, since it was not strong enough to motivate the "believing" authorities to openly profess Jesus and risk being expelled from the synagogue by the Pharisees. John's judgment that these individuals "loved the praise of men more than the praise of God" brings to mind Jesus' condemnation of the leaders "who receive glory from one another and to not seek the glory that comes from the only God."

Since Jesus had closed his public ministry and certainly would not be seeking out an audience, it is clear that the discourse recorded in this last section of chapter 12 is not in its original location. It is appropriately placed here however, at the conclusion of Jesus' public ministry, as a summary of his teachings. Time and again throughout his ministry Jesus refers to the oneness of purpose and activity which he shares with the Father. He came into the world to do his Father's will, to carry out his work and to preach his teaching. It is this absolute unity which allows Jesus to say that the person who believes in him in reality believes in the one who sent him. It is because Jesus can truly say that he and the Father are one, that he can also say that the person who sees Jesus also sees the Father. Jesus is in very truth the visible manifestation of the Father in this world.

Jesus is sent into the world as light, a light which brings life to human beings and saves them from the evil and the death which are symbolized by darkness. He comes into the world not to condemn the world but to save it. Even if someone hears Jesus' word and fails to observe it, Jesus himself does not have to condemn him. The word which he has spoken is his judge now, and will be his judge on the last day. Since Jesus' words themselves bring life, people bring damnation upon themselves by rejecting them.

Jesus again stresses the oneness between himself and his Father in terms of his own obedience to the commandment of the Father, who has told Jesus what to say and what to speak. The words and the deeds which Jesus performs in obedience to the Father are the source of eternal life for humanity. We are reminded here of Jesus' discourse in which he points to himself as the bread of life inasmuch as he is the bearer of divine revelation (6:35-50). The choice could not be any more clear. To believe in Jesus and his Father, the source of the revelation disclosed in Jesus' words and deeds, is to accept life. To reject that revelation is to freely call down darkness, death and condemnation upon one's self.